Other Books by Amitai Etzioni

A Responsive Society (1991)

The Moral Dimension:
Toward a New Economics (1988)

Capital Corruption:
The New Attack on American Democracy (1984)

An Immodest Agenda:
Rebuilding America Before the Twenty-First Century (1983)

Genetic Fix:
The Next Technological Revolution (1973)

The Active Society:
A Theory of Societal and Political Processes (1968)

Political Unification:
A Comparative Study of Leaders and Forces (1965)

Modern Organizations (1964)

A Comparative Analysis of Complex Organizations (1961)

The Spirit of Community

THE REINVENTION OF AMERICAN SOCIETY

Amitai Etzioni

A TOUCHSTONE BOOK
Published by Simon & Schuster
New York London Toronto Sydney Tokyo Singapore

TOUCHSTONE
Rockefeller Center
1230 Avenue of the Americas
New York, New York 10020

First Touchstone Edition 1994
Published by arrangement with Crown Publishers, Inc.

TOUCHSTONE and colophon are registered trademarks of
Simon & Schuster, Inc.

Manufactured in the United States of America

3 5 7 9 10 8 6 4

Library of Congress Cataloging-in-Publication Data
is available.
ISBN 0-671-88524-3

The following publishers have generously given permission to use quotations
from previously published works: From *A Pac of Lies: The Commodore Savings Case*
by Byron Harris; reprinted with permission of *The Wall Street Journal*, © 1989
Dow Jones Company, Inc.; all rights reserved. From a letter to Ann Landers, *The
Washington Post*, Sept. 26, 1991; permission granted by Ann Landers and Creators
Syndicate. From *Two Messes: One of Trash, One of Bureaucracy*, by Sarah Bartlett,
Nov. 29, 1991; copyright © 1991 by The New York Times Company; reprinted
by permission. From personal correspondence; Christmas card written by Joseph
Duffey and Anne Wexler, Dec. 1991; reprinted by permission. From *Rights Talk:
The Impoverishment of Political Discourse* by Mary Ann Glendon, copyright © 1991
by Mary Ann Glendon; reprinted with the permission of The Free Press, a Division of Macmillan, Inc. From *Rebuilding The Good Society* by Patrick F. Fagan;
copyright © 1991 by Patrick F. Fagan; reprinted with permission. From *A Class
Divided: Then and Now* by William Peters; copyright © 1987 by William Peters;
reprinted by permission of the publisher, Yale University Press.

To the newest Etzionis:
Danielle, my granddaughter,
Hedva and Ruthi, my daughters-in-law,
and Pat Kellogg, whose husband I am.
This is for your generations.

Communitarianism.

Cartoon by Niculae Asciu, May 24, 1992. Copyright © 1992 by The New York Times Company. Reprinted with permission.

Contents

Part II
Too Many Rights, Too Few Responsibilities

Part III
The Public Interest

Introduction ♦ A New Moral, Social, Public Order— Without Puritanism or Oppression

We Hold These Truths

E hold that a moral revival in these United States is possible without Puritanism; that is, without busybodies meddling into our personal affairs, without thought police controlling our intellectual life. We *can* attain a recommitment to moral values—without puritanical excesses.

We hold that law and order can be restored without turning this country of the free into a police state, as long as we grant public authorities some carefully crafted and circumscribed new powers.

We hold that the family—without which no society has ever survived, let alone flourished—can be saved, without forcing women to stay at home or otherwise violating their rights.

We hold that schools *can* provide essential moral education—without indoctrinating young people.

We hold that people can again live in communities without turning into vigilantes or becoming hostile to one another.

We hold that our call for increased social responsibilities, a main tenet of this book, is not a call for curbing rights. On the contrary, *strong rights presume strong responsibilities.*

We hold that the pursuit of self-interest can be balanced by a commitment to the community, without requiring us to lead a life of austerity, altruism, or self-sacrifice. Furthermore, unbridled greed can be replaced by legitimate opportunities and socially constructive expressions of self-interest.

We hold that powerful special-interest groups in the nation's capital, and in many statehouses and city halls, can be curbed without limiting the constitutional right of the people to lobby and petition those who govern. The public interest *can* reign, without denying the legitimate interests and the right to lobby of the various constituencies that make up America.

We hold these truths as Communitarians, as people committed to creating a new moral, social, and public order based on restored communities, without allowing puritanism or oppression.

The Communitarian Thesis

The Communitarian assertions rest upon a single core thesis: Americans—who have long been concerned with the deterioration of private and public morality, the decline of the family, high crime rates, and the swelling of corruption in government—can now act without fear. We can act without fear that attempts to shore up our values, responsibilities, institutions, and communities will cause us to charge into a dark tunnel of moralism and authoritarianism that leads to a church-dominated state or a right-wing world.

Chapter and verse are in the body of the book, but let me introduce the Communitarian approach by way of an example: Airline pilots, school bus drivers, and others who directly hold people's lives in their hands can be required to be tested for drug and alcohol use. This would significantly enhance our safety, without testing every Dick, Jane, and Harry, from employees of the Weather Bureau to children in kindergarten. Beyond the important details (such as, should police officers also be tested? will the samples be collected in the presence of others?) are matters of principle, such as how we can restore a civil society (in this case, enhance public safety) while upholding our constitutional rights and moral traditions.

The Communitarian movement—which is an environmental movement dedicated to the betterment of our moral, social, and political environment—seeks to sort out these principles. And

Communitarians are dedicated to working with our fellow citizens to bring about the changes in values, habits, and public policies that will allow us to do for society what the environmental movement seeks to do for nature: to safeguard and enhance our future.

America in the Early Nineties

From time to time there's a finding of social science that may by itself be of limited importance but illuminates a major conundrum: A study has shown that young Americans expect to be tried before a jury of their peers but are rather reluctant to serve on one. This paradox highlights a major aspect of contemporary American civic culture: a strong sense of entitlement—that is, a demand that the community provide more services and strongly uphold rights—coupled with a rather weak sense of obligation to the local and national community. Thus, most Americans applauded the show of force in Grenada, Panama, and in the Persian Gulf, but many were reluctant to serve in the armed forces or see their sons and daughters called up.

First prize for capturing this anticommunitarian outlook should be awarded to a member of a television audience who exclaimed during a show on the savings and loan mess, "The taxpayers should not have to pay for this; the government should," as if there really were an Uncle Sam who could pick up the tab for us all.

A 1989 study by People for the American Way notes:

> Young people have learned only half of America's story. Consistent with the priority they place on personal happiness, young people reveal notions of America's unique character that emphasize freedom and license almost to the complete exclusion of service or participation. Although they clearly appreciate the democratic freedoms that, in their view, make theirs the "best country in the world to live in," they fail to perceive a need to reciprocate by exercising the duties and responsibilities of good citizenship.

Only one out of eight (12 percent) of the respondents felt that voting was part of what makes a good citizen. When asked what was special about the United States, young people responded: "Individualism and the fact that it is a democracy and you can do whatever you want." And: "We really don't have any limits."

The imbalance between rights and responsibilities has existed for a long time. Indeed, some argue that it is a basic trait of the American character. However, America's leaders have exacerbated this tendency in recent years. In 1961 President John F. Kennedy could still stir the nation when he stated: "Ask not what your country can do for you. Ask what you can do for your country." But Presidents Ronald Reagan and George Bush, backed up by some Democrats in Congress, proposed a much less onerous course: they suggested that ever-increasing economic growth would pay for government services, and taxpayers would be expected to shell out less—implying that Americans could have their cake and eat it, too.

In many other areas, from public education to the war on illegal drugs, facile, nontaxing "solutions" have been offered. Thus it has been suggested that we can improve our education system without additional expenditures simply by increasing parental choices among schools. Choice, it is claimed, will "drive the bad schools out of business." And how should we deal with the demand for illicit drugs? "Just say no."

Harvard legal historian Lawrence Friedman points to a particularly troubling mismatch of rights and responsibilities: a tendency among Americans in recent years to claim rights for themselves and to leave responsibilities to the government. It is therefore necessary to reiterate that sooner or later the responsibilities we load on the government end up on our shoulders or become burdens we bequeath to our children.

A Four-Point Agenda on Rights and Responsibilities

Correcting the current imbalance between rights and responsibilities requires a four-point agenda: a moratorium on the minting of most, if not all, new rights; reestablishing the link between rights and responsibilities; recognizing that some responsibilities do not entail rights; and, most carefully, adjusting some rights to the changed circumstances. These pivotal points deserve some elaboration.

A Moratorium

We should, for a transition period of, say, the next decade, put a tight lid on the manufacturing of new rights. The incessant issuance of new rights, like the wholesale printing of currency, causes a massive inflation of rights that devalues their moral claims.

When asked whether certain things are "a privilege that a person should have to earn, or a right to which he is entitled as a citizen," most Americans (81 percent) considered health care a right (versus 16 percent who said it was a privilege). Two-thirds (66 percent) considered adequate housing a right (as opposed to 31 percent who called it a privilege). Indeed, why not? Until one asks, as there are no free lunches, who will pay for unlimited health care and adequate housing for all? The champions of rights are often quite mum on this question, which if left unanswered makes the claim for a right a rather empty gesture.

Tajel Shah, the president of the U.S. Student Association, claims that higher education "is a right, not a privilege." A fine sentiment indeed. It would, however, be more responsible if she at least hinted at how this right is to be paid for—in whose ledger the entailed obligation is to be entered.

In Santa Monica, California, men were found dealing drugs in public women's rooms on the beaches and in parks. To combat the abuse, the city council passed an ordinance that prohibited men and women from using the opposite sex's facilities unless they were in urgent need (which was defined as a line of three or more in front of them). This did not satisfy a local activist, Gloria Allred, who saw in the ordinance a violation of a woman's right to urinate in any public facility, at any time. Referring to a similar ordinance in Houston, Texas, she stated: "Little did I know that such a nightmare might soon be reenacted in this fair city." Ms. Allred warned: "This is the first step down a long dark road of restricting women's rights in the name of public safety."

Death-row inmates at San Quentin have sued to protect their reproductive "rights" through artificial insemination. An attorney in the case reports that "these inmates believe that they are being subjected to cruel and unusual punishment because not only are they being sentenced to die, but future generations of their family are being executed also. . . ."

Lisa Dangler, a mother in Yorktown, New York, sued the local school district for not admitting her son into the high school honor society. She argued that his rejection reduced his chances of being accepted by a select college and medical school. She further claimed that he was being punished because the Danglers were outspoken critics of the school—and hence his rejection was actually a violation of the family's right of free speech. A jury rejected her suit. The presiding judge stated that if the jury had ruled in Ms. Dangler's favor, he would have overturned the verdict. He added: "By attempting to elevate mere personal desires into constitutional rights and claiming denial of their civil rights whenever their desires are not realized, these persons are demeaning the essential rights and procedures that protect us all."

The American Bankers Association took out a full-page ad in *The Washington Post* (when Congress was considering putting a cap on the interest banks may charge credit-card holders) that bore the headline WILL CONGRESS DENY MILLIONS OF AMERICANS THE RIGHT TO KEEP THEIR CREDIT CARDS?

Once, rights were very solemn moral/legal claims, ensconced in the Constitution and treated with much reverence. We all lose if the publicity department of every special interest can claim that someone's rights are violated every time they don't get all they want. Suspending for a while the minting of new rights, unless there are unusually compelling reasons to proceed, will serve to restore the special moral standing and suasion of rights.

We need to remind one another that *each newly minted right generates a claim on someone*. In effect, new rights often arouse or play upon feelings of guilt in others. There is a limited amount of guilt, however, that one can lay upon other people before they balk. Unless we want to generate a universal backlash against rights, we need to curb rights inflation and protect the currency of rights from being further devalued.

Moreover, the expression of ever more wants, many quite legitimate, in the language of rights makes it difficult to achieve compromises and to reach consensus, processes that lie at the heart of democracy. A society that is studded with groups of true believers and special-interest groups, each brimming with rights, inevitably turns into a society overburdened with conflicts. Columnist John Leo of *U.S. News & World Report* declares: "Rights talk polarizes debate; it tends to suppress moral discussion and consensus building. Once an agenda is introduced as a 'right,' sensible discussion and moderate positions tend to disappear."

Even if lawyers and judges realize among themselves that individual rights are limited by the rights of others and the needs of the community, as the language of rights penetrates into everyday discourse, the discourse becomes impoverished and confrontational. It is one thing to claim that you and I have different interests and see if we can work out a compromise; or, better yet, that we both recognize the merit or virtue of a common cause, say, a cleaner environment. The moment, however, that I claim a *right* to the same piece of land or property or public space as you, we start to view one another like the Catholics and Protestants in Northern Ireland or the Palestinians and Israelis in the Middle East.

A return to a language of social virtues, interests, and, above all, social responsibilities will reduce contentiousness and enhance social cooperation.

People treat rights-based arguments, unlike many others, as "trump cards" that neutralize all other positions. Cass R. Sunstein, professor of jurisprudence at the University of Chicago, put it well when he pointed out that rights can "be conclusions masquerading as reasons." For example, he writes, those who defend even the most extreme kinds of what he labels violent pornography state that it is a form of free speech, period. Sunstein suggests that perhaps a person is entitled to this particularly abusive form of speech. But, he argues, an individual's entitlement should be established in detailed argumentation that would weigh the right at issue against the rights of those who are hurt by the given act, rather than simply asserting that it is a right, as if its evocation closed off all debate.

Mary Ann Glendon, a Harvard Law professor and leading Communitarian, shows that we treat many rights the way we treat property, which we tend to view as intrinsically "ours" and which we are therefore free to do with as we wish. Actually, we readily accept that there are many things we may not do with things we own, such as burning leaves, which may endanger others, or playing the stereo loud enough to be heard five blocks away. To put it differently, we all know on one level that our liberties are limited by those of others and that we can do what we want only *as long as we do not harm others*. Rights talk, however, pushes us to disregard this crucial qualification, the concern for one another and for the community. Soon "I can do what I want as long as I do not hurt others" becomes "I can do what I want, because I have a right to do it."

A telling case in point is the opposition to seat belts and motorcycle helmets. Libertarians have long argued adamantly that the government should not require people to use these safety devices. They blocked the introduction of seat belt and motorcycle helmet laws in many jurisdictions and ensured the repeal of such regulations in several localities where they had been in place. The main libertarian argument is that people have a right to do with their lives what they wish, including endangering them. People are said to be the best judges of what is good for them, because they will have to live with the consequences of their acts. Therefore we should treat people as adults and not as children, without paternalism. (Some libertarians apply the same idea to the use of narcotics.)

Reckless individuals, however, do not absorb many of the consequences of their acts. Drivers without seat belts are more likely than those wearing belts to lose control of their cars in an accident and hurtle into others. They are also more likely to die and leave their children for society to attend to and pick up the pieces. And, of course, they draw on our community resources, from ambulance services to hospitals, when they are involved in accidents, for which they pay at best a fraction of the cost. To insist that people drive safely and responsibly is hence a concern for the needs of others and the community; there is no individual right that automatically trumps these considerations.

Aside from a temporary suspension in the minting of new rights, *there are several rights,* some recently generated and some of long standing, *that deserve reexamination.* It makes little sense, for example, to refer to rights of inanimate objects, as law professor Christopher Stone did some years back in an environmental flourish:

> It is no answer to say that streams and forests . . . cannot speak. Corporations cannot speak either; nor can states, estates, infants, incompetents, municipalities or universities. . . . One ought, I think, to handle the legal problems of natural objects as one does the problem of legal incompetents—human beings who have become vegetable. . . . On a parity of reasoning, we should have a system in which, when a friend of a

natural object perceives it to be endangered, he can apply to a court for the creation of a guardianship.

Others have pointed out that many builders use sand from beaches, that cities cut into them to create new harbors, and that utilities use them for their power plants—all of them benefiting from beaches and contributing to their erosion. But instead of turning to the language of responsibility to protect beaches, legal scholars, among them a Los Angeles lawyer who specializes in the environment, have advanced the notion that sand has rights! It is difficult to imagine a way to trivialize rights more than to claim that they are as common as sand.

Stone is correct that one can find a way to appoint a lawyer not merely for everybody, but also for everything, and surely many objects—say, a majestic mountain—deserve some protection, even command some respect. (Corporations are different because they are combinations of humans and hence are more akin to communities than to animals or stones.) None of this, however, proves that we have to consider them as if they command rights. The difference between granting them some consideration versus rights is that to grant them rights puts them on the same plane as humans—and we should grant humans a higher moral standing than brooks and sand. Note that *consideration for the objects themselves is secondary*. The stunning mountain requires protection so that other humans may find it stunning, and not for its own sake. Therefore we have an *interest* in protecting it; but to accord it the higher status of commanding a right interferes with our dealing with it in a dispassionate way. We must and can find ways to recognize the value of things and to respect them without imbuing them with rights. Let's just say that they deserve our respect and command our care.

Rights Presume Responsibilities

Claiming rights without assuming responsibilities is unethical and illogical. Mary Ann Glendon puts it well: "Buried deep in our rights dialect," she writes, "is an unexpressed premise that we roam at large in a land of strangers, where we presumptively have no obligations toward others except to avoid the active infliction of harm." She notes in *Rights Talk*:

Try, for example, to find in the familiar language of our Declaration of Independence or Bill of Rights anything comparable to the statements in the Universal Declaration of Human
Rights that "everyone has duties to the community," and that
everyone's rights and freedoms are subject to limitations "for
the purposes of securing due recognition and respect for the
rights and freedoms of others and of meeting the just requirements of morality, public order and the general welfare in a
democratic society."

The Constitution, while not nearly as explicit on obligations to the
community as the other documents cited, does open with the quest
"to form a more perfect Union" and speaks of the need to "promote the general welfare" for that purpose.

To take and not to give is an amoral, self-centered predisposi-
tion that ultimately no society can tolerate. To revisit the finding
that many try to evade serving on a jury, which, they claim, they
have a right to be served by, is egotistical, indecent, and in the long
run impractical. Hence, *those most concerned about rights ought to be the
first ones to argue for the resumption of responsibilities.* One presumes the
other. Much of the following discussion about the conditions under
which moral commitments can be strengthened in the family,
schools, and in communities speaks directly to the shoring up of
our responsibilities. Indeed, many of our core values entail concern
for others and the commons we share. As we restore the moral
voice of communities (and the web of social bonds, the Communitarian nexus, that enables us to speak as a community), we shall
see, we will also be more able to encourage one another to live up
to our social responsibilities.

Responsibilities Without Rights

Although it is difficult to imagine rights without corollary responsibilities, we must recognize that we have some duties that lay
moral claims on us from which we derive no immediate benefit or
even long-term payoff. Our commitment to a shared future, especially our responsibility to the environment, is a case in point. We
are to care for the environment not only or even mainly for our
own sakes (although we may desire some assurance of potable
water, breathable air, and protection from frying because the ozone

layer is thinning out). We have a moral commitment to leave for future generations a livable environment, even perhaps a better one than the one we inherited, certainly not one that has been further depleted. *The same observations hold true for our responsibility to our moral, social, and political environment.*

Careful Adjustments

Finally, some areas in which legal rights have been interpreted in ways that hobble public safety and health need to be reinterpreted. Thus, the Fourth Amendment outlaws *unreasonable* searches and seizures. The question of what is deemed reasonable versus unreasonable is subject to change over time. In several areas of public life, the times now call for a modest increase in what we can reasonably be asked to do for the sake of the community, for public safety and public health.

Radical Individualists, such as libertarians and the American Civil Liberties Union (ACLU), have effectively blocked many steps to increase public safety and health. Among the measures they systematically oppose are sobriety checkpoints (which can play an important role in reducing slaughter on the highways), *all* drug testing (even of those who have the lives of others directly in their control), and limiting the flood of private money into the pockets, drawers, and war chests of local and national elected representatives.

Having presented this fourth part of the Communitarian agenda before scores of groups, my colleagues and I have learned that this element of balancing rights and responsibilities is the most controversial. Hence a special discussion (in part two of this book) is dedicated to showing that such adjustments can be made—if the set of principles spelled out is followed—without opening the floodgates to a police state or excessive intrusion by public health departments. On the contrary, *the best way to curb authoritarianism and right-wing tendencies is to stop the anarchic drift by introducing carefully calibrated responses to urgent and legitimate public concerns* about safety and the control of epidemics.

Moral Reconstruction

Social responsibility is but one of the core virtues that need reaffirmation. We require a general *shoring up of our moral foundations.*

Since the early sixties, many of our moral traditions, social values, and institutions have been challenged, often for valid reasons. The end result is that we live in a state of increasing moral confusion and social anarchy. Once we were quite clear about what young couples were supposed to do—and refrain from doing—even if many of them did not fully live up to these expectations. The trouble now is not that the traditional family was undermined; it did deserve a critical going-over. The trouble is that no new concept of the family—of responsibility to children, of intimacy, and of commitment to one another—has emerged to replace the traditional form. (The fate of two books by Betty Friedan illustrates the difference: *The Feminine Mystique*, which was critical of the traditional family, was all the rage in the 1960s and early 1970s. Her second book, *The Second Stage*, published in 1981, which advocated the restructuring of the family, fell on deaf ears.) Moral transitions often work this way: destruction comes quickly. A vacuum prevails. Reconstruction is slow. This is where we are now: it is time to reconstruct, in the full sense of the term—not to return to the traditional, but to return to a moral affirmation, reconstructed but firmly held.

Once schools transmitted the moral and social values of previous generations to the young. Granted, these values were complacent, a bit authoritarian, and rather discriminatory. Did we shake them up! But this was the easy part, as destruction often is. Now we are all too often left with educational rubble. Schools are so overwhelmed simply by maintaining order and passing on elementary knowledge and skills that they have neither the time nor the inclination to attend to their most important mission: transmitting a core of values to the next generation.

In the fifties we were quite clear what our attitude toward authority figures should be: a great deal of respect and only a modicum of questioning. Parents, ministers, doctors, labor leaders, presidents—all commanded a fair amount of unchallenged moral authority to tell right from wrong, to guide the young and perplexed. The silent generation may well have been too silent and too compliant. It was largely blind to racial and gender discrimination, and it seems to have been genuinely unaware that millions of Americans lived in abject poverty. (It would take the undeniable data in Michael Harrington's *The Other America,* which was heralded by President John F. Kennedy, for poverty in America to be discovered.)

Since the 1950s we have cut our authority figures down to size. In the mid-sixties still nearly one-half of Americans expressed high confidence in the leaders of most institutions, from the military to Congress and from the press to corporations. Over the past twenty-five years, however, the proportion of Americans who have confidence in their leaders has dropped significantly. Public officials are daily skewered in the press. Once a venerated figure, Christopher Columbus has been brought down from his pedestal to be tried in the court of public opinion. Is he a national hero or a conquering murderer? asked *The New York Times* on Columbus Day 1991. Others, from George Washington to Martin Luther King, Jr., are being treated less kindly. Public opinion polls show that a majority of Americans believe that those in power do not care about their constituents. We are bereft of clear leadership in most matters, especially moral matters.

Liberal friends, who read a draft version of this book, expressed concern about the use of the term *moral*. Americans don't like to be told about morals, said one, and it sounds like preaching. Another suggested that the term reminds him of the Moral Majority. I do not mean to preach, but to share a concern and perhaps an agenda. I am sorry if I remind people of the Moral Majority, because I believe that although they raised the right questions they provided the wrong, largely authoritarian and dogmatic, answers. However, one of the purposes of this book is to retrieve for the realm of democratic discourse good, basic terms that we have allowed to become the political slogans of archconservatives and the right wing. Just because a Pat Robertson talked about family values, community, and morality when he tried to keep social conservatives in the Bush camp during election campaigns should not mean that the rest of us should shy away from applying these pivotal social concepts. And just because some abuse these terms to foment divisiveness and hate, and to attack all intellectuals or liberals as if they were one "cultural elite," hostile to all that is good in America, should not lead us implicitly to accept this notion. Just as we should not give up on patriotism because some politicians wrap themselves with the flag when it suits their narrow purposes, so should we not give up on morality because some abuse it to skewer their fellow community members.

Now we need to concern ourselves with shoring up the social foundations of morality, so that communities can again raise their moral voices, families can educate their youngsters, and schools can graduate individuals who will become upstanding members of their communities. We will attend to the question of whose values will prevail as the discussion unfolds. Here the emphasis is on the ability to articulate and sustain any set of values in a social world that has largely lost this capacity. This is the subject of the first part of the Communitarian agenda and of this book: shoring up the underpinnings of moral values.

As rights exploded and responsibilities receded, as the moral infrastructure crumbled, so did the public interest. True, special interests have always been with us. Moreover, pluralism—the rich fabric of various groupings, subcultures, and viewpoints—is a major foundation of the freedom that is the proud hallmark of this country, a country that was created by people fleeing enforced homogeneity.

But since the sixties, the forces that combined all the plurals into one mosaic—one society and one nation—have waned. The notion of a shared community or public interest, which balances but does not replace the plurality of particular interests, has been eroded. Political parties, vying over their conception of the public good, have been largely pushed aside; they have been replaced on center stage by myriad special interests and a Congress that is deeply indebted to them. Now all too often the dominant interests are not those of major segments of the population, such as consumers, workers, and industrialists. Instead they are those of groups that represent narrow, self-serving goals, such as parking lot owners seeking a special tax deduction, beehive owners in quest of a government subsidy, and organizations of sugar farmers, office equipment makers, and thousands of others. Their subsidies, tax concessions, special credits, and such consume large chunks of the public budget. Among them they are eating up the country's wealth and sapping its energy, leaving little for the projects that serve the commonweal—that is, all of us and our shared future. This is the subject of the third part of the Communitarian agenda and of this book: underwriting the public interest.

We, the Communitarians

Who are we? In 1990 a group of fifteen ethicists, social philosophers, and social scientists met in Washington, D.C., at the invitation of the author and his colleague, William Galston. As we explored matters that afflict our society, we expressed our distaste for the polarization of debate and the "sound bite" public life, the effects of teledemocracy. We were troubled by pressures to be labeled either conservative or liberal, pro-life or pro-choice, for or against the death penalty. We found that a person is under duress either to be for free trade or risks being labeled a Japan basher; either you are for immigration (presumably unlimited), or you are called a racist (because some of those who seek to limit immigration, seek to limit certain kinds of people); and so on. (I refer to this malaise as "the curse of either/or.") Many issues, we suggested, could not be properly discussed using such simplistic, stark, oppositional terms. And we saw the reaction to every group and speaker, "if you are not for us, you must be against us," as unnecessarily divisive, as antagonistic to the spirit of community.

More deeply, we were troubled by the finding that many Americans are rather reluctant to accept responsibilities. We were distressed that many Americans are all too eager to spell out what they are entitled to but are all too slow to give something back to others and to the community. We adopted the name *Communitarian* to emphasize that the time had come to attend to our responsibilities to the conditions and elements we all share, to the community.

As Communitarians we also recognized a need for a new social, philosophical, and political map. The designation of political camps as liberals or conservatives, as left or right, often no longer serves. We see at one extreme Authoritarians (such as the Moral Majority and Liberty Bell). They urge the imposition on all others of moral positions they believe in, from prayer in schools to forcing women to stay in the kitchen. At the other end we see Radical Individualists (libertarians such as the intellectuals at the Cato Institute; civil libertarians, especially the American Civil Liberties Union; and laissez-faire conservatives), who believe that if individuals are left on their own to pursue their choices, rights, and self-interests, all will be well. We suggest that *free individuals require a community,* which backs them up against encroachment by the state and sustains morality by drawing on the gentle prodding of kin, friends, neighbors, and other community members, rather than building on government controls or fear of authorities.

In January 1991 we published our first statement in the form of a new publication, a quarterly we named *The Responsive Community: Rights and Responsibilities.* It was a poorly timed move. The United States was in the midst of a recession, and people were preoccupied with making ends meet. Moreover, the countdown toward the war in the Persian Gulf had started; in fact, the war was launched within a week after our first issue appeared.

Nevertheless our ideas generated a tremendous response, indicating that the time was ripe for a change in course toward community rebuilding. First came the press. While we were still struggling with the premier issue of *The Responsive Community*, *BusinessWeek* got wind of our work and afforded our ideas a full page.

The magazine began by reporting the struggle of Ramona Younger, a black community activist who supports a local antiloitering law aimed at street corner drug dealers. "The system is not working for the decent law-abiding people, it is working for the perpetrators," she stated in an affidavit filed in Alexandria, Virginia. The ACLU and the National Association for the Advancement of Colored People were challenging the ordinance as racist and as an infringement of individual rights. But Younger argued that her ordinance is a helpful tool for those trying "to get the drug business off our streets." *BusinessWeek* noted:

> Younger has company in her concerns. An emerging group, sometimes called "communitarians," believes that the cause of the individual has gotten out of hand, jeopardizing community needs and public safety. For some in this movement, the problem is overemphasis on individual rights. Others are more troubled by what they see as rampant, irresponsible individualism throughout American society.

As our presses turned, *The Washington Post* shared with its readers in the nation's capital the new beginning:

> Communitarianism is not an organized movement but a catchword for a line of thought that Etzioni said seeks a middle ground between extreme libertarians who make personal rights an absolute and authoritarians who, he said, have sometimes talked of suspending constitutional rights to fight AIDS and drugs.

While the initial stories focused on our primary theme—rights and responsibilities—John Leo, in a column in *U.S. News & World Report* soon after the issue was released, captured well our community-building, restoring-the-moral-foundations theme:

One thing to note is that communitarianism is not the agenda of the right in new clothing, though it obviously has much in common with social conservatism. Here, for instance, is a communitarian perspective on plant closings: If a steel plant shuts down in Youngstown, why should the suddenly unemployed workers be left alone to pay the price for what is, predictably, the occasional result of our economic system?

Leo went on to explain:

In Japan and in Western nations not infected by American hyperindividualism, society pays heavily to retrain or relocate workers, partly out of a sense of justice, partly to avoid the negative social effects of plant closings—chiefly alcoholism and severe family stress.

He was the first to call attention to a misunderstanding that dogged us from the first day:

Community ethics have been used for so long to mask prejudice or to exclude minorities that communitarian thinking is likely to be suspect. But it is not simply majoritarianism. It does not exalt the group over the individual. It asks for social responsibility and laws based on connectedness. New York Mayor David Dinkins likes to refer to the city's racial and ethnic groups as "a gorgeous mosaic." A nice image, but as financier Felix Rohatyn replied, a mosaic needs some sort of glue to hold the pieces together.

The *Chronicle of Higher Education,* a publication that is widely read on college campuses, followed suit. Then *Time* magazine weighed in with a full-page story. Many others followed. We were on the map within months, not because we are brighter or better than the next person, but because Communitarian thinking is a way of approaching our condition whose time has come.

Community leaders, colleagues, ministers and rabbis, and fellow citizens sent us a most encouraging stream of mail. They offered suggestions and even volunteered to join in to help make the movement happen. Most astonishing, two foundations (which must usually be courted long and hard before they write a check) called us to ask if we would accept their contributions to our cause. (We readily acquiesced.)

On November 18, 1991, at a 1960s-style teach-in, we took the next step and issued a Communitarian platform, summarizing our approach and listing our basic positions (included at the back of the book). Seventy community leaders, from a wide variety of walks of life, joined us in signing the platform, which gave it more public recognition. As active citizens we shared the Communitarian platform with those in office, those running for office, and with those to whom they are accountable: our fellow citizens. At the teach-in we saw the first signs of interest not only in the public at large, but among our elected officials; four senators—two Democrats (Al Gore and Daniel Patrick Moynihan) and two Republicans (Dave Durenberger and Alan Simpson)—joined us for the teach-in. Strong letters of support followed from Senator Bill Bradley of New Jersey and Secretary of Housing and Urban Development Jack Kemp.

Although all this attention is gratifying, the future of Communitarian ideas and ideals lies not with Washington but with our fellow citizens, with you. What America needs, above all, is a change in the way we approach things, what we value and what we devalue, *a change of heart*. True, some of the matters at hand can be addressed through changes in public policy, but first and foremost we need a change in philosophy, a new way of thinking, a reaffirmation of a set of moral values that we may all share. This book is about this framework, these values, the Communitarian approach.

Be a Communitarian: Join the Movement

I am quite certain that success has not gone to our heads. We realize that despite the long way we have come in less than three years, much more ground remains to be negotiated. There are many issues that must be sorted out. This is not a task for thinkers and ethicists, although they do have their place. It is one in which all must participate, in communities and nationwide, in a grand dialogue about new and renewed directions. As these directions are identified, we must back them up, within our communities, across the land, and in Washington, D.C. *Ideas do not soar on their own wings.* If we are to have a more decent world, you and I must actively advance Communitarian ideas and ideals across neighbors' fences, in town hall meetings, in political debates, during call-in radio shows, and, above all, in our own lives. At issue is how to take care of our children, what we should ask of teachers in school (even if our children graduated long ago or if we do not have any), and what we can reasonably and fairly ask of other members of our neighborhood and what they can ask of us.

Please do not just read this book. Please try to respond. We in the Communitarian movement are keen to hear from you, and we hope you will tell others about the Communitarian framework. You may find some of the Communitarian ideas and ideals discussed here engaging enough to move you to explore and develop them further in conjunction with others and to lead the way by organizing Communitarian groups. If we are to enhance a richer set of values, the country needs groups of people concerned with bolstering our families, schools, and neighborhoods—our communities on the local and national levels—as the main conduits of a moral revival.

When social scientists examine the ways in which we may significantly alter a society as complex and as free as ours, they often conclude that the government is too heavy-handed, costly, and inappropriate an agency to confront most moral and many social issues. But when social scientists ask what social forces *have* profoundly shaped and reshaped our values and social lives, they regularly come up with the one and the same response: *social movements.* Thus, even if you think that the environmental movement has progressed too far or hasn't gone far enough, there is no question that it has permanently changed the way we live and deal with the world that surrounds us. Similarly, the civil rights movement of the sixties ensured that black Americans would have an effective right to vote and opened for minorities elected offices all over the country, including the Deep South. And in the eighties neoconservatives played a significant role in guiding us to rethink the liberal propensity to rely on federal bureaucracies to solve our problems. *What America needs now* is a major social movement dedicated to enhancing social responsibilities, public and private morality, and the public interest. We need you, your friends, your neighbors, and others we can reach to join with one another to forge a Communitarian movement.

You are certainly entitled to know more about what I am suggesting you get involved in. This book is my response. The Communitarian approach and agenda are laid out in three parts in the pages that follow. First, we discuss how we may reraise our moral voice—implant it in renewed families, cultivate it in schools, and shore it up in communities. Communities themselves need some major fixing if they are to provide the social foundation for a life that is more cognizant of the values we all share. Second, we examine how we can save the moral and civil order of communities from those who would mint ever more rights but who shy away from assuming responsibility. Specifically we discuss where to redraw the line between saying "Give me" and asking what you can do for your community. Third, we look critically at the political system. That is, how did it happen that interest groups captured so much of the national and local systems of governance and what we need to do to reenergize the public interest—the one that represents the community at large.

PART

I

Shoring Up Morality

1 ♦ The Moral Voice

The State of the Union's Morality

I N the fifties we had a clear set of values that spoke to most Americans, most of the time, with a firm voice. These values were often discriminatory against women (who were not allowed into many clubs, to have credit in their own name, or to advance far in their jobs) and against minorities, from blacks to Jews. They were also at least a bit authoritarian. When your doctor told you that you needed surgery, you did not even think of asking for a second opinion. When your boss ordered you around at work, you did not mention that the Japanese invite their workers to participate in decision making. When your priest, labor leader, or father spoke, he spoke with authority. Indeed, often such figures of authority expected unquestioning obedience. (When I addressed the board of the United Steelworkers in the early sixties at the Greenbrier Hotel in White Sulphur Springs, West Virginia, no board member so much as peeped until the head of the union, the forceful I. W. Abel, spoke and set the tone of the discussion that ensued.)

In the sixties all these voices and the values they spoke for were deeply challenged—as they ought to have been. That challenge, though, is *not* the reason for the moral predicament we find ourselves in these days in both private and public realms. The problem is that the waning of traditional values was not followed by a solid affirmation of new values; often nothing filled the empty spaces that were left when we razed existing institutions. The result is rampant moral confusion and social anarchy. We often cannot tell right from wrong—or cannot back up what we do believe in. Thus, while traditional authority figures were challenged, the new form of "participatory democracy" that was supposed to replace them remained largely a vague slogan. Above all, the young these days are bombarded with incessant violent, sexual, and commercial messages, but they hear relatively few credible, morally reaffirming voices.

The eighties tried to turn vice into virtue by elevating the un-bridled pursuit of self-interest and greed to the level of social virtue. It turned out that an *economy* could thrive (at least for a while) if people watched out only for themselves (although this is by no means as well documented as many economists suggest, and it is certainly not what the classic economist Adam Smith favored). But it has become evident that a *society* cannot function well given such self-centered, me-istic orientations. It requires a set of dos and don'ts, a set of moral values, that guides people toward what is decent and encourages them to avoid that which is not.

I often ask my students whether if they had a severe cash short-fall—in plain English, if they needed money badly—they would consider selling a kidney (the going price is about $10,000 in Europe). They look at me as if the old man has finally lost his senses, and I am proud of them. Their reaction is what we require in more areas. *We need to return to a society in which certain actions are viewed as beyond the pale,* things that upright people would not do or even consider: to walk out on their children, file false insurance claims, cheat on tests, empty the savings accounts of others, or force sexual advances on unwilling employees. We also need to return to a state in which there are a fair number of positive compelling commit-ments—the dos rather than the don'ts—that are beyond debate and dispute. When a sick child cries at night, a parent rushes to help. There is no need to consult clergy or a book by Kant to determine what one's duty is under such clear, elementary conditions. This is what Tocqueville and Communitarian sociologist Robert Bellah mean by "habits of the heart": values that command our support because they are morally compelling.

Communitarians do not suggest that we return to the traditional values of the fifties. We do not favor, say, a return to the "Leave It to Beaver" family (the father at work, the mother shut in the kitchen), but to a communitarian family—one in which both parents are actively and deeply involved in their children's upbringing. Similarly, Communitarians favor not a return to authoritarian leadership, but a climate that fosters finding agreed-upon positions that we can favor authoritatively.

We do require a set of social virtues, some basic settled values, that we as a community endorse and actively affirm. Thus, if we are to maintain our edge in an increasingly competitive world, workers will have to come to their jobs drug free and sober, stay sober all the time they are on the job, and give a day's work for a decent day's pay. We must reaffirm that expressions of hate toward members of other ethnic or racial groups, not to mention violent behavior, are intolerable. And although we may disagree on exactly how far we should go in protecting our shared environment (for example, what rights do spotted owls have?), we will most certainly express our disapproval of those who flush their engine oil down the drain, refuse to sort their garbage, or wash their cars and water their lawns when the town's water reservoir is low and falling. At the same time, we will continue to debate other values that are contested, seek changes in the prevailing consensus, and even rebel if we feel we are pushed too far, by moral claims or a choir of our peers.

The eighties was a decade in which "I" was writ large, in which the celebration of the self became a virtue. (The period was not unique, however, since such tendencies run far and deep in our national tradition.) Now is the time to push back the pendulum. The times call for an age of reconstruction, in which we put a new emphasis on "we," on values we share, on the spirit of community.

This is our particular American course. The people of China, Eastern Europe, and Japan for that matter may well need to move in the opposite direction: to make more room for self-expression, to slash excessive government control, and to roll back severely enforced moral codes that suppress creativity and impinge on individual rights. But this is not our problem at this stage of American history. To worry now about excessive "we-ness" is like suggesting in the depths of winter that we shouldn't turn on a space

Drawing by Mankoff. Copyright © 1991 by The New Yorker Magazine, Inc.

heater because it might make us sweat. People can freeze to death
that way. Our society is suffering from a severe case of deficient
we-ness and the values only communities can properly uphold;
restoring communities and their moral voice is what our current
conditions require.

When Communitarians argue that the pendulum has swung too
far toward the radical individualistic pole and it is time to hurry its
return, we do *not* seek to push it to the opposite extreme, of encouraging a community that suppresses individuality. We aim for a
judicious mix of self-interest, self-expression, and commitment to
the commons—of rights *and* responsibilities, of I and we. Hence the
sociological recommendation to move from "I" to "we" is but a
form of shorthand for arguing that a strong commitment to the
commons must now be *added* to strong commitments to individual
needs and interests that are already well ensconced. Balancing the
me-istic forces with a fair measure of resumed we-ness will bring

our society closer to a balanced position, without a significant tilt toward either side, a society able to steer a stable course.

Enter the Nineties

The nineties opened with a growing awareness that the previous decades had left in their wake a hodgepodge of notions but few firmly established moral positions. Social attitudes toward sex often speak volumes about how a society approaches moral and social matters in general. These days many parents are uncertain about what to say to their children about sexual matters. Ever since we gave up, in effect, on the notion that "one should save oneself for marriage," we talk vaguely about the need to have a "committed relationship" before intercourse. Many provide their kids with little more guidance than vague suggestions, such as "never on the first date" and "at least do it safely." No one should be surprised, then, that in contemporary America nearly one in seven American children has lost his or her virginity by the age of thirteen. Millions of teenagers see little meaning in life other than to have a child, without having a serious commitment to their infants. Marriage for many has become a *disposable* relationship. It is all too often entered into like a rental agreement—with an escape clause that if it does not suit the parties involved, they may look for another apartment. We are no longer clear if and when we ought to marry or if fidelity in marriage is to be expected. And if we beget children, it is unclear what we owe them.

The moral condition of other areas is similarly a source of concern. Almost half of Americans surveyed report chronic malingering at work and calling in sick when they are not sick; one-sixth admit that they have abused drugs or alcohol while at work. Six out of ten (59 percent) admit to having used physical force against another person—and fewer than half (45 percent) regret it. Twenty-five percent of Americans say they would abandon their families for money, and 7 percent admit freely that they would kill someone if paid enough. The moral patrimony of the eighties has been the proliferation of cost-benefit analysis into realms in which it has no place; it has devalued matters such as life, companionship, and integrity that ought not to be subject to such superficial quantification.

In public life one scandal follows closely on the heels of the previous one, as the terms of our moral covenant with our elected representatives are hazy. Do we expect public figures to serve as role models for the rest of us? We still chastise some in public life for having had an extramarital affair or for smoking a joint of marijuana (or for having lied about it), as we did Governor Bill Clinton, Senator Gary Hart, and Supreme Court nominee Douglas H. Ginsburg. But for decades we tolerated others who were obsessive womanizers and adulterers (such as Senator Edward Kennedy). We complained about elected representatives who kited checks or accepted money from special interests in the form of expensive junkets and sizable honoraria, but we reelected the same people year after year. More recently we have replaced these representatives with often rather similar persona.

Concomitantly, Americans' faith in the country's political system has dropped sharply. A 1991 poll found that almost half of all Americans (46 percent) believed that quite a few government officials were crooked, up from under 30 percent in the late 1950s. Further, 54 percent felt that the level of ethics and honesty had fallen in the past decade, and 59 percent didn't think that "public officials care much what people like me think," twice the number compared with the late fifties.

In the financial markets there is great confusion about whether insider trading is unethical, a practice that has caught the public eye. Other dubious practices are rampant, from "cornering the market" to churning accounts. James B. Stewart, an editor of *The Wall Street Journal* (hardly a hotbed of left-wing radicals), called his book about the markets *Den of Thieves*. (If you need more documentation, see Michael Lewis's *The Money Culture* or read *The Wall Street Journal* during any given week.)

Too many businesspeople no longer accept the responsibility of *stewardship,* at the very least to leave their communities no worse off than they found them. They no longer see it as their duty to reach beyond furthering self or corporate advancement or to serve as trustees of a social undertaking. Speculation, cronyism, bribery, and raiding of corporate coffers have left numerous savings and loans, banks, insurance companies, and pension funds teetering on the brink of insolvency and have shattered public confidence, which in turn damages the country's economic performance. Deregulated airlines have become less safe and monopolistic. Drug companies have continued to market drugs and devices such as silicone breast implants, artificial heart valves, and pacemakers long after they had found them to be unsafe. The list goes on.

Some argue that there is no pervasive moral erosion with America today but that we have become more attentive to moral abuses. For instance, they point out that there is less discrimination now against minorities and women than there was thirty years ago, not to mention compared with earlier periods. Instead of deliberate discrimination and disenfranchisement to the point of lynching, there are scores upon scores of black elected officials, and sheriffs, even in the Deep South. American males are learning that rape is a crime of violence and not something that women subconsciously ask for; they are even becoming more aware of the meaning of sexual harassment.

Others point out that matters are much worse in other countries, and not just in the Third World. Fair enough. We should acknowledge that we have made progress and that our standards in many areas are higher than those of countries such as Italy and France (say, in tax morality) and Japan (outright corruption and cronyism). This takes away nothing from the observation that in private matters such as family relations and business transactions and in public spheres from elected office to voluntary organizations, our moral foundations *are* crumbling, and shoring up is overdue. The fact that some others in some areas are less ethical than we are does not belie the fact that our morality in key areas has been corroded.

Similarly, it is true that throughout history, parents, especially fathers, have run off and left their children behind. But since the sixties we have witnessed a mass exodus of both parents from the home to the workplace. The members of the younger generation cannot learn the difference between right and wrong if they're left alone at home while their parents are out pursuing their careers and do not find the time required to educate them. Traders have surely shortchanged customers, and merchants have tipped the scales in their favor from the first days bazaars were open. But no economy can thrive when greed is so overpowering that few have a motive to invest in the long run and the highest rewards go to those who engage in financial manipulations rather than constructive enterprises.

Elected representatives may well have had extramarital affairs ever since the Founding Fathers met in Philadelphia, and many may well have imbibed more liquor than is proper for anyone. But the fact is that the personal conduct of many of today's elected officials provides a rather poor role model for us to emulate, and many legislators are in the pockets of special interests to an extent that is highly troubling to anyone concerned about the integrity and well-being of American democracy.

To put it in more general terms: *No society can function well unless most of its members "behave" most of the time because they voluntarily heed their moral commitments and social responsibilities.* There can never be enough police and FBI, IRS, and customs agents, inspectors, and accountants to monitor the billions of transactions that occur every day. And who will guard the guardians? Even if half the society were to police the other half, who would police this vast police to ensure that *it* obeyed the law? The only way the moral integrity of a society can be preserved is for most of the people, most of the time, to abide by their commitments voluntarily. The police powers of the government should be called upon only as a last resort to deal with the small number of sociopaths and hard-core recalcitrants, those who do not have moral commitments or sufficient impulse control to heed those commitments.

Unfortunately the record shows, even after only a cursory examination of our world, that from drug abuse to corporate crime, illegal and immoral behaviors have broken through this important line of voluntary self-restraint. Large segments of the population do not voluntarily do what they are supposed to do. It follows that we must shore up our moral foundations to allow the markets, government, and society to function properly again.

Morality as a Community Affair

Conscience Is Not Enough

How do we shore up morality? How can we encourage millions of individuals to develop a stronger sense of right and wrong? First, it is essential to reiterate that morality does not soar on its own wings. True, the ultimate custodian of moral conduct is a person's own conscience. However, individuals' consciences are neither in-born nor—for most people—self-enforcing. We gain our initial moral commitments as new members of a community into which we are born. Later, as we mature, we hone our individualized versions out of the social values that have been transmitted to us. As a rule, though, these are variations on community-formed themes. Thus, many Americans are more socially concerned and active than other nationalities, not because of differences in genes or basic human nature, but because social concern and activism are major elements of this country's moral tradition. If we were living instead in traditional Korea, the same energy would be dedicated to, say, ensuring that we conducted ourselves properly toward numerous relatives. That is, the mainspring of our values is the community or communities into which we are born, that educated us (or neglected to educate us), and in which we seek to become respectable members during our adult lives.

Most important for the issue at hand is the sociological fact that we find reinforcement for our moral inclinations and provide reinforcement to our fellow human beings, through the community. We are each other's keepers. As Common Cause founder John Gardner writes:

> Families and communities are the ground-level generators and preservers of values and ethical systems. No society can remain vital or even survive without a reasonable base of shared values. . . . They are generated chiefly in the family, schools, church, and other intimate settings in which people deal with one another face to face.

When the term *community* is used, the first notion that typically comes to mind is a place in which people know and care for one another—the kind of place in which people do not merely ask "How are you?" as a formality but care about the answer. This we-ness (which cynics have belittled as a "warm, fuzzy" sense of community) is indeed part of its essence. Our focus here, though, is on another element of community, crucial for the issues at hand: *Communities speak to us in moral voices. They lay claims on their members.* Indeed, they are the most important sustaining source of moral voices other than the inner self.

Communitarians, who make the restoration of community their core mission, are often asked which community they mean.

The local community? The national community? The sociologically correct answer is that communities are best viewed as if they were Chinese nesting boxes, in which less encompassing communities (families, neighborhoods) are nestled within more encompassing ones (local villages and towns), which in turn are situated within still more encompassing communities, the national and cross-national ones (such as the budding European Community). Moreover, there is room for nongeographic communities that crisscross the others, such as professional or work-based communities. When they are intact, they are all relevant, and all lay moral claims on us by appealing to and reinforcing our values.

But, we are asked, given the multiple communities to which people belong (the places where they live and work, their ethnic and professional associations, and so on), can't a person simply choose at will which moral voice to heed? Aren't people using the values of one community to free themselves from obligations that others may press on them—leaving them free to do what they fancy? It is true that you can to some extent play these multiple affiliations against one another, say, spend more time with friends at work when people in the neighborhood became too demanding. However, societies in which different communities pull in incompatible directions on basic matters are societies that experience moral confusion; have moral voices that do not carry. We need—on all levels, local, national—to agree on some basics.

The Community as a Moral Voice

How can the moral voice of the community function when it is well articulated and clearly raised?

I lived for a year on the Stanford University campus. Not far from the house I rented was a four-way stop sign. Each morning I observed a fairly heavy flow of traffic at the intersection. Still, the cars carefully waited their turns to move ahead, as they were expected to. The drivers rarely moved out of turn, and in those cases when they did, the offenders often had out-of-state license plates. The main reason for the good conduct: practically everyone in the community knew who was behind the wheel. If someone rushed through, he or she could expect to be the subject of some mild ribbing at the faculty club, supermarket, or local movie theater (such as "You must have been in an awful rush this morning"). This kind of community prodding usually suffices to reinforce the proper behavior that members of the community acquire early—in this case, observing safe traffic patterns.

When I first moved to a suburb of Washington, D.C., I neglected to mow my lawn. One neighbor asked politely if I needed "a reference to a good gardener." Another pointed out that unless we all kept up the standards of the neighborhood, we would end up with an unsightly place and declining property values. Soon after I moved into a downtown cooperative building, the tenants were sent memos that reminded us to sort our garbage. Various exhortations were used ("It is good for the environment"), and a floor representative was appointed to "oversee" compliance. I never found out what the representative actually did; the very appointment and reminders seemed sufficient for most residents to attend to their trash properly.

It might be said that I have lived in middle-class parts. It is well established, however, that many working-class and immigrant communities—to the extent that they are intact—uphold their values. These are often further modulated and backed up by the ethnic groups. Thus the specific values may differ from a Cuban to an Irish neighborhood, or from an Asian to a black one, but all communities sustain values. Their concerns may vary from what is the proper way to conduct a wake or a confirmation to how much help a new immigrant can expect or whether a local shopkeeper will hire illegal aliens. But it is mainly in instances in which there is no viable community, in which people live in high-rise buildings and do not know one another, in some city parts in which the social fabric is frayed, and in situations in which people move around a lot and lose most social moorings, that the social underpinnings of morality are lost.

The examples of moral voices that carry that I have cited so far are about matters of limited importance, such as lawns and garbage. Hence, community responses to those who disregard the shared values have been appropriately mild. When people misbehave in more serious ways, the community's response tends to be stronger, especially when the community is clear about what is right and wrong. If someone's child speeds down the street as though there were no tomorrow or throws beer bottles at passersby, the rebuke is appropriately sharper. People may say to parents "We are all deeply troubled about what happened the other day when you were not home" or "For the sake of the safety of all of us, we [meaning you] must find a way to ensure that this will not happen again." Basketball star David Robinson once explained to a TV interviewer that instead of telling everybody that "you are great," he "gets into the face" of those who need to be told right from wrong. Americans brought up on Dale Carnegie, anxious never to give offense, may find such an approach a bit moralistic. Well, as I see it, *what we need now is less "how to win friends and influence people" and more how to restore the sway of moral voices.*

Most important, the moral voice does not merely censure; it also blesses. We appreciate, praise, recognize, celebrate, and toast those who serve their communities, from volunteer fire fighters to organizers of neighborhood crime watches. Members of a neighborhood constantly share tales of how wonderful it was that this or that individual organized a group to take care of the trees on the side of the road, rushed to welcome the new families that escaped from Iran, or whatever. It is these positive, fostering, encouraging, yet effective moral voices that we no longer hear with sufficient clarity and conviction in many areas of our lives.

The Fear of Moral Claims

Often when I speak about the need to shore up the moral voice of our communities, I observe a sense of unease. Americans do not like to tell other people how to behave. I first ran into the fear many liberal people have of formulating and expressing moral claims, of articulating the moral voice of the community, when I taught at Harvard. A faculty seminar was conducted on the ethical condition of America. The first session was dedicated to a discussion of what our agenda should be. I suggested a discussion of the moral implications of the decline of the American family. Nobody objected, but nobody picked up on the idea, either; it was politely but roundly ignored. When I later asked two members of the seminar why my suggestion had been accorded such a quiet burial, they explained that they (and presumably other members of the seminar) were uncomfortable discussing the subject. "If a high-profile group of ethicists at Harvard would form a consensus on the matter, it might put a lot of pressure on people, and it might even be used to change the laws [on divorce]."

Sociologist M. P. Baumgartner found that in an American suburb he studied in the 1980s, people who observed minor violations of conduct often simply ignored them rather than express their displeasure. If the violations were somewhat serious, people tended to ostracize the offenders without explanation. If they did confront a miscreant—say, a person who burned chicken feathers in his backyard and stank up the neighborhood, mowed the lawn early in the morning, or left a barking dog out at night—they were likely to ask him to cease the behavior as a *favor* to them, rather than labeling it as something a decent person would not do.

This disinclination to lay moral claims undermines the daily, routine social underwriting of morality. It also hinders moral conduct in rather crucial situations.

During a conference on bone-marrow transplants, a psychiatrist argued that it was not proper to ask one sibling for a bone-marrow donation for another sibling, despite the fact that making such a donation does not entail any particular risk. His reason was that the sibling who refused might feel guilty, especially if as a result the brother or sister died. On the contrary, a Communitarian would argue that siblings should be asked in no uncertain terms to come to the rescue. If they refuse, they *should* feel guilty.

When I discuss the value of moral voices, people tell me they are very concerned that if they lay moral claims, they will be perceived as self-righteous. If they mean by "self-righteous" a person who comes across as without flaw, who sees himself as entitled to dictate what is right (and wrong), who lays moral claims in a sanctimonious or pompous way—there is good reason to refrain from such ways of expressing moral voices. But these are secondary issues that involve questions of proper expressions and manner of speech.

At the same time we should note that given our circumstances, our society would be much better off if some of its members sometimes erred on the side of self-righteousness (on which they are sure to be called) than be full of people who are morally immobilized by a fear of being considered prudish or members of a "thought police." I personally regret occasions I did not speak up about some foul tricks Japan plays on us, because I feared being called a Japan basher; I should have called it the way I saw it. And I realize that when I speak of the value of the two-parent family, many of my single-parent friends frown. I do not mean to put them down, but their displeasure should not stop me or anybody else from reporting what we see as truthful observations and from drawing morally appropriate conclusions. It is my contention that *if we care about attaining a higher level of moral conduct than we now experience, we must be ready to express our moral sense,* raise our moral voice a decibel or two. In the silence that prevails, it may seem as if we are shouting; actually we are merely speaking up.

As more and more of us respond to the claims that we ought to assume more responsibilities for our children, elderly, neighbors, environment, and communities, moral values will find more support. Although it may be true that markets work best if everybody goes out and tries to maximize his or her own self-interest (although that is by no means a well-proven proposition), moral behavior and communities most assuredly do not. They require people who care for one another and for shared spaces, causes, and future. Here, clearly, it is better to give than to take, and the best way to help sustain a world in which people care for one another—is to care for some. The best way to ensure that common needs are attended to is to take some responsibility for attending to some of them.

To object to the moral voice of the community, and to the moral encouragement it provides, is to oppose the social glue that helps hold the moral order together. It is unrealistic to rely on individuals' inner voices and to expect that people will invariably do what is right completely on their own. Such a radical individualistic view disregards our social moorings and the important role that communities play in sustaining moral commitments. Those who oppose statism must recognize that communities require some ways of making their needs felt. They should welcome the gentle, informal, and—in contemporary America—generally tolerant voices of the community, especially given that the alternative is typically state coercion or social and moral anarchy.

True, there have been occasions in the past when community voices were stridently raised to justify coercion. More than forty years ago, for example, America experienced the nightmare of McCarthyism. Likewise the memory of the real Ku Klux Klan (today's Klansmen are largely a defanged and pathetic bunch) serves to warn us against the excesses of community. A colleague asks: "What if the community demands that children with AIDS not be allowed to attend public schools, or that a family of color not be allowed to buy a home in a neighborhood?" (One might add, what if the community decided to burn books?) In response I suggest that no community has a right to violate higher-order values, values that we all should share as a society, or even humanity, values that prescribe rules of behavior such as "Do unto others only as you wish others would do unto you."

Moreover, we do constantly need to be on guard against self-centered communities, just as we need to watch out for self-centered individuals. (I'll discuss ways to be on guard later in this book.) However, we do not forgo cars just because some drive them dangerously. The same holds, many times over, for the moral voices of communities. The fact that those voices are to be raised in moderation, and only in ways that do not violate overarching values, should not hide the fact that we cannot be a civil and decent society without a moral voice. Try the following mental experiment: Ask yourself what the alternatives are to the exercise of moral voices. There are only two: a police state, which tries to maintain civic order by brute force, or a moral vacuum in which anything goes.

Look also at the historical condition we are in. As we have seen, at this particular stage in our history signs of moral deficiencies abound, while incidents of excessive moralism are few and far between. The fact is that many thousands of communities keep all kinds of books in their libraries, while each year not more than a handful try to ban them; and most of them are stopped from proceeding by those who are committed to our liberties. True, ugly and deeply disturbing incidents of racial hatred and other forms of bigotry (such as gay bashing) continue, especially in some cities. Unfortunately they grab headlines, leaving the impression that they are the norm. Actually there are hundreds of places in which people of different backgrounds, orientations, and persuasions work and live together peacefully. In short, excessive moralism is not exactly our current problem.

In principle there is no reason to deny that there are always the twin dangers of too much and too little social pressure. As when we ride a bike, we need to lean in the opposite direction of where the course of social history is tilting us. The bulk of the evidence shows that in recent decades we have been tilting too far in the direction of letting everybody do their own thing or pursue their own interests and have concerned ourselves too little with our social responsibilities and moral commitments. It is time to set things aright.

What About "Coercion"?

Many Radical Individualists *confuse the right to be free from government intrusion with a nonexistent "right" to be exempt from the moral scrutiny of one's peers and community.* Any form of social encouragement or pressure is quickly branded "coercion." Jonathan Rauch, who is writing a book on this subject, discusses the uproar that ensued at Georgetown University Law School after publication of a campus newspaper article that had alleged that the school admits blacks who are much less qualified than whites. The uproar was interpreted correctly as pressure on the law school to treat all applicants as equal. Whether or not one agrees with this position, all we have here is speech. Those who objected to this view, however, were quick to brand it as violence. One student declares that the "article is assaultive. People were injured." On another occasion, Duke professor Stanley Fish commented: "[President Bush] talks about the assault on free speech on campus. . . . What he doesn't note is that the speech that is being assaulted is itself assaultive speech. . . ."

As I see it, suasion is not coercion, because coercion entails the use of force. Moral suasion carries no threat of imprisonment, deportation, physical harm to one's loved ones, or even destruction of property. As a result, the ultimate decision of how to conduct oneself when one is subject to suasion, as distinct from coercion, rests with the individual. Ultimately, most times if a person does not accede to the community's moral urgings, nobody will make the person "behave." He or she may not be invited over for coffee or be asked to sit at the head of the table during community celebrations, and people may even refuse to chat over the back fence or at the store or bar, but typically this is more or less as far as it goes.

Branding these moral expressions "coercion" and putting them in the same category as taking someone by the scruff of the neck and carrying him off, say, to a forced labor camp until he toes the line is to confuse the normal social give-and-take with the tactics of a police state. True, sometimes moral suasion turns into violence (although these are the exceptions to the rule); we must oppose such violence with the full conviction of our moral voice, but without eliminating the essential moral expressions.

It is crucial not to confuse strong moral expressions with the use of violence, precisely because we do not want to allow the first to spill over into the second. Thus, Anne Sinclair, a French television journalist, confounds the two realms when she asks (given all the attention that has been paid to American politicians' extramarital affairs) if "one [can] still court a woman in America in 1992 without moral terrorism winning a complete victory." Whether or not you believe that sexual adventurism should disqualify a person from public office is a completely legitimate, appropriate topic. Use of terror to advance your values in a democratic society is illegitimate and abhorrent.

Much of what Communitarians favor has little to do with laws and regulations, which ultimately draw on the coercive powers of the state, but with being active members of a community. Whether the activity is learning cardiopulmonary resuscitation (or CPR, which allows someone to restart a failing heart) or forming or joining a neighborhood crime watch, members of communities make them work for one another. In the past—and, to a lesser extent, today—ethnic associations bore a great deal of the burden of absorbing new immigrants. These seriously social activities nourish vital parts of the community, making its members true participants in its shared life and allowing them to draw significant parts of their inner lives and satisfaction from serving one another and their common causes.

Does that mean that every act of moral observance is completely and purely voluntary? The answer is yes, if by "voluntary" acts we mean those propelled by moral voices within the community that are neither forced nor motivated by the threat of a lawsuit or a gun, nor accompanied by a fist or other violence, nor driven by the state. If by "voluntary" we mean, however, that people do right only out of the goodness of their hearts, that inner drives and pangs of conscience are the wellsprings of their actions, then moral acts egged on by moral voices of the community do not qualify.

Take the example of a charity fund-raiser. People of means are invited to participate, knowing full well that they will be asked to make hefty contributions to pay, say, for soup kitchens and mobile clinics for the homeless. They attend the function in part because they feel it is morally proper to contribute, in part because they like the recognition, and in part because they expect to spend the time with friends and maybe even make some new business contacts—or find a date. During the event they come under some social "pressure" to contribute more than they had originally intended to give—assuming they came with a clear limit in mind, which is often not the case. Perhaps it's the excitement or because others have contributed more and they are embarrassed to be less generous—the result is that they end up pledging more than they had intended, to a cause to which they were committed long before they came to the fund-raiser. It would be foolish to call such behavior "coerced." We should not be troubled by such mild social pressure; it is an essential part of the moral life of a community. Only when it is used for immoral purposes (for example, to pressure teenagers to become sexually active when they are unwilling) or becomes excessive (such as excommunicating people for their beliefs) need we concern ourselves.

To put it differently, to the extent that we have lost community, we need to rebuild it, not only because community life is a major source of satisfaction of our deeper personal needs, but because the social pressures community brings to bear are a mainstay of our moral values.

"The Puritans Are Coming"

In the early nineties Communitarians began to call for a moral recommitment and were gratified by the positive response we received. But as soon as there were signs that Americans were again inclined to lay moral claims on one another and to express their moral concerns somewhat more firmly, critics raised the specter of a moral police. They dubbed the fledgling movement "neopuritanism" and depicted our rather gentle proddings as the work of zealots and meddlesome busybodies.

A summer 1991 cover story in *Time* magazine railed against the dangers of busybodies "humorlessly imposing on others arbitrary (meaning their own) standards of behavior, health and thought." The London *Economist* cautioned against dangers associated with trying to legislate our social problems out of existence. Both labeled this new wave of American morality a form of puritanism. Let me first acknowledge that puritanism is a potential danger for the Communitarian movement. Puritanism, at its worst, was a rigid social order maintained through fear and conformity and denying dissent. Even in our age a community may get carried away and make its moral consensus too tight and too imposing, as one can readily see in Saudi Arabia, where women must robe almost their entire bodies and cannot go out alone if they are single. In Iran, until recently, special officials called *komitehs* patrolled the streets to ensure that no sign of hair showed from beneath the *chador,* not to mention other parts of the female anatomy. In an earlier period in the United States, such excesses were found in Salem, Massachusetts, where, some argue, puritanism led to witch-hunts, as depicted in Arthur Miller's play *The Crucible.*

Critics are correct to point to the hypothetical danger that a small number of American ayatollahs could impose their capricious moral perspective on the rest of the community through loyalty oaths, condemnations, and excommunications. There have already been some attempts to limit the teaching of evolution (by insisting that creationism be given equal standing in schools), to impose specific prayers in public schools, and to close abortion clinics. But because the religious Right is generally in disarray—televangelism has been rocked by a series of salacious scandals, and the Moral Majority is an increasingly irrelevant minority—America is currently experiencing significantly less intolerance from these quarters than was often true in the past. Note, for instance, that juries refused to convict museum directors who displayed what Senator Jesse Helms (and quite a few other Americans) considered to be obscene pictures and paintings. (I should add that in my judgment the question of whether taxpayer money should be used to pay for such exhibits is a legitimate question. However, nothing should be done—and rather little is done—to prevent creating or displaying works of which many may disapprove.) The pressure to "bring God back into the classroom" (as if He needed an invitation from a government agency or a summons from a board of education to be present) is a matter we heard much more about in earlier decades than in the nineties. And no Pat Robertsons presented themselves as preacher-politicians in the 1992 presidential election.

When I discuss these matters on radio call-in shows, someone invariably brings up the fact that a few extreme pro-lifers attempted to close abortion clinics by throwing bombs, setting fires, and other acts of violence. (Similar acts have been committed by some extreme advocates of animal rights.) As I see it, this is not reflective of the way contemporary America typically deals with moral issues or questions of public policy. On the contrary, on most issues—from the right to health care to questions of what is the proper character for our elected officials to the amount of aid we should give to Israel or to Russia—debates are just that: debates. Moreover, the moral voices that have been raised recently—Communitarian early birds—tend to reflect the consensus of the community rather than the notions of isolated busybodies and moralizers. Thus we agree with one another that creationism will not be taught in public schools, that there will be no prayers in public schools, and so on. A new community campaign such as "Friends don't let friends drive drunk" is another case in point. So are neighborhood crime watches, which continue to spring up across the country. While Radical Individualists keep warning us that these community activists will turn into vigilantes and chase minorities out of the neighborhood, the fact is that such incidents are very rare among the thousands of such neighborhood associations. The abortion issue is unusual in that the two camps are locked into an uncompromising, I-am-right/you-are-evil confrontation.

These days it is much more common to find so-called communities that have lost most of their moral convictions and in which practically anything goes and most people attend to their own knitting, caring little about what goes on around them.

No matter what the Radical Individualists claim, such rare incidents do not constitute nationwide trends. Thus a Penn State student sees in arguments that the placement of Goya's *Naked Maja* in a classroom constituted sexual harassment (a claim made by one professor), "a puritanism [that] has created false and poor conceptions. . . . This prudishness is making it impossible for some people to accept a great (and old) work like the *Naked Maja*." An isolated incident such as this does not make an American cultural pattern.

To demonstrate that America has become "the punitive society," the London *Economist* writes that Americans "reprimand a neighbor for kissing her boyfriend good night on the steps of her house and so lowering the tone of the block (as happened recently in California)." While I am sure that sooner or later everything conceivable happens once or twice in California, this incident constitutes no American pattern. Indeed, the storm of unfavorable publicity surrounding the event suggests just the opposite: the busybodies were widely reprimanded, and kissing in California and elsewhere continues unabated on doorsteps and in quite a few other places.

The *Economist* sites another example of rising American punitiveness: "if you lose your job you can sue for the mental distress of being fired." (No time or place was mentioned.) Although it is true that one can sue for practically any reason, it is extremely unlikely that a case could be won on such grounds.

True, there are a few potentially more disturbing incidents. To assess them properly, it is necessary to distinguish among three realms that are often lumped together: new or renewed values foisted by members of the community on one another; values imposed by corporations on their employees; and values that are underwritten by law.

Puritanism Within Communities

In some communities members put strong pressure on those who live and work within their confines to be religiously committed. They allow some leeway in terms of which religion their members may adhere to, but these communities will express concern, if not dismay, over those who are atheists or agnostics. (Nor will the followers of Islam or Buddhism be nearly as welcome as those who subscribe to the various Christian denominations.) Or local moral pressures may lock in some other value—for instance, making all those who are not married after a certain age feel inferior. But as long as these preferred moral expressions do not lead to discrimination against those who do not abide by them, not to mention coercion, they do not amount to puritanism. Those who wish to follow other courses may join other communities, form their own communities—or put up with the fact that many people in a given community will avoid social contact with them. This may sound somewhat intimidating until one realizes that one may change one's community without changing one's residence, by joining a differ-ent social club, place of worship, and so on.

   The best way to minimize the role of the state, especially its policing role, is to enhance the community and its moral voice. If most of us, most of the time, observed the speed limit, especially near schools and where children play, there would be much less need for police. If we basically paid our share of the taxes due, there would be less need for IRS agents and auditors. If divorced fathers paid agreed-upon amounts of child support, there would be no need for the state to go after them. There are always some who violate what is right, and hence the state is unlikely to wither away, at least until very far-reaching and fundamental changes occur in human nature. However, such limited use of the state, for a handful of miscreants, is not the issue. What we must try to avoid is relying on the state to maintain social order, which can be achieved more humanely and at less cost by the voluntary observance of those values we all hold dear, such as driving without endangering others and paying our share of the communities' burdens. In short, the more people gen-erally agree with one another about what is to be done and encour-age one another to live up to these agreements, the smaller the role that coercive authority will play and the more civil the community.

Corporations and Their Puritanical Tendencies

The critics of the new morality, those who evoke the specter of neopuritanism, point to corporations that use their economic power to force their employees to behave. Businesses, they say, are insist-ing that their employees refrain from smoking, avoid drug abuse, lose weight, exercise, and so on. They bring up the case of a secu-rity guard at the *Los Angeles Times* who was dismissed, despite an excellent performance record, because he was overweight. And they tell the story of Janice Bone, from Wabash, Indiana, who lost her job at a company called Ford Meter Box. Why? Because she violated a company rule against smoking on or off the job. How did the company know? It insisted on a urine test, in which nicotine was found. Indeed, there are many similar cases.

   Some of these measures may be prudent and hardly smack of neopuritanism. Thus, if a guard's potbelly is so overwhelming that he cannot give chase, a corporation may ask the guard to lose some weight.

Moreover, corporations that explicitly inform persons who apply for jobs, before they are retained, that the job entails, say, drug testing leave the choice up to the employee whether or not he or she wishes to join such a workplace. (Economic coercion enters here only if there are no other jobs to be had, which is true only for a small proportion of the labor force.)

True, according such a free choice does not automatically render ethical and proper all corporate requirements. The courts have already ruled that corporations (and other parties) may not impose conditions of employment that are unconstitutional. For example, no one may sell a person as if he or she were a slave. Even if a person were to consent to such a condition, it would still be legally invalid and unenforceable. When the requirements are constitutional, however, prior notification that the job entails, say, computer monitoring of the quality of the work carried out adds to the legitimacy of the claims. There is nothing in the Constitution to prevent companies from insisting that their employees be sober and not high on drugs. (The Constitution bars *unreasonable* search and seizure, but drug tests for a large number of categories of employees have been repeatedly ruled reasonable by the courts.)

Much of the conduct at issue has clear consequences for others, and corporations may legitimately take it into account. For example, smoking affects not merely the smoker, but his or her co-workers; drunken pilots endanger not only themselves, but the lives of the airlines' passengers; and so on. Note that reference is being made to conduct that may significantly affect work or the public interest. I will turn to a full-scale discussion of the ways we may tell what is significant and where to draw the line when I examine the balance between rights and responsibilities (in part II of this book).

Much more problematic is the question of whether corporations may ban behavior that occurs outside the workplace. As a general rule, these prohibitions are appropriate only if employees' private behavior significantly affects their on-the-job performance. For example, studies show that alcohol consumption impairs behavior as long as twenty-four hours later. Hence pilots may be expected not to drink for a given period before they come to work, even if it means placing restrictions on what they may consume in their "free" time. Drugs that lead to unexpected bouts of hallucination or paranoia, such as PCP and LSD, may be banned at any time, at least until we know more about the duration of their effects. By the same criteria, private behavior that cannot be shown to affect on-the-job performance should not be corporations' business.

Finally, there remains the question of the propriety of corporations trying to control private behavior that affects only health care costs, a tab that they pick up. For example, a small property-development firm in Atlanta prohibits its employees from engaging in "hazardous activities and pursuits" such as skydiving, mountain climbing, and motorcycling. Best Lock Corporation of Indianapolis forbids alcohol consumption by its employees, even after work. The city of North Miami has a policy against hiring smokers. So does Turner Broadcasting. Fortunoff's, a retailer, charges employees who smoke $12.50 more a week for health insurance costs. Both Texas Instruments and U-Haul International also have monthly health insurance surcharges for smokers. Some states have responded by passing legislation prohibiting employer discrimination based on off-the-job smoking or some other legal off-the-job activity.

Should corporations attempt to regulate this type of behavior? Probably not. In fact, this may be a good place to limit the reach of corporate morals. An important criterion for corporate intervention—protecting the life and limb of others besides the offender—is not met, and if we go farther down this road, there is no stopping. Most behavior affects health costs in some way, and if we endorse this kind of paternalism, soon we'll see corporations insisting that we go to bed early, floss and brush our teeth regularly, engage only in heterosexual intercourse with one partner, and meditate frequently to reduce stress.

In short, when private behavior directly affects job performance, corporations may step in. Otherwise they should refrain from regulating the private affairs of their employees. This does not mean that anything goes after hours, only that the proper people to deal with private behavior are those who share in it: fellow family members, neighbors, and the community in which the behavior takes place.

By Force of Law: Shades of Authoritarianism?

Radical Individualists are particularly troubled by America's alleged proclivity to impose the new morality by force of law. They equate such laws with authoritarian tendencies. Government controls, states the *Economist*, are nothing more than an archaic form of Eastern European social engineering. Ira Glasser, the executive director of the American Civil Liberties Union (ACLU), wrote the following to *The Wall Street Journal* in response to a Communitarian article I had written:

> It is ironic indeed that at a time when the early American idea of individual rights as the highest purpose of government is reasserting itself all over the world—in the Soviet Union and elsewhere—Prof. Etzioni would choose to revive in this country the profoundly dangerous and statist notion that individual rights and the common good occupy distinct and oppositional spheres. If this is communitarianism, who needs it?

Actually, a world of difference separates Eastern Europe's former Communist party regimes from ours. Laws in the United States are arrived at democratically and not imposed by a tyrannical government. They are limited in scope and are neither omnipresent nor totalitarian. Moreover their enforcement is subject to public scrutiny, democratic approval, and constitutional checks; gulags, secret police, and torture chambers are alien to the American scene.

Second, laws do represent, in every society, a proper method of expressing social and moral values and of signaling conduct that the community considers proper or abhorrent—even when these laws are rarely enforced through fines, jail sentences, or other coercive means. Mary Ann Glendon explains in *Rights Talk*:

> At the very least, judges and legislators need to be more conscious of the radiating pedagogical effects of their activities in a law-saturated society. Lawmakers and law-sayers have more responsibility today than ever before to consider how their words will be understood—not only within a professional community schooled to distinguish between law and morality,

but by a wider public that experiences these spheres as overlapping and interpenetrating.

Thus we do not approve of adultery, and our laws used to say so,
even if they were typically only "on the books." When we changed
the laws that apply to divorce to make it "no fault," far from being
viewed as a technical change or as way to make divorce less costly,
many considered the new law to be one more indication that the
community was less troubled by easy divorce than it had been. For
much the same reason, if we were now to enact somewhat stricter
divorce requirements, it would signal that we were restoring our
respect for the family. It is important, then, to recognize the *ex-
pressive power* that law holds for the community's moral concerns
and for influencing what is deemed appropriate and inappropriate
behavior.

Third, the law as a deterrent has its place in any moral order.
Morality rests on intricate interactions among three factors: individual conscience, the moral voice of the community, and the state.
Each one helps to sustain the others. Hence, while it is best to build
up individual consciences and community voices, communities
must on occasion fall back on the law. Without punishing those
who do serious injury to our commonly held values—child abusers,
toxic polluters, fathers who renege on child support, corporations
who market unsafe drugs—no moral order can be sustained. We do
not have to love the coercive side of the law, but we cannot fail to
recognize its place as a last resort.

One example will have to stand for numerous others that could
be cited: To enhance public safety, there must be fewer drunken
drivers. To combat drunk driving we need, among other things,
more people who fully embrace the notion of a designated driver
(the way Scandinavians do)—that is, choosing one person per car
who will not consume alcohol during an outing or party. This
practice is best introduced as a social and moral expectation. For
example, if both a husband and wife consumed alcohol at a party,
they would be subject to social criticism (unless, of course, they
carpooled). Those who stated with pride (as if they were saying
"Look how responsible I am!") that they were abstaining—because
they were designated drivers—would gain social approbation. I do
not mean a standing ovation, but the kind of informal cues—such

as a nod or a word of support—that we are quite familiar with, but the importance of which we tend to overlook.

For those who do not pay attention to these Communitarian cues, however, we need to support sobriety checkpoints (rather than fight them, as the ACLU does) to help enforce the new social and moral tenets. Ultimately the changed moral valuation of drunk driving will significantly reduce the need for such checkpoints. Whatever state action is needed is to be limited to buttressing new or renewed moral values and those endorsed by the consensus of the community.

I do not dispute that authorities sometimes get carried away and impose laws in an authoritarian, even brutal, manner; the clubbing of Rodney King comes to mind. We need to be vigilant to protect one and all from such excesses. We cannot, however, oppose the rule of law because it is sometimes abused, any more than we can oppose government-subsidized school lunches just because people are sometimes force-fed.

Consensus with Rights (without Majoritarianism)

Another fear voiced by Radical Individualists is that the restoration of a consensus about what is virtuous—and urging it upon the members of the community—will lead to "majoritarianism." For those who evoke it, especially the ACLU, the term *community* conjures up not merely the specter of "thought police" or of a minority of extremists imposing their immoderate views on the community, but a fear of a majority imposing its view on minorities or dissenting individuals. Some fear, for example, that the community would ban from public and school libraries books the majority dislikes. Note that the concern here is not that some local goon or national tyrant would take over, but that ordinary citizens would instruct their duly elected city council or school board to institute policies that violated basic rights.

The charge of majoritarianism was leveled specifically against Communitarians when we started a new publication, *The Responsive Community: Rights and Responsibilities*. ACLU's Ira Glasser told *BusinessWeek* that "communitarian really means majoritarian. The tendency is to make constitutional rights responsible for the failure to solve social problems."

Professor Tibor Machan of Auburn University, a philosopher close to Radical Individualism, writes:

> Communitarians wish to place community and individual on a collision course, saying there is some kind of balance that is needed between the rights of individuals and the rights of the community. But if we consider that community means simply a lot of other people other than oneself, this simply makes for majority rule. And if we consider that such other people usually leave it to a few who will speak out in their behalf, that again means that we will have a few community representatives dictating to the rest of us what we must do, what our "responsibilities" are.

Actually, American society has both constitutional and moral safeguards against majoritarianism that Communitarians very much respect. These safeguards basically work by *differentiation,* by defining some areas in which the majority has not and ought not to have a say and those in which it does and should. We are not simply a nose-count majoritarian democracy, but a constitutional one. That is, some choice, defined by the constituencies, are out of realm for the majority.

Clearest among these is the Bill of Rights, which singles out matters that are exempt from majority rule and from typical democratic rule making and in which minority and individual rights take precedence. The First Amendment, which protects the right of individuals to speak freely whether or not the majority approves of what they have to say, is a prime example of an area explicitly exempt from majority rule or consensus building. It does not matter if most, some, or none of us agrees with you; *you* have a basic right to state what you please. Similarly, the majority may not deny any opposition group the right to vote; even Communists were not banned even in the days when they were most hated and feared. We are all entitled to a trial by jury of our peers, whether we are members of the majority or the minority. And that is the way it ought to be.

The Constitution and our legal traditions and institutions indicate clearly, however, that other matters are subject to majority rule. Thus Americans must pay their taxes, drive with a license, and refrain from abusing children. It is inconceivable, and there is no moral and legal support for the notion, that everybody would be allowed to decide for himself whether or not he wished to obtain a license, how much taxes he would choose to pay, and so on. (On still other matters, we require a special majority—say, a two-thirds vote; these are matters that are not as fully set aside as individual and minority rights, but are more weighty than routine policy matters, such as overriding a presidential veto or proposing an amendment to the Constitution.)

There is more here than meets the eye. This constitutional differentiation between the realms of minority and individual rights and where the majority is to rule is not merely a matter of legal provisions. It is backed up by beliefs that many Americans hold dear. That is, differentiation is upheld not merely in courts of law, but also, most times, is underwritten by community consensus. Thus, when in the early nineties about 130 universities moved to ban racial slurs and thereby limit free speech, very few of the challenges to this approach found their way into the courts. The primary voices of opposition to any such codes were raised by editorial writers, authors (such as Arthur M. Schlesinger, Jr., in *The Disuniting of America* and Dinesh D'Souza in *Illiberal Education*), columnists (from George Will to Nat Hentoff), and many others who together comprise the main opinion leaders of America. They evoked a moral claim: We must continue to allow free expression of ideas, words, and sentiments even if it hurts the feelings of minorities and women. The majority ought not to decide what can be said; it is the right of each individual to speak freely. They carried the day in the court of public opinion. The so-called hate codes did not spread to most universities; several were canceled, and those that are in place are rarely enforced. (In the summer of 1992, the Supreme Court invalidated many of these codes.)

A similar mobilization of public opinion on the side of free speech occurred when an art show that contained sexually explicit sadomasochistic and homoerotic photographs, taken by Robert Mapplethorpe, came under attack. Among the photos in question were one that depicted one man urinating into another's mouth; three that showed penetration of a man's anus with various objects; one that showed a finger inserted in a penis; and two that showed children with their genitals exposed. Another source of controversy

was a show that included a photograph by Andres Serrano entitled
"Piss Christ," which depicted a crucifix in a jar filled with the
artist's urine.

Many Americans consider such artwork abhorrent. But the
moral support for free speech prevailed, and the freedom to display
these pictures was sustained largely through community voices and
not legal steps. Christina Orr-Cahall, the director of the Corcoran
Gallery of Art in Washington, D.C., had to resign after a months-
long debate that ensued after she canceled the Corcoran's exhibit of
the Mapplethorpe photographs. The director of the Contemporary
Arts Center in Cincinnati and the museum itself were acquitted by
a jury on charges of pandering to obscenity by displaying the Mapplethorpe show. In short, community consensus need not conflict,
indeed may underwrite, protection from the majority when and
where it is called for.

We should also note that minority and individual rights within
a given community are protected by the values of the society at
large. Thus some communities may wish to prohibit selling houses
to members of minorities; others bash lesbians and gay men; and so
on. However, societywide values come into play to alert the communities' members that their inclinations violate fundamental values we share as a community of communities, as a society. And if
moral suasion does not suffice, legal procedures are available to
challenge local policies that violate overarching values to which the
whole society is committed. For instance, as recently as the late
1980s a federal court forced the city of Yonkers, New York, to end
its patterns of housing segregation, which were favored by the
Yonkers City Council and, most likely, by most of the city's residents.

In Conclusion

We have seen that although American society is more moral than
many others, and still has high standards in some areas, in all too
many matters moral confusion or emptiness reigns. As no society
can thrive without a moral order, especially if heavy reliance on the
state is to be avoided, the moral voice—carried by communities
that are intact or reconstituted—must be reraised. The moral voice
is the main way communities keep moral order, other than relying

on individual consciences. Although there is a possibility that such voices may be raised too stridently, on most issues we are currently whispering at best. Moreover too many fear laying moral claims on one another, lest they be considered self-righteous. As I see it, just as we do not avoid swimming because some people drown, we should not hesitate to raise our moral voice, albeit guarding against excesses. Two major factors help keep moral voices within bounds: the Bill of Rights and those overarching values we all share that no majority or community may override.

We turn next to questions of how one refurbishes the moral order of communities: What is to morality as infrastructure is to the economy? What are the foundations that undergird morality? And how can they be shored up?

2 ◆ The Communitarian Family

Children as a Communitarian Act

AKING a child is a moral act. Obviously it obligates the parents to the child. But it also obligates the parents to the community.

We must all live with the consequences of children who are not brought up properly, whether bad economic conditions or self-centered parents are to blame. Juvenile delinquents do more than break their parents' hearts, and drug abusers do more than give their parents grief. They mug the elderly, hold up stores and gas stations, and prey on innocent children returning from school. They grow up to be useless, or worse, as employees, and they can drain taxpayers' resources and patience. In contrast, well-brought-up children are more than a joy to their families; they are (oddly, it is necessary to reiterate this) a foundation of proud and successful communities, those whose future is promising. Therefore, *parents have a moral responsibility to the community to invest themselves in the proper upbringing of their children, and communities—to enable parents to so dedicate themselves.*

"Well," you may say, "the Millers tried all they could, and though two of their children grew up swell, the youngest one is a terror. Parents can do only so much." Fair enough. Fulfilling the moral responsibility of parenthood does not guarantee success; it demands only that parents do their best. (I deal with corporations and the government a bit later in the book.)

A word about proper upbringing: I do not mean merely feeding children, cleaning their rear ends, and making sure that they do not roam the streets. These custodial responsibilities are obvious and quite well reflected in our laws. As psychology professor Urie Bronfenbrenner writes: "Basic medical services and adequate diet, while essential, are not enough by themselves to insure normal physical and psychological development. . . . Beyond health care and nutrition, certain other essential requirements must also be met."

Our culture wraps newborn infants in a pink mist. Actually those newborn "cute babies" are animals with few human traits; left to their own devices, they will crawl on all fours and bark. We know from studies of children who have been monstrously deprived of human contact—hidden away in attics, denied basic warmth and cuddling—that they lack the most basic human attributes, from walking erect to being able to talk. And if all that children receive is custodial care and morally careless education, their bodies will mature, but their souls will not. If the moral representatives of society do not fill the inborn vacuum, television and the streets will. We are all too familiar with, and frequently bemoan, the results of this type of "education." Now I will examine one of the root causes: like charity, education—or the lack thereof—begins at home. In order for education to start at home, there must be a home.

The Parenting Deficit

I rarely discuss this matter in public or with friends without someone exclaiming: "Hey, you're dumping on women!" or "You believe that women must stay at home and attend to the family's children! Women have the same right as men to work outside the home!" As I see it, this is *not* the issue; the issue is the dearth of parental involvement of both varieties: mothers and fathers.

Consider for a moment parenting as an industry. As farming declined, most fathers left to work away from home. Over the past twenty years millions of American mothers have sharply curtailed their work in the "parenting industry" by moving to work outside the home. By 1991 two-thirds (66.7 percent) of all mothers with children under eighteen were in the labor force and more than half (55.4 percent) of women with children under the age of three. At the same time a much smaller number of child care personnel moved into the parenting industry.

If this were any other business, say, shoemaking, and more than half of the labor force had been lost and replaced with fewer, less-qualified hands and still we asked the shoemakers to produce the same number of shoes of the same quality (with basically no changes in technology), we would be considered crazy. But this is what happened to parenting. As first men and then women left to work outside the home, they were replaced by some child care services, a relatively small increase in baby-sitters and nannies, and some additional service by grandparents—leaving parenting woefully shorthanded. The millions of latchkey children, who are left alone for long stretches of time, are but the most visible result of the parenting deficit.

Is this the "fault" of the women's movement, feminism, or mothers per se? Obviously not. All women did was demand for themselves what men had long possessed, working outside the home not only for their own personal satisfaction, but because of what they often perceived as the economic necessity. Whatever the cause, the result is an empty nest. Only it isn't the small fry who grew up and took off: it is the parents who flew the coop. Those who did not leave altogether increased their investment of time, energy, involvement, and commitment outside the home.

Although parenting is the responsibility of both parents—and may well be discharged most effectively in two-parent families immersed in a community context of kin and neighbors—*most important is the scope of commitment*. Single parents may do better than two-career absentee parents. Children require attention, as Robert Bellah and the other authors of *The Good Society* declared. Kids also require a commitment of time, energy, and, above all, of self.

The prevalent situation is well captured by a public service commercial in which a mother calls her child and reassures him that she has left money for him next to the phone. "Honey, have some dinner," she mutters as the child takes the twenty-dollar bill she left behind, rolls it up, and snorts cocaine. One might add that the father didn't even call.

The fact is that parenting cannot be carried out over the phone, however well meaning and loving the calls may be. It requires physical presence. The notion of "quality time" (not to mention "quality phone calls") is a lame excuse for parental absence; it presupposes that bonding and education can take place in brief time bursts, on the run. *Quality time occurs within quantity time.* As you spend time with one's children—fishing, gardening, camping, or "just" eating a meal—there are unpredictable moments when an opening occurs and education takes hold. As family expert Barbara Dafoe Whitehead puts it: "Maybe there is indeed such a thing as a one-minute manager, but there is no such thing as a one-minute parent."

The Institutionalization of Children

Is the answer to the parenting deficit building more child care centers? After all, other societies have delegated the upbringing of their children, from black nannies in the antebellum South to Greek slaves in ancient Rome. True enough. But in these historical situations the person who attended to the children was an adjunct to the parents rather than a replacement for them and an accessory reserved mostly for upper-class families with leisure. A caregiver remained with the family throughout the children's formative years and often beyond; she was, to varying degrees, integrated into the family. The caregiver, in turn, reflected, at least in part, the family's values and educational posture. Some children may have been isolated from their parents, but as a rule there was a warm, committed figure dedicated to them, one who bonded and stayed with them.

Today most child care centers are woefully understaffed with poorly paid and underqualified personnel. Child care workers are in the lowest tenth of all wage earners (with an average salary of $5.35 per hour in 1988), well below janitors. They frequently receive no health insurance or other benefits, which makes child care an even less attractive job. As Edward Zigler, a professor of child development at Yale, put it: "We pay these people less than we do zoo keepers—and then we expect them to do wonders." The personnel come and go, at a rate of 41 percent per year at an average day care center.

Bonding between children and caregivers under these circumstances is very difficult to achieve. Moreover, children suffer a loss every time their surrogate parents leave. It would be far from inaccurate to call the worst of these facilities "kennels for kids." Sure, there are exceptions. There are a few fine, high-quality child care centers, but they are as rare and almost as expensive as the nannies that some truly affluent households can command. These exceptions should not distract us from the basically dismal picture: substandard care and all-too-frequent warehousing of children, with overworked parents trying frantically to make up the deficit in their free time.

Government or social supervision of the numerous small institutions and home facilities in which child care takes place to ensure proper sanitation and care, even to screen out child abusers, is difficult and is often completely neglected or only nominally carried out. We should not be surprised to encounter abuses such as the case of the child care home in which fifty-four children were left in the care of a sixteen-year-old and were found strapped into child car seats for the entire day.

Certainly many low-income couples and single parents have little or no choice except to use the minimum that such centers provide. All we can offer here is to urge that before parents put their children in such institutions, they should check them out as extensively as possible (including surprise visits in the middle of the day). Moreover, we should all support these parents' quest for additional support from corporations and government if they cannot themselves spend more on child care.

Particularly effective are cooperative arrangements that require each parent to contribute some time—four hours a week?—to serve at his or her child's center. Not only do such arrangements reduce the center's costs, they also allow parents to see firsthand what actually goes on, ensuring some measure of *built-in accountability*. It provides for continuity—while staff come and go, parents stay. (Even if they divorce, they may still participate in their child care center.) And as parents get to know other parents of children in the same stage of development, they form social bonds, which can be drawn upon to work together to make these centers more responsive to children's needs.

Above all, age matters. Infants under two years old are particularly vulnerable to separation anxiety. Several bodies of data strongly indicate that infants who are institutionalized at a young age will not mature into well-adjusted adults. As Edward Zigler puts it: "We are cannibalizing children. Children are dying in the system, never mind achieving optimum development." A study of third-graders by two University of Texas researchers compared children who returned home after school to their mothers with children who remained in day care centers:

> children who stayed at the day care centers after school were having problems. They received more negative peer nominations, and their negative nominations outweighed their positive nominations. In addition, the day care third-graders made lower academic grades on their report card and scored lower on standardized tests. There was some evidence of poor conduct grades.

Unless the parents are absent or abusive, infants are better off at home. Older children, between two and four, may be able to handle some measure of institutionalization in child care centers, but their personalities often seem too unformed to be able to cope well with a nine-to-five separation from a parent.

As a person who grew up in Israel, I am sometimes asked whether it is true that kibbutzim succeed in bringing up toddlers in child care centers. I need to note first that unlike the personnel in most American child care centers, the people who care for children in kibbutzim are some of the most dedicated members of the work force because these communities consider child care to be a very high priority. As a result, child care positions are highly sought after and there is little turnover, which allows for essential bonding to take place. In addition, both parents are intimately involved in bringing up their children, and they frequently visit the child care centers, which are placed very close to where they live and work. Even so, Israeli kibbutzim are rapidly dismantling their collective child care centers and returning children to live with their families—because both the families and the community established that even a limited disassociation of children from their parents at a tender age is unacceptable.

There is no sense looking back and beating our breasts over how we got ourselves into the present situation. But we must acknowledge that as a matter of social policy (as distinct from some individual situations) we have made a mistake in assuming that strangers can be entrusted with the effective personality formation of infants and toddlers. Over the last twenty-five years we have seen the future, and it is not a wholesome one. With poor and ineffective community child care, and with ever more harried parents, it will not suffice to tell their graduates to "just say no" and expect them to resist all temptations, to forgo illegal drugs and alcohol, and to postpone sexual activity. If we fervently wish them to grow up in a civilized society, and if we seek to live in one, let's face facts: it will not happen unless we dedicate more of ourselves to our children and their care and education.

Equality Within the Communitarian Family

Who needs to bond with children? *Both* parents. It is no accident that in a wide variety of human societies (from the Zulus to the Inuits, from ancient Greece and ancient China to modernity), there has never been a society that did not have two-parent families. Societies have varied a great deal in the roles they assigned to other members of the family (aunts, uncles, grandparents) and in the educational roles of other members of the tribe. They have also varied a great deal in the specifics of the relationship between the parents and between the parents and the child. But in the hundreds of known societies throughout recorded history, two-parent families have been the norm.

To be quite clear: To argue that the two-parent family is "better" than the single-parent family is in no way to denigrate single parents. It's akin to saying that for most purposes a two-bedroom home is better than a one-bedroom home. Moreover, just because most people prefer a two-bedroom home does not mean that those who have a home with only one bedroom are in it only or firstly by their choice.

There are several compelling reasons why two-parent families are the most suitable form for children. First, child care and education are highly labor-intensive, demanding tasks. Young children are a very needy bunch. They can soak up huge amounts of care, attention, and love. Second, parenting works best when there is a division of the educational labor. One parent may be more supportive, the source of emotional security that all children require if they are to dare to grow up in a threatening world. The other parent may be more achievement-oriented, pushing children to extend themselves beyond the comfortable cradle of love.

In the United States mothers have historically often fulfilled the former role, while fathers have typically adopted the latter. But the *two-piston engine of effective education* can work the other way around. Indeed, in some contemporary families children are cuddled by their fathers and disciplined by their mothers. What matters most is the two-parent mode. True, some single parents can shift back and forth between the supportive and achievement-oriented modes of parenting quite successfully. But this is difficult to accomplish on top of the other difficulties faced by a single parent, who is often the sole breadwinner as well.

Another essential feature for a family effectively to carry out its parenting mission is a *mutually supportive educational coalition*. The parents, as educational agents, must be mutually supportive because their specific educational goals are in part contradictory. Goading children to achieve generates stress ("Did you prepare for your math test yet?"), while reassuring them generates a relaxation response ("Don't overdo it—Rome wasn't built in a day"). Hence, only if the parents are basically in agreement can they make education work and avoid being unwittingly played off one against the other by their children, to the detriment of education. (This is, of course, a major reason divorced parents have such a hard time working together to bring up their children, even when they have joint custody.)

The sequence of divorce followed by a succession of boy- or girlfriends, a second marriage, and frequently another divorce and another turnover of partners often means a repeatedly disrupted educational coalition. Each change in participants involves a change in the educational agenda for the child. Each new partner cannot be expected to pick up the previous one's educational post and program. The educational input that each adult provides is deeply affected by his or her total personality and upbringing. As a result, changes in parenting partners means, at best, a deep disruption in a child's education, though of course several disruptions cut deeper into the effectiveness of the educational coalition than just one. (The discussion presumes, somewhat optimistically, that new partners are willing to get involved in the first place.)

The ill results are reflected in the following statistics, which are but a sample of the many that could be cited. A 1991 study by the National Center for Health Statistics found that children living in single-parent families and stepfamilies were more likely to fail in school and to require treatment for emotional and behavioral disorders as compared with children living with both biological parents. The incidence, for example, of children who needed to repeat a grade varied from only 12 percent among children living with both biological parents to nearly twice as many (22 percent) among those who were living with stepfamilies (and with divorced mothers) and 30 percent who were living with never married mothers. The incidence of children suspended from school was 4 percent among "intact" families, 9 percent among stepfamilies, 11 percent among children living with divorced mothers, and 15 percent among children living with never married mothers. Some social scientists point out that these differences reflect economic differences—for instance, that divorced parents are less well off than those who are married. But this factor itself reflects the decline of the family. The dismembering of the family thus hits children like a one-two punch: first directly, by disrupting the educational coalition of the parents, and second indirectly, by dividing them between two households that are more costly to run than one.

When I testified on these matters before a U.S. Senate committee, then-Senator Jeremiah Denton (R–AL) asked me: "Are you implying that single parents *cannot* bring up a child properly?" I answered: "As I read the social science findings, it would be preferable to have *three* parents per child, or to draw upon grandparents and child care staff to supplement, but not to replace, their two parents. Parenting is a heavy-duty load for single parents to carry entirely on their own, especially if they are employed full-time outside the household." I should have added that the sad fact is that most divorced fathers quickly fade away as parents, and that fathers who were never married to their children's mothers infrequently play a parental role.

The Valuation of Children

When Communitarians discuss parental responsibilities we are often asked: "How can we have more time for the kids if we need to work full-time just to make ends meet?" Our response requires an examination of the value of children as compared to other "priorities."

Nobody likes to admit it, but between 1960 and 1990 American society allowed children to be devalued, while the golden call of "making it" was put on a high pedestal. Recently, college freshmen listed "being well off financially" as more important than "raising a family." (In 1990 the figures were 74 percent versus 70 percent, respectively, and in 1991 they were 74 percent versus 68 percent.) *Kramer vs. Kramer,* a novel and movie that both captured the era and helped popularize its values, stressed the right of women to find themselves, to discover their identities, and to follow their careers the way men do.

Some blame this development on the women's rights movement, others on the elevation of materialism and greed to new historical heights. These and other factors may have all combined to devalue children. However, women are obviously entitled to all the same rights men are, including the pursuit of greed.

But few people who advocated equal rights for women favored a society in which sexual equality would mean a society in which all adults would act like men, who in the past were relatively inattentive to children. The new gender-equalized world was supposed to be a combination of all that was sound and ennobling in the traditional roles of women and men. Women were to be free to work any place they wanted, and men would be free to show emotion, care, and domestic commitment. For children this was not supposed to mean, as it too often has, that they would be bereft of dedicated parenting. Now that we have seen the result of decades of widespread neglect of children, the time has come for both parents to revalue children and for the community to support and recognize their efforts. Parents in a Communitarian family, in the "age of we," are entitled not just to equal pay for equal work, equal credit and housing opportunities, and the right to choose a last name, they also must bear equal responsibilities—above all, for their children.

A major 1991 report by the National Commission on Children, in effect, is a national call for revaluation of children. Joseph Duffey, the president of the American University, and Anne Wexler, a leading liberal, have also expressed the renewed commitment. "Perhaps, in the end," they wrote, "the great test for American society will be this: whether we are capable of caring and sacrificing for the future of children. For the future of children other than our own, and for children of future generations. Whether we are capable of caring and sacrificing that they might have a future of opportunity." In the 1950s, mothers who worked outside the home were often made to feel guilty by questions such as "Doesn't Jenny mind eating lunch in school?" By the 1980s the moral voice had swung the other way. Now women, not to mention men, who chose to be homemakers were put down by such comments as "Oh, you're *not* working," the implication being that if one did not pursue a career outside the house, there was nothing to talk to you about. We need to return to a situation in which *committed parenting is an honorable vocation*.

One major way that commitment may be assessed is by the number of hours that are dedicated to a task over the span of a day. According to a 1985 study by a University of Maryland sociologist, parents spent an average of only seventeen hours per week with their children, compared with thirty in 1965. Even this paltry amount of time is almost certainly an overstatement of the case because it is based on self-reporting. And although guilt is not a social force I recommend building on, if any finger pointing is to be done, a finger should be pointed at those who, in effect, abandon their children to invest themselves whole hog in other pursuits.

And we all need to chip in. Many parents point to the great difficulty they have in teaching their children right from wrong. They remind us that they are fighting a culture that bombards their kids with unwholesome messages: that it is supremely important to keep up with the Joneses; that you can discharge your human duties and express your feelings by buying something; that violence and raw sex are as pervasive and corrosive as shown on TV and in music tapes, discs, and records. A community that is more respectful of children would *make parenting a less taxing and more fulfilling experience*.

This revaluation of the importance of children has two major ramifications. First, potential parents must consider what is important to them: more income or better relationships with their children. Most people cannot "have it all." They must face the possibility that they will have to curtail their gainful employment in order to invest more time and energy into their offspring. This may hurt their chances of making money directly (by working fewer hours) or indirectly (by advancing more slowly in their careers).

Many parents, especially those from the less endowed classes, argue that they both desire gainful employment not because they enjoy it or seek self-expression, as many Radical Individualists would have it, but because they "cannot make ends meet" otherwise. They feel that both parents have no choice but to work full-time outside the home if they are to pay for the rent, food, clothing, and other basics. A 1990 Gallup poll found that one-half of those households with working mothers would want the mother to stay home if "money were not an issue." (The same question should have been asked about fathers.)

This sense of economic pressure certainly has a strong element of reality. Many couples in the nineties need two paychecks to buy little more than what a couple in the early seventies could acquire with a single income. This problem will be with us at least until the American economy starts to grow faster. There are millions of people in America these days, especially the poor and the near poor, who are barely surviving, even when both parents do work long and hard outside the home. If they have several children and work for the minimum wage (often without medical insurance), they may need to draw on the support of others just to stay afloat. A growing number of working-class families and some of those in the lower reaches of the middle class have also fallen on hard economic times. And surely many single women must work to support themselves and their children. But at some level of income, which is lower than the conventional wisdom would have us believe, parents do begin to have a choice between enhanced earnings and attending to their children.

There is considerable disagreement as to what that level might be. Several social scientists have shown that most of what many more endowed people consider "essentials" are actually purchases that their cultures and communities tell them are "essential," rather than what is objectively required. They point out that objectively people need rather little: shelter, liquids, a certain amount of calories and vitamins a day, and a few other such things that can be bought quite cheaply. Most of what people *feel* that they "must have"—from VCRs to shoes that match their pocketbooks to $150 Nike sneakers to designer frames for their sunglasses—is socially conditioned. This is further documented by the fact that what is considered "necessary" varies a great deal within the society and over time. Some people cannot live without fancy jeans. Others "need" pink flamingoes on their front lawns (and the lawns themselves!). A colleague who lives in a suburb of New York City was miffed by my implied criticism of people who are so preoccupied with consumer goods that they do not attend adequately to their children. In his letter to me, he observed that because he and his wife had worked long hours outside the household, they were able to buy cars for their children. Well, the children might just have been better off if they'd had to walk or bike but had more time with their parents. In short, although there may be conflicting notions regarding how high an income level is sufficient for people to satisfy their basic needs, there is clearly a level at which they are able to make choices.

A colleague who read an earlier version of these pages suggested that the preceding line of argument sounds as if social scientists wish to cement the barriers between the classes and not allow lower-class people to aspire to higher status. Hardly so. They are arguing not that people should lead a life of denial and poverty, but that they have, and make, choices all the time, whether or not they are aware of this fact. They choose between a more rapid climb up the social ladder and spending more time with their children. Communitarians would add that in the long run parents will find more satisfaction and will contribute more to the community if they heed their children more and their social status less. But even if they choose to order their priorities the other way around, let it not be said that they did not make a choice. Careerism is not a law of nature.

We return then to the value we as a community put on having and bringing up children. In a society that places more value on Armani suits, winter skiing, and summer houses than on education, parents are under pressure to earn more, whatever their income. They feel that it is important to work overtime and to dedicate themselves to enhancing their incomes and advancing their careers. We must recognize now, after two decades of celebrating greed and in the face of a generation of neglected children, the importance of educating one's children.

Take a couple of successful young professionals—lawyers, perhaps—who are planning to have a child. They need to decide whether they will continue to invest themselves entirely in their work—putting in long hours at the office, taking briefcases full of work home at night, seeing and entertaining clients on the weekends—or whether they will lighten up on their workload once the child is born. (Lightening up, of course, will reduce their billable hours, and hence their income, and may even delay the time it takes for them to make partner.) They must further decide how much parental leave they are going to take, whether they will try to work different schedules so that at least one of them can be at home at most times, and whether one or both of them will try to work more at home than in the office. (These choices will, in turn, be deeply affected by what their law firms will welcome or at least tolerate; but the firms, too, are likely to be influenced by changing societal values.) All these decisions reflect more the tension between commitment to a child and to career and money; they also show that even if both parents choose to remain gainfully employed full-time, they still have several options in terms of the relative intensity of their commitment to their children versus other values. I am sorry that Dan Quayle stirred up such a fuss about single mother Murphy Brown; it would have been more positive to point to the Huxtables. Here are two professionals, a lawyer and a doctor, both working full-time but very dedicated to their children and one another.

Ah, you say, you are talking about yuppies: *they* have choices. Well, first of all, they too have children. And others have similar choices, although to reiterate, the lower the income and assets, the more limited and harder these choices are.

Inner Joy

Although the shift from consumerism and careerism to an emphasis on children is largely one of values, it has some rewarding payoffs. Corporations keep complaining, correctly, that the young workers who present themselves on their doorsteps are undertrained. A good part of what they mean (and I address this in more detail later on) is a deficiency of character and an inability to control impulses, defer gratification, and commit to the task at hand. If businesses would cooperate with parents to make it easier for them to earn a living and attend to their children, the corporate payoffs would be more than social approbation: they would gain a labor force that is much better able to perform. The community, too, would benefit by having members who are not merely more sensitive to one another and more caring but also more likely to contribute to the commonweal. Last but not least, parents would discover that although there are some failures despite the best intentions and strongest dedication, and although there are no guarantees or refunds in bringing up children, *by and large you reap what you sow*. If people dedicate a part of their lives to their kids, they are likely to have sons and daughters who will make them proud and fill their old age with love.

Ann Landers published a letter by a person who attended his class reunion and was in the dumps because he did not have the material success of many of his classmates. This triggered many replies, of which the following is a fair sample:

> My husband is probably one of the guys he admires. We have moved six times in ten years, always for a better-paying, more prestigious job. Each move requires establishing new friendships and becoming part of the community. I dream of staying in one place long enough for my children to develop ongoing relationships, but I know it will never happen.
>
> We drive the BMW that "Class of '73" admires as a status symbol. Actually, we have two. Sounds wonderful? Not really. What I wouldn't give for a husband who is satisfied with his job, his salary, and the city we live in.

Ethicists have a device that helps people sort out their priorities. They ask you to consider what you would like to have written on your tombstone, how you would like to summarize your life's work. Would you prefer to have it written that you had made more money than you ever believed possible, more than your schoolmates or neighbors? Or would you rather be remembered for helping to bring up some lovely human beings, your children? Having actively participated in bringing up five lovely children, I would conclude that kids are not pieces of property that you add to your acquisitions and then turn over to a staff. As the great ethicist Immanuel Kant would have put it, children are ends in themselves, persons of full value—like you and me.

The community—that is, all of us—suffers the ill effects of *absentee* parenting. For example, according to a study by social scientist Jean Richardson and her colleagues, eighth-grade students who took care of themselves for eleven or more hours a week were twice as likely to be abusers of controlled substances (that is, smoke marijuana or tobacco or drink alcohol) as those who were actively cared for by adults. "The increased risk appeared no matter what the sex, race, or socioeconomic status of the children," Richardson and associates noted. The study found that 31 percent of latchkey children had two or more drinks at a time, compared with 17 percent for supervised children; 27 percent of the latchkey children expected to get drunk in the future, compared with only 15 percent of the others. And students who took care of themselves for eleven or more hours per week were one and a half to two times more likely "to score high on risk taking, anger, family conflict, and stress" than those who did not care for themselves, a later study by Jean Richardson and her colleagues found.

James Q. Wilson, discussing Travis Hirschi's *Causes of Delinquency,* reports:

> The number of delinquent acts, as reported by the children themselves, was powerfully influenced by the children's attachment to the parents. The closer the mother's supervision of the child, the more intimate the child's communication with the father, and the greater the affection between child and parents, the less the delinquency. Even when the father held a low-status job, the stronger the child's attachment to him, the less the delinquency. Other factors also contributed to delinquency, such as whether the child did well in and liked school, but these factors were themselves affected by family conditions.

Other studies point to the same dire consequences.

Gang warfare in the streets, massive drug abuse, a poorly committed work force, and a strong sense of entitlement and weak sense of responsibility are, to a large extent, the product of poor parenting. True, economic and social factors also play a role. But a lack of effective parenting is a major cause, and the other factors could be handled more readily if we remained committed to the importance of the upbringing of the young. The fact is, given the same economic and social conditions, *in poor neighborhoods one finds decent and hardworking youngsters right next to antisocial ones. Likewise, in affluent suburbs one finds antisocial youngsters right next to decent, hardworking ones.* The difference is often a reflection of the homes they come from.

What Can We Do?

What we need now, first of all, is to return more hands and, above all, more voices to the "parenting industry." This can be accomplished in several ways, all of which are quite familiar but are not being dealt with nearly often enough.

Given the forbearance of labor unions and employers, it is possible for millions of parents *to work at home.* Computers, modems, up- and downlinks, satellites, and other modern means of communication can allow you to trade commodities worldwide without ever leaving your den, to provide answers on a medical hot line from a corner of the living room, or to process insurance claims and edit books from a desk placed anywhere in the house.

If both parents must work outside the household, it is preferable if they can arrange to *work different shifts,* to increase the all-important parental presence. Some couples manage with *only one working full-time and the other part-time.* In some instances two parents can *share one job* and the parenting duties (for example, the post of Washington deputy bureau chief for the *St. Louis Post-Dispatch* is shared by a couple). Some find *flextime* work that allows them to come in late or leave late (or make some other adjustments in their schedule) if the other parent is detained at work, a child is sick, and so on.

These are not pie-in-the-sky, futuristic ideas. Several of the largest corporations already provide one or more of these family-friendly features. DuPont had in 1992 two thousand employees working part-time and between ten thousand and fifteen thousand working flextime. IBM has a "flexible work leave of absence" plan that allows employees to work up to three years part-time and still collect full-employment benefits. Avon Products and a subsidiary of Knight-Ridder newspapers have their own versions of these programs, and the list goes on.

Public policies could further sustain the family. Child allow-ances, which are common in Europe, could provide each family with some additional funds when a child is born. Others suggest a pro-gram, modeled after the GI Bill, that would give parents who stay home "points" toward future educational or retraining expenses.

These measures require a commitment on the part of parents, to work things out so that they can discharge more of their parenting responsibilities, and on the side of corporations and the govern-ment, to make effective parenting possible.

The debate over whether parents should be allowed three months of unpaid leave is ridiculous, a sign of how much we have lost our sense of the importance of parenting. A bill considered in Congress in 1991 would have mandated only twelve weeks of *unpaid* leave and only for companies with more than fifty employees. The bill passed Congress, but President Bush vetoed it. Even *Working Mother* mag-azine, in its yearly listing of the best companies for working par-ents, requires that a company provide protection of a new mother's job for only *six weeks* after childbirth to qualify for the *best* rating! The U.S. Navy used to discharge women who became pregnant. Now it allows them six weeks of paid maternity leave, after which they are expected to return to work. They are expected to resume sea duty four months after giving birth!

No one can form the minimal bonding a newborn child requires in such woefully brief periods of time. A typical finding is that in-fants who were subject to twenty hours a week of nonparental care are insecure in their relationship with their parents at the end of the first year and more likely to be aggressive between the ages of three and eight. (One can disagree with all findings. Some social scientists argue that these data are the effects not of child care but of poor child care. But it is not accidental that we have often had inadequate child care. To provide quality child care would cost more than many women or men earn.) If children who are two years or younger are too young to be institutionalized in child care centers, a bare mini-mum of two years of intensive parenting is essential.

The fact that this recommendation is considered utopian is trou-bling, not merely for parents and children, but for all who care about the future of this society. Let's state it here unabashed: Cor-porations should provide six months of paid leave and another year and a half (eighteen months) of unpaid leave. (The costs should be shared by the employers of the father and the mother.) Of the eighteen months, the government should cover six months from public funds (many European countries do at least this much), and the rest should be absorbed by the family.

Given increased governmental support and corporate flexibility, each couple must work out its own division of labor. In one family I know, the mother is a nurse and the father a day laborer. She is earning much more, and he found it attractive to work occasionally outside the home while making the care of their two young daughters his prime responsibility. He responds to calls from people who need a tow truck; if the calls come while his wife is not at home, he takes his daughters with him. I met them when he towed my car. They seemed a happy lot, but he was a bit defensive about the fact that he was the home parent; he giggled when he spoke about the way his domestic life was structured. The community's moral voice should fully approve of this arrangement rather than expect that the woman be the parent who stays at home. At the same time there should be no social stigma attached to women who prefer to make raising children their vocation or career. We need more fathers and mothers who make these choices; stigmatizing any of them is hardly a way to encourage parenting. Reelevating the value of children will help bring about the needed change of heart.

Is the American Family an Endangered Species?

Scientists are all too familiar with factoids. Factoids are "facts" that many people believe to be true but are not. Thus it is a factoid that if a lemming jumps off a cliff, all the others in tow will take a dive. It is a factoid that Inuits have a large number of terms for snow (because, it is said, snow is much more important in their lives than in ours). And it is a factoid that the American family is a goner, that only 14 percent (or 6 percent or 7 percent) of all American families fit the traditional format. Radical Individualists use these dismal statistics to bolster their argument that the nuclear family cannot be resurrected because it has been replaced by a wide variety of other "families," from single-parent households to gay couples. Ruth Messinger, currently the Manhattan Borough president, put the figure vividly, saying that the "mythical nuclear family today describes only one in seventeen American families." Representative

Mary Jane Gibson stated in a hearing before the Massachusetts State Legislature that fewer than 10 percent of American families resemble the familiar "Ozzie and Harriet" model of mother as caregiver and father as breadwinner. They maintain that the nuclear family has changed from being the basic cell of the societal body to serving as just one among several "life-style" options.

To get at the truth behind this factoid, one must note that Radical Individualists' definition of the family includes elements that have been historically associated with nuclear families but are not essential to them. By their definition a family "must have" a father, who is the sole wage earner; a mother, who is a full-time homemaker; and *two* children. This arrangement is hardly necessary for the family to discharge its prime responsibility: to lay the basic foundations for the moral education of the next generation. Hence, these are, in effect, antifamily statistics, figures that are used to belittle the family.

Actually, the majority of preschool children (about 78 percent) live in functioning families of one kind or another: 33 percent in families in which the father works outside the house and the mother is at home; 29 percent in which both parents work full-time; and 16 percent in which the married mother works part-time. The two-parent family is less common than it used to be, but it is far from dying out.

Should We Curb Divorce?

If two-parent families were just one option among many, there would be no reason to be concerned about the high rate of divorce. But since the evidence strongly suggests that intact families are to be preferred, divorce becomes more problematic. One first notes that divorce removes parents from their children, often completely. Most fathers ignore their offspring from first marriages shortly after they set up new families, if not before. Even in the period soon after divorce, only one-sixth of all children see their fathers even once a week; close to one-half do not see them at all. After ten years practically two-thirds have *no contact*. Single mothers, who are typically the custodial parents, are even more subject to economic pressures that diminish parenting than their married counterparts. In addition, divorce has detrimental effects all its own, as children

Cartoon by Eleanor Mill. Reprinted with permission of Eleanor Mill.

often become pawns in bitter conflicts and entangled in cross loyalties. As a result, many feel—quite understandably—abandoned and unloved.

After divorce, children are also frequently faced with a bewildering rotation of their parents' boyfriends or girlfriends. Many of these transients develop some kind of relationship with the children; then they too vanish, for reasons that the children cannot fathom and all too often presume to be their fault. If and when they finally have stepparents, children often find that the second marriages are even less stable than the first. And although some stepparents develop remarkably close relations with their stepchildren, much more common are the tense relations mythologized in tales such as Cinderella.

True, social science studies of the effects of divorce have produced conflicting findings, and one can always further question any and all findings. Douglas Besharov, a family expert at the American Enterprise Institute, has this to say about the finding that people are happier in marriage than on their own: "Well, maybe people who are happier enter marriages." But much evidence indicates that dismembering the family is harmful under most circumstances. Claire Berman, the author of *Adult Children of Divorce Speak Out,* contends that among children of divorce "a hole in the heart is universal. There is a sense of having missed out on something that is a birthright, the right to grow up in a house of two parents." Personally I do not know of a single instance in which the children were not harmed by divorce, although there are significant differences in the extent of harm, and clearly some rotten marriages can cause as much harm as (or even more harm) than divorce.

Family expert David Popenoe effectively summarizes the problem divorce poses for children in his discussion of the "new familism":

> It is a fact that much of the voluntary family breakup occurring recently has a negative impact on children. Certainly, I have never met the child who did not want to be raised, if possible, by both biological parents who stayed together and cooperated in child-rearing at least until the child's maturity (and hopefully for life).

In her book *Second Chances: Men, Women, and Children a Decade After Divorce,* Judith Wallerstein reports that children entering adolescence immediately following their parents' divorce are particularly vulnerable.

> In our study, one out of three of the young men and one in ten of the young women between ages nineteen and twenty-three at the ten-year mark are delinquent, meaning they act out their anger in a range of illegal activities including assault, burglary, arson, drug dealing, theft, drunk driving, and prostitution. Many of these children got involved in one episode of breaking the law before age eighteen, but a disturbing number of them continue this delinquency pattern into their early twenties.

She adds:

The kind of misbehavior that we see—abuse of drugs and alcohol, petty vandalism, and the like—is widespread in our society, divorce or no divorce. Although such misbehavior emerges in children of divorce, the more frequent pattern in their lives is one of underachievement, low self-esteem, and inhibition of anger related to feelings of rejection.

Other studies found the effects of divorce on children to be apparent in their academic, social, moral, and physical development as well as their emotional development. Teenagers from homes with a stepparent or a single parent are more likely to drop out of school than teenagers from families in which both natural parents are present. A 1991 study by researchers at Princeton and Johns Hopkins universities found that "growing up in a single-parent family has negative consequences for a student's grade point average, school attendance, and . . . educational attainment." The researchers found the same effects in children who were growing up in stepparent families. A national health survey shows that children from single-parent families or stepfamilies were two to three times more likely to have had emotional or behavioral problems than those who had both of their biological parents in the home.

Thirty percent of two-parent elementary school students were ranked as high achievers, while only 17 percent of one-parent students were, according to a study by the National Association of Elementary School Principals. Conversely, 23 percent of the two-parent students were low achievers, while 38 percent of the one-parent students were. The children of one-parent families were more likely to be truant, late, disciplined, and to drop out of school. Furthermore, 70 percent of juveniles in state reform institutions were children of one-parent or no-parent families.

Psychiatrist James M. Herzog of the Children's Hospital Medical Center in Boston studied the effects of the absence of an active father figure on young children. His findings imply that the father's absence may have specific and long-range consequences for the way young children deal with aggressive drives. Among the seventy-two children of divorce whom he studied, the absence of the father was especially disruptive for the children, almost all of them boys between one and a half and five years old. The very youngest typically had nightmares about monsters; those three to five years old were apt to be highly macho, hyperaggressive, and preoccupied with ideas of stern male discipline. In children of both sexes aged five to seven years old, depression—which is aggression turned inward—was the more common result. Herzog suggests that parents monitor and absorb a variety of feelings and conflicts for one another and that this interaction creates a "protective shield" that allows both to be caring, effective parents. When the father leaves, this shield tends to break down and leave the children vulnerable.

Children of divorce carry within them the seed of later trouble. Children who were under sixteen years of age at the time of their parents' divorce or separation were more likely to get divorced themselves, according to a 1987 study by University of Texas sociologists Norval Glenn and Kathryn Kramer.

Indeed, a surprising finding is that divorce deeply hurts not merely young children, but also adolescents and even older offspring. Affective disorder is from one and a half to two times as likely to occur in women whose parents had separated than among those whose parents had stayed together, according to a study of three thousand adults by British psychiatrist Bryan Rodgers.

There may be alternative explanations for some of these findings, and they are far from universally accepted. For example, Jessie Bernard, a distinguished sociologist and feminist, reviewed several early studies of stepchildren; she found a more varied and complex picture than the studies cited above. Moreover, economic background factors deeply confound the picture. Single parents are often poorer than married ones, and hence it is hard to distinguish between the effects of poverty and the presence of only one effective parent. And to reiterate, there are some marriages for which divorce is the preferred solution. The most reasonable conclusion, based on a whole body of data, rather than dwelling on this or that study, *is that divorce should not be banned or condemned, but that it should be discouraged. Easy divorces for parents are not in the interest of children, the community,* or as we shall see, the adults involved.

Changing the Moral Voice

There is no magic pill that one can prescribe that will make married people get along better with one another, and there is no lever that ought to be pulled that will again make divorce a source of stigma.

There are, however, ways to encourage young people to enter marriage more responsibly, help sustain and enrich those marriages that are in place, and at the same time reflect the moral voice of the community that marriages are not to be treated as disposable relations.

Before Marriage

To avoid the rush to divorce, we need to further slow the rush to marriage. Many churches and synagogues are pointing the way. Priests, ministers, and rabbis are refusing to marry couples who walk in off the street. They insist that the prospective bride and groom first attend some group counseling sessions and learn the secrets of joint decision making, mutual respect, budget making, and so on.

In Modesto, California, sixty-three religious leaders agreed to enforce a four-month *waiting period* for couples planning to marry, which must include at least two counseling sessions. The statement announcing the policy argued that "couples who seriously participate in premarital testing and counseling will have a better understanding of what the marriage commitment involves. . . . We acknowledge that a wedding is but a day; a marriage is for a lifetime." At Modesto's First Baptist Church, there is an eight-month waiting period. During this time, the prospective bride and groom meet at least eight times with a church instructor. The minister for singles at the church says that half of the couples who took the course in the past six years decided not to marry. The minister called the program "effective divorce prevention."

These waiting periods may well be too long for some. Time by itself is not as important as opportunities for couples to explore the depth of their commitment, to establish if they have the basic communication skills that stable and satisfactory relations require, and to develop these communication skills if they are deficient.

If the community starts to counsel young people about marriage earlier, those seeking to marry would be better prepared. One way this could be achieved is if *schools offered more courses on human relations*. These would help to improve all human interactions, not merely the relations between married people. Americans are a rather assertive, litigious people. We know all too well how to confront, to be contentious, and to guard our turf and rights. It seems we would all be better off if we learned less abrasive and more socially beneficial ways of resolving differences. This is a subject that can be taught, although it is often better taught through role playing than through lectures. In such courses people learn to attack issues rather than one another; to avoid bringing up past events when a recent matter is under review; and to set specific times during which to discuss certain matters. Studies show that about the same number of conflicts occur in "good" and "bad" marriages; the difference is that the partners in solid and relatively happy marriages have developed less bruising and more effective means of dealing with their differences. (*The Intimate Enemy,* by George R. Bach and Peter Wyden, provides a popular discussion of one approach.)

Two psychologists, John Gottman and Lowell Krokoff, conducted a study that examined the development of marriages over a three-year period. The researchers found that partners may be able to deescalate fights by paraphrasing one another's arguments and searching for a solution rather than continuing to disagree. As Gottman notes, "Couples who have healthy fights develop a kind of marital efficacy that makes the marriage stronger as time goes on."

Howard Markman, a psychologist who runs a project at the University of Denver to train couples to handle conflict, found that couples who learn how to argue well were unhappy at first but became more satisfied later. The divorce rate after six years for couples who had undergone the training was half that of couples who had not.

Another way to proceed is to arrange for what a law professor called "precommitments," which in effect would add to the existing marital vows. Professor Elizabeth Scott of the University of Virginia School of Law suggests that couples who are about to marry or are already married would agree with one another that if they reached a point where they considered divorce, they would 1. delay their decision for two to three years; 2. participate in marital counseling; and 3. accept that the spouse seeking a divorce would make extra economic sacrifices.

Finally, laws may be changed to require a waiting period for couples who seek to get married to allow more time for second thoughts in times when impulses run high. Note also that easy divorce makes people enter marriage too easily. And as they expect it likely not to last, they invest less of themselves to make it work.

Thus divorce breeds still more divorce. For the same reason, entering marriage more responsibly is going to make it more durable, which in turn will enhance the couples' commitments to make their marriage succeed.

During Marriage

The ritual of the family meal—which was once as integral to Americans' daily routine as tooth brushing—has been recently extolled by a list of eminent social observers, from Robert Bellah and his colleagues to an assistant secretary of the U.S. Department of Health and Human Services. Bellah and company approach the family meal with reverence:

> The family meal . . . is the chief family celebration, even a
> family sacrament. . . . If everyone joins in the common tasks,
> husband as well as wife, and children, too, as much as they are
> able, then the family can enjoy at least several common meals
> a week, celebrate the pleasure they have in each other's pres-
> ence and the good things they have mutually helped to pre-
> pare. Mealtime, as anyone who has ever had children knows,
> can also produce conflicts; but learning how to resolve them,
> to listen and be listened to, is part of the indispensable educa-
> tional function of the common meal. We can be sure that
> having a common meal, and one to which all contribute, re-
> sults in a warmer family and an enhancement of everyone's
> capacity for attention.

And Patrick F. Fagan of the U.S. Department of Health and Human Services argues that one of the "actions and reforms" needed in the area of family is

> that families return to the common practice of family dinner
> together, to have at least one hour together each day, talking
> about the usual trivia which make up most normal days. Fa-
> ther's presence is crucial for it to be a family hour. Workplace
> expectations of fathers will need to adapt accordingly.

This is but one example out of many ways to enhance marriage. Others include programs run by religious organizations (such as marriage "encounters"), renewal of vows, and marriage counseling.

Before Divorce

The adoption of "braking" mechanisms that foster extensive consideration before divorce proceedings begin has been suggested by William Galston, a leading Communitarian who previously served as the issues director of Walter Mondale's 1984 presidential campaign. One of the measures he suggests has also been recommended by Britain's Law Commission. A couple would be required to use the nine months after they informed a court of their decision to divorce to settle the important details of the divorce. Issues involving their children would take precedence, and the couple would have to decide these before they would be allowed to return to court and be granted a divorce. The idea is that this would encourage parents to concentrate on the results of a family breakup and possibly discourage the divorce.

Another method of using waiting periods to discourage divorce is currently being debated in Oklahoma. The Oklahoma State Legislature has proposed measures that would make couples think twice about divorce and remarriage: a recent bill would require that couples who get a divorce wait nine months before remarrying.

I support such waiting periods, albeit reluctantly. First of all, I dislike the idea of regulating human conduct with ever more laws and regulations. Second, a cooling-off period of as little as thirty days may not suffice, and it may very well be impractical to insist on a longer waiting period. I would, however, use Galston's proposal as an example to make a general point about the Communitarian role of law.

We tend to think of laws as coercive, punitive, and deterring. This is all quite true. They correctly bring to mind courts, jails, and fines. Therefore their use as a social tool should be minimized. But there is another use for laws. They can serve to communicate and symbolize those values that the community holds dear. This is one reason Communitarians do not wish to see the legalization of the use of narcotics. It would send the wrong message by implying that the community approves of people being in a drug-induced stupor.

In her book *Abortion and Divorce in Western Law*, Mary Ann Glendon discusses the difference between the messages being sent to Europeans and to Americans through their varying laws that address divorce. Although many Europeans still view divorce as something to be avoided, for many Americans divorce has become more socially acceptable. Specifically it was the implementation of no-fault divorce laws that has detracted from the significance of marriage vows. No-fault divorce was advocated originally as a practical solution to the problem of expensive, messy divorces and as a way to remove the government from people's personal lives. But it has had the effect of sanctioning divorce; it sends a moral message that marriage is a relationship that exists primarily for the fulfillment of the individual spouses. If it ceases to perform this function, no one is to blame and either spouse may terminate it at will. In this way, Glendon concludes, current divorce laws serve to inform the community that marriage is no longer a permanent contract.

Women were among the most outspoken advocates of no-fault divorce because they believed it would strengthen their rights. Ironically, as Lenore Weitzman explains in her book *The Divorce Revolution,* the major effect of the change has been to harm the woman's bargaining position and to make divorce more financially rewarding for the noncustodial parent, usually the father.

The moral seal of approval on no-fault divorce, combined with the generally unequal division of assets, sends a clear message to men, who are more likely to initiate divorce, that abandoning their responsibilities to their families is acceptable to the community. If divorce is to be discouraged, this moral message is to be reversed and its economic consequences changed accordingly.

Economic sanctions

Galston argues that it is insufficient merely to express unequivocally society's moral opinion. "Mandatory declarations—laws with teeth—are typically needed to convince citizens that the community is serious about its professed standards of responsibility. From drunk driving to racial discrimination, vigorous enforcement backed by sanctions has proved essential in changing behavior."

David T. Ellwood of Harvard University, in his book *Poor Support,* suggests that the system of providing child support should be modified so that all parents have a responsibility to their children, whether they live with them or not. To this effect, he suggests that both parents' Social Security numbers should be registered on a child's birth certificate, so that it would be possible to find either parent if he or she left the child. He further suggests that all absent parents be required to allot a portion of their income to the support of their children and that these payments be withheld from their paychecks like Social Security. Failure to make these payments would be considered "an offense comparable to tax evasion." In this way the responsibility of absent parents would be clearly expressed and enforced. The increased responsibilities of absent fathers, Ellwood suggests, would reduce the "financial incentive to create single-parent families."

Another measure, it seems to me, would be in case of divorce, to divide the family's assets not between fathers and mothers, but three ways, with the third part going to whoever is the custodial parent (typically the mother). The size of the third part would depend on the number and ages of the children. As far as I can determine, this is an idea that has not been discussed, let alone implemented by policy makers, so far. However, it is much in line with Mary Ann Glendon's widely recognized notion of "children first," the idea that their needs should take precedence in any divorce arrangements.

Other students of public policy favor positive economic incentives to make it easier for families to dedicate themselves to children and to make parents, mainly fathers, less inclined to walk out. Many European societies provide parents with such an allowance for each child they have, as well as numerous services from health care to counseling. Two economists, C. Eugene Steuerle and Jason Juffras, suggest a $1,000 refundable tax credit for every child, which in effect would serve as a form of child allowance. Over the years, taxes have taken an ever-larger bite out of family income. In 1950 only 2 percent of gross annual income was paid in the form of federal income and payroll taxes by a median-income family. Nowadays the figure hovers at more than 20 percent. In turn, the personal exemption has shriveled: if it were as valuable as it was in 1950, it would be nearly $7,000; instead it is only a little more than $2,000.

Unfortunately, during the 1992 election campaign, the income tax exemption for children was the focus of debate because President Bush advocated increasing it rather than instituting a child allowance. If we proceed in that direction, parents who both work outside the household will be favored over those households in which one of the parents (or both, in part) stay home to attend to the children. The reason is that while child allowances (or tax credits, if properly crafted) are allotted to all parents, tax exemptions help only those who have taxable incomes. This excludes the poor and those with relatively low incomes. And it provides much more of a benefit for the rich than for those less well off, especially to families in which more time is dedicated to parenting and less to generating income. A public policy that relies on child allowances is the one that is truly pro-family.

Welfare laws need to be revised, too. At present, in nearly every jurisdiction, welfare payments are cut off if a recipient marries a working person, thus discouraging marriage. Just as we have practically eliminated most of the marriage penalty that used to exist in the tax law (and the rest should be removed), marriage of those on welfare should be welcomed rather than penalized.

Also, other states should follow those fourteen states in which welfare agencies have changed their policies and are working to maintain families rather than simply ignoring them. The Family Preservation Program in New York City provides every two welfare families covered by the program with a caseworker who works with them as many as twenty hours a week. The caseworker arranges for home-based services such as parent training, job skills development, and homemaking. The cost is $8,000 a year per family, compared to $20,000 a year per child in foster care.

More generally, Karl Zinsmeister, a writer on family affairs, points out:

> Interventions must operate through and with parents, not around them. Day care programs, for instance, ought to require classroom participation by each parent on a rotating basis. Child counseling should include parents. Unless undertaken cautiously, well-intentioned public efforts to compensate for parental remoteness can have the inadvertent effect of apologizing for, and increasing, such remoteness.

When all is said and done, if we wish to communicate that we care more about sustaining families than we did in the heyday of permissiveness, alternative life-styles experimentation, and antifamily ideology, we should make divorce less easy. This can be achieved without returning to the days when divorce was illegal, which led to all kinds of unwholesome social practices—from living with one person while being married to another to quickie divorces in other countries (a policy that discriminated against those who could not afford a trip to the Dominican Republic or Mexico).

Such changes in divorce laws will not save all marriages; nothing could achieve such a goal, nor should it be attempted. But we should offer incentives that would make staying married and attending to one's children more attractive. And we should go after parents who cease to pay for their children after divorce, both because it is their duty and to make divorce less lucrative. My main concern, though, is not with incentives or punishments, but with the need for a change of heart: people need to enter marriage more responsibly and be more committed to making it work.

Marriage and the Childless Couple

So far the discussion has deliberately focused on parents' responsibility to children. People who have kids ought to strive to make their marriages work and should avoid divorce as often as possible. But what about couples that choose not to have children or whose children have left the nest? Mary Ann Mason, in her book *The Equality Trap,* confronts this issue head on. She argues that we should have, in effect, two kinds of marriages, one for those with children (much more binding) and one for those without. As she sees it, childless marriages fall under the category of "relationships," and the emphasis in these should be on the freedom of the individual. Such relationships could be governed by a contract, provided it was written and carefully constructed.

Behind her idea is a libertarian concept of human nature. She sees adults as individuals who, in situations that do not affect children, are capable of "playing their own game." Social philosopher Michael Novak characterizes this libertarian view of marriage:

> The central idea of our foggy way of life, however, seems unambiguous enough. It is that it is solitary and brief, and that its aim is self-fulfillment. Next come beliefs in establishing the

imperium of the self. Total mastery over one's surroundings, control over the disposition of one's time—these are necessary conditions for self-fulfillment. . . . In such a vision of the self, marriage is merely an alliance.

Sometimes a cultural theme is captured in a few lines, such as these from *Newsweek*: "Stuck marriages often break up—or worse, don't. Many go on to become what Dr. William B. Phillips, an Atlanta family counselor, calls the 'American Gold Watch Marriage'—short on excitement and fulfillment but long on security." The implied value judgment is stark: it puts excitement and fulfillment above security and continuity and the stability that it implies. One is entitled to make such a choice, but need we assume that it is automatically, across the board, the better of the two options? Many married people who are not devotees of pop psychology seem to feel otherwise, as their continued "stuck" behavior indicates.

In contrast with this idealization of the individual as an autonomous being, strong social science data show that people who are isolated and not involved in sustained relationships (of which marriage is the primary category) are more likely to be physically and mentally ill. The unmarried have higher mortality rates than the married (from all causes of death). A study of more than 2,500 adults found that the mortality rate among isolated men was 3.87 times higher than that of men with a high level of social relations (marriage, contact with extended family, and so on). Women who had a low level of social integration had a mortality rate that was nearly twice as high as that of women with a high level of social integration. Four other similar studies found that socially isolated individuals had a mortality rate that was between 1.07 to 4.0 times that of highly social individuals. The influence of social networks rivals such known physical factors as "cigarette smoking, blood pressure, blood lipids, and physical activity." Survivors of heart attacks who lived alone were nearly twice as likely to suffer a second attack within six months as those who lived with a companion.

Married people do not simply live longer, stay healthier, and exact fewer community costs. A 1991 study by Lawrence A. Kurdek at Wright State University of more than 6,500 adults found that "married persons reported greater happiness and less depression than persons who were not currently married." Another study found that divorced women were more likely to abuse alcohol than were married women.

The underlying reason for these phenomena is that most people deeply need one another. They need bonding—not as much as children, who are only partially formed persons—but still a great deal. In isolation most people become unformed, if not unglued. And although people can have a variety of relationships, with friends and kin and pets, for most these are supplements to or inadequate substitutes for the stable and institutionalized bonds that marriage provides.

Sociologists Peter and Brigitte Berger explain:

> Marriage is designed to provide a "haven" of stable identity and meaning in a social situation where these are very scarce commodities. Here there is the norm of mutual concern for all aspects of the individual's life. Further, it is here that two individuals are in a position to construct a "world of their own," again something that is not easy to do elsewhere amid the complexities of modern life.

The power of the marital bond comes into sharp relief when one spouse has a chronic or terminal illness. Under such circumstances the other spouse will usually stick by through thick and thin, providing love and care. There are numerous reports of husbands who visited their wives in nursing homes day in and day out for years; wives, too, have been known to patiently nurse their husbands after strokes and through long bouts with cancer and Alzheimer's disease. In contrast, most friendships (there are, of course, exceptions) do not carry such a bond of mutual support. Friends, however well meaning, tend to visit less and less frequently, and the time and attention that they afford is rather limited compared with that of a spouse.

We should avoid here as elsewhere "the either/or" curse. To suggest that most adults thrive on bonding is not to suggest that their individuality needs to be lost as they become immersed in a relationship. A person who becomes steeped in a relationship need not find, as women did in traditional families, that he or she is under pressure to suppress his or her ambitions, even to become a family fixture—a wife and mother, but not a person in her own right. To suggest a higher valuation of the we-ness of being a couple (and a partner-parent) does not entail giving up a personal identity. Boundaries can be worked out that define the couple's (and family's) "we" zone (for instance, shared meals) and the individuals' "I" zones (my studies, your football game). Sustaining marriage requires only that the we-ness be significant and that conflicts between the "I" zones of various family members (and between the "I" zones and the "we" zone) be worked out with an eye to maintaining the union. It does *not* entail suppressing the "I" zones.

Because people outside lasting relationships are often damaged in every sense of the term, the moral voice of the community should repeat what our forefathers and -mothers knew a long time ago: people are born as halves and gravitate toward one another to find their completion. We do not mean to ostracize those who remain single as "aging bachelors" and "spinsters," and we can be less concerned and agitated about childless divorces than about those that involve children. But we poorly serve the community, and the many persons involved, if we fail to communicate that together is better for most people, most of the time.

In Conclusion

Having a child is not merely a personal, private matter. It is an act that has significant consequences for the community. Hence those who bring children into the world have a social obligation to attend to their moral education. Children have no inborn moral values, and unless these values are introduced, they will not become civil members of the community. The best way to educate most infants (up to at least two years) is through bonding with their parents. Child care centers, especially the kind that are most common in the United States, are a poor substitute. Therefore it is important that parents who have satisfied their elementary economic needs invest themselves in their children by spending less time on their careers and consumeristic pursuits and more time with their youngsters. The community should enable parents to do this—by encouraging paid leave, flextime, and other such measures—and express its support for such an ordering of priorities. This is not an indirect way of suggesting that mothers should stay home; both parents share the responsibility to attend to their children. The community should not stigmatize but appreciate those who do.

3 ♦ The Communitarian School

Character Formation and Moral Education

IF the moral infrastructure of our communities is to be restored, schools will have to step in where the family, neighborhoods, and religious institutions have been failing. In the Communitarian's ideal world, children would come to school with their basic characters well formed and their values sufficiently internalized. Children already enrolled in school would have their character traits further reinforced at home (traits that had been instilled at an early age). Under such conditions, teachers would be able to concentrate on passing on information and skills—on what is called "cognitive development"—rather than be charged with dealing extensively with personality development and introduction of values.

But this is not the case in contemporary America. Youngsters are enrolled in many public schools—and quite a few private ones—with their characters underdeveloped and without a firm commitment to values. The basic reason is that the families have been dismembered or the parents are overworked or consumed by other concerns and ambitions. As a result, the children tend to be poor students. Moreover, if their lack of character and moral values are not attended to while at school, they will graduate to become deficient workers, citizens, and fellow community members. The moral deficit among the young is not limited to inner-city schools, in which violence and drug abuse are common and in which the basic conditions for learning are often missing. Nationwide, one out of twenty (5.3 percent) pupils carries a gun. Many public schools now find that they need to install metal detectors at their entrances and hire security guards. The number of young Americans killed by firearms was more than twice as high in 1990 as it was in 1970 (2,162 versus 1,059). An indication of the dire state schools are in is that we debate whether students should be allowed to carry beepers—by which they are summoned to deal drugs.

Although there are long lists of what our youngsters require, we Communitarians argue that two requirements loom over all others, indeed are at the foundation of most other needs: to develop the basic personality traits that characterize effective individuals and to acquire core values. In the sizable educational literature on the subject, both are sometimes referred to as "developing character."

Cracking the Summer Reading Lists.

We mean by *character* the psychological muscles that allow a person to control impulses and defer gratification, which is essential for achievement, performance, and moral conduct. The *core values,* which need to be transmitted from generation to generation, contain moral substances that those with the proper basic personality can learn to appreciate, adapt, and integrate into their lives: hard work pays, even in an unfair world; treat others with the same basic dignity with which you wish to be treated (or face the consequences); you feel better when you do what is right than when you evade your moral precepts.

Character Formation

There is little mystery as to what proper character development entails. In essence, it is acquiring the capacity to control one's impulses and to mobilize oneself for acts other than the satisfaction of biological needs and immediate desires. Workers need such self-control so that they can stick to their tasks rather than saunter into work late and turn out slapdash products, becoming able to observe a work routine that is often not very satisfying by itself. Citizens and community members need self-control so that they will not demand ever more services and handouts while being unwilling to pay taxes and make contributions to the commons, a form of citizen infantilism. And self-control—together with a growing sense of commitment to values—makes people more tolerant of those from different ethnic, racial, and political backgrounds. Such tolerance is a major foundation of democratic societies and polities.

When we look at the violent ways people in other countries—from India to Somalia, from Yugoslavia to Ireland—"deal" with their differences, we realize the importance of instilling in each new generation of youngsters, and those who join us from other cultures, the capacity to hold impulses in check. Impulse control is even more essential for a democratic society than the often cited prerequisites of being politically informed and voting regularly. The only reason we can focus on these features of democracy is that we implicitly assume that character formation is well attended to. However, interethnic violence in places such as Los Angeles, New York City, and Miami alerts us to the fact that character formation requires unrelenting commitment—not only in faraway places, but in our urban centers and quite a few suburbs, towns, and villages.

Education proceeds by tying gratification to the development of qualities that are socially useful and morally appropriate. That is, by relating satisfaction to completing a task, taking other people's feelings into account, playing by the rules, and so on, one acquires the ability to abide by moral tenets and to live up to one's social responsibilities.

Certainly education can draw too much of the ego's energies into the inner mechanisms of self-control. This is what we mean when we refer to being "uptight"—people who are obsessed with their careers or achievements and are unable to relax or show affection. Such excessive self-control has concerned social scientists in the past, especially in the sixties, and has led to a call for less education and more unbounded expression for the ego (the days of "let it all hang out"). Excessive self-control, however, is uncommon in contemporary America; indeed, many youngsters come to school with a rather deficient capacity to guide themselves. The fact that a larger proportion of the young find it very difficult to be punctual, get up in the morning, do homework on their own, and complete tasks in an orderly and timely fashion—these are but the most visible indications of a deeper deficiency: insufficient self-control.

As a result, schools are left with the task of making up for undereducation in the family and laying the psychic foundation for character and moral conduct. This is where the various commissions that have studied educational deficits missed a major point. By and large they argued for loading students with more hours of science, foreign language, math, and other skills and bodies of knowledge. *But you cannot fill a vessel that has yet to be cast.*

Self-Discipline as a Master Key

To illustrate what is at issue, let us look at a specific incident. A young secretary I retained was asked to form a list using the telephone Yellow Pages. When she was unable to do so, it became clear that she had neither a command of the English alphabet nor an understanding of the principles of categorization and subcategorization involved.

Such an inability would usually be considered a cognitive deficiency, a result of poor teaching or low IQ. But if you ask why it should be so difficult to teach someone a list of twenty-six items and the principles of a very simple classification system, you soon realize that something quite different is amiss. More is at issue than the fact that no one ever took the time and trouble to teach the person involved, and many others like her, what the alphabet contains and how classifications work. Nor is it usually a question of IQ level for most pupils, because so little comprehension or intelligence is involved. To gain a "feel" for what is at issue, a reader who is familiar with the Yellow Pages may wish to consider what it would take if she or he were required to memorize, say, a twenty-six-digit telephone number. A considerable amount of effort is entailed, but it is *not* a cognitive effort; instead it takes concentration, impulse control, self-motivation, and an ability to face and overcome stress (in order to resist distractions and accept the "routine" work involved in memorizing). This element of psychic organization—the ability to mobilize and commit psychic energy to a task—is what those who are not learning well seem to lack most. It is what seems to account for their "inability" to do elementary computation (to memorize a few rules and discipline oneself to adhere to them, for example) or to write a coherent paragraph (to remember the rules of punctuation, that sentences have nouns, and so on—not necessarily effective writing, just straight English exposition).

School administrators, elected officials, and numerous commissions that have studied why Johnny can't read have found it easier and less controversial to focus on matters that can be measured, such as math and vocabulary tests, and have shunned those that raise moral issues. They have, for example, largely ignored such matters as the state of the character of our youngsters and the effects of such practices as permissiveness, grade inflation, and automatic grade promotion.

Discipline, Self-Discipline, and Internalization

How do we educate for character? Parents and educators often stress the importance of *discipline* in character formation and in the moral education of the new generation of Americans. In several public opinion surveys, teachers, school administrators, and parents rank a lack of discipline as the number one problem in our schools. They correctly perceive that in a classroom where students are restless, impatient, disorderly, and disrespectful, where rules and routines cannot be developed and maintained, learning is not possible.

Unfortunately discipline, as many people understand it, takes on an authoritarian meaning. A well-disciplined environment is often considered one in which teachers and principals "lay down the law" and will brook no talking back from students, who "show respect" by rising when the teacher enters the room and speak only when spoken to. Mayor Sharon Pratt Kelly of Washington, D.C., even suggested that schools ought to reexamine the use of corporal punishment. Indeed, in quite a few states physical punishment is still considered an effective way to maintain discipline. Moreover, the Supreme Court upheld a lower court that had maintained that schoolchildren were not protected by the Constitution from corporal punishment. The justices let stand a Texas law that authorizes the use of corporal punishment "short of deadly force."

If discipline is achieved by such authoritarian means, youngsters will behave as long as they are closely supervised and fear punishment. But as soon as the authorities turn their backs, they will misbehave. Moreover, their resentment at being coerced will express itself in some form of antisocial behavior. This is because the discipline is linked to punishment rather than to a commitment to doing what is right and avoiding what is wrong.

What the pupil—and the future adult—requires is *self-discipline,* the inner ability to mobilize and commit to a task he or she believes in and to feel positive—that is, self-rewarded—for having done so.

Internalization occurs in structured environments, but not under authoritarian conditions. Close, continuous, external supervision and punitive environments are counterproductive. What is required is a school structure made up of educating figures, rules, and organization of tasks that motivate students by providing clear guidelines. These must be both firmly upheld and be reasonable and *justified,* so that students can understand and accept the need to abide by them.

There is some social science evidence to support my thesis, although it is relatively scarce and somewhat indirect. The following findings are drawn from a study by James S. Coleman and his associates, one of the largest and most systematic studies in the field. Coleman and his colleagues studied 58,728 sophomores and seniors in 1,016 public, private, and parochial schools. They found that the single factor that separated effective from ineffective schools was the existence of discipline—and that the discipline had to be perceived by the students as legitimate rather than capriciously imposed. The latter point is of great importance: without a sense that the requirements introduced are sound and proper, students will not internalize discipline and hence their character will not benefit.

Educational requirements, in turn, must be clearly stated and the link between requirements and goals be fully explained. Curricula can be neither arbitrary nor subject to the whim of an individual teacher. To foster self-discipline, assignments need to be "doable," appropriately checked, and properly rewarded. When they are excessive and mechanical (such as the time one of my sons was required in high school to memorize the names of all the Indian tribes that resided in America), or when rewards are allocated according to irrelevant criteria (such as teacher favoritism, social status, or undue parental influence), requirements become dictates and not sources of involvement and ways to internalize commitments, to build self-discipline.

Moral Education

Character formation lays the psychic foundation for the ability both to mobilize to a task and to behave morally by being able to control impulses and defer gratification. However, character formation per se does not educate one to a specific set of virtues or values; it is without specific moral content. It provides the rectitude to tell the truth even if the consequences are unpleasant, but it does not teach the value of being truthful. It enables a person to refrain from imposing his sexual impulse on an unwilling partner, but it does not teach him that it is morally unacceptable to rape. Trying to develop character without attention to sharing of values with the young is like trying to develop the muscles of an athlete without having a particular sport in mind. It follows that if those who are being educated are to become committed to moral values, youngsters must acquire not only the capacity to commit—the psychological muscle that moral conduct requires—but also the values that direct the exercise, the application of the moral capacity. To the extent that the family no longer provides these values, the community turns to schools to teach the young to tell right from wrong.

Such moral education should be an integral part of all teaching. Richard McCloud, a Fairfax County, Virginia, teacher, put it well:

> When I read and study the Declaration of Independence to my junior students. . . I am not teaching historical facts as an end in themselves. Instead, I am implicitly teaching Thomas Jefferson's commitment to freedom and high moral standards. Molière's *Tartuffe* has much to say to my seniors about hypocrisy and deceit; Twain's *Huck Finn* speaks of common decency and friendship.

The Opposition

Unfortunately, schools, especially public ones, have been extremely reluctant to engage openly in moral education. School administrators claim that they are overloaded as it is. The public demands that they cover ever more subjects, in more depth. They are saddled with many problems the family and community are unable to cope with, such as teen pregnancy, drug and alcohol abuse, and violence; and they are understaffed and underfunded.

Moreover, moral education is very controversial. (This is especially true of public schools, which are attended by 88 percent of American students.) Boards of education find it is much safer politically not to include moral education in their agenda. Typically, a school counselor in Teaneck, New Jersey, explained, in reference to a hypothetical moral discussion among students: "If I come from the position of what is right and what is wrong, then I'm not their counselor."

"Whose morals are you going to teach?" is a kind of trump question that is often raised to stop all further exploration of the subject. Opponents of moral education frequently depict its advocates as Authoritarians who would impose their values on one and all. To bolster their argument, critics often cite cases of the banning of books or attempts to institute prayer in public schools. They call attention to instances such as one in Dallas, Texas, where school administrators had teachers rip out an offending page from a school textbook that referred to male genitals and bodily functions. In another example, school administrators at Simsbury High School in Simsbury, Connecticut, canceled the showing of Michael Cristofer's *The Shadow Box*, a Pulitzer Prize-winning play, after students refused to alter objectionable parts of the script.

Opponents of moral education also alarm us by bringing up instances in which Authoritarians tried to promote moral education by fostering Christian dogma in schools through the imposition of prayers. These are perceived to be but the opening wedge. If schools agree to mandated prayers, they argue, soon these groups will insist on selecting "appropriate" reading material, which will lead to the teaching of unscientific creationism. This, in turn, will be followed by outright religious indoctrination. Such suggestions concern followers of different religions, those who are agnostic or atheist and those who, while favorable to Christianity, wish to keep church and state separated. I would add that reciting a prayer a day (or even several) provides no more assurance that those in the classroom pews will be morally upright than repeating the Pledge of Allegiance makes the graduates of our schools true patriots. Moral education does not come that easily.

Although such instances do pertain to the transmission of values in the schools, they most certainly do not concern the kind of value education Communitarians are referring to. Reference here is to numerous values we share as a community—such as the inappropriateness of racial and gender discrimination, the rejection of violence, and the desirability of treating others with love, respect, and dignity. If we would transmit to the young in schools only these shared values, our world would be radically improved.

The Limits of Moral Reasoning

Among those schools that have overcome the opposition and turned to moral education (so far only a minority of public schools), there are quite a few that teach ethics in ways that, sadly, leave much to be desired. They have sought refuge in something called "moral reasoning," a highly cognitive approach built on the works of psychologists Jean Piaget and Lawrence Kohlberg, who were largely interested in developing moral *reasoning*, but not value internalization. In these classes youngsters learn, at best, to argue about moral issues, but no attempt is made to enhance their moral commitments. Moral commitment requires helping young people feel more strongly about those values they already have (or acquire in schools), which can be achieved by using stories, drama, role-playing, videotapes, "courts," visiting places where homeless people hang out or a polluted lake, and other such educational devices that are evocative and not merely informative.

A typical course on moral reasoning starts with something called "values clarification." In a typical lesson, students are asked to list what is dear to them—money, reputation, and power—and then to rank these pursuits in terms of which they hold most important. They fail—and are thus considered in need of moral tutoring—only if they have difficulty in deciding what is up and what is down in *their* scale of interests.

They are further helped to clarify their preferences through exercises such as the lifeboat drill. In this exercise students are told to imagine that they are in a lifeboat with a group of people that includes a scientist, an artist, a teacher, and a general (the list may vary). The boat is overloaded, and they must decide whom they would cast overboard first, second, and so on. In this way the students' values are revealed. For instance, do they rank art higher than arms? (Usually the teachers are cast off first and the kids themselves last.) As long as the pupils are clear on their preferred tossing order, and hence by implication their values, their moral education is considered properly advanced.

Under moral reasoning per se, nobody is supposed to discuss the question whom they *should have* cast overboard first or ask why there aren't enough lifeboats to begin with. More deeply, I question whether such extreme examples (what ethicists call "limit situations") really prepare one for real-life moral choices. And as columnist William Raspberry notes, learning *about* ethics is not the same as learning ethics itself. "Nobody ever had an epiphany," he noted in a different context, "while cramming for a comparative religion final."

In more advanced classes (and some that are taught on the college level), students learn to argue at even more elevated levels. They are taught about various ethical theories like utilitarianism and deontology, about autonomy and beneficence, and so on. Students are expected to sort out from many conflicting claims which course to follow. Thus, in one case, prepared by the University of Minnesota and used in a discussion of ethics, a social worker visits the home of an ill person. The patient tells her visitor that if her condition deteriorates further, she will use her gun "long before anyone puts me into a nursing home." The question is, should the social worker report the suicide threat to the authorities and have the gun removed? It is then suggested that because of "the principle of autonomy, the client's wishes are to be respected" and the social worker is not to intervene. But if someone put more weight on beneficence, the gun would be removed.

Such values clarification and development of moral reasoning may be helpful if and when they are provided to people who already have evolved moral commitments. They can help such people sort out how specifically to express and apply their generalized sense that they ought to do what is right and to order various moral values when these do not readily dovetail with one another. But for youngsters whose moral commitments are underdeveloped, such classes tend to become idle debating clubs. "Because the typical course in applied ethics concentrates on problems and dilemmas, the students may easily lose sight of the fact that some things are clearly right and some clearly wrong, that some ethical truths are not subject to serious debate," notes Christine Hoff Sommers, a professor of philosophy at Clark University. In moral reasoning, teachers are typically expected to be passive discussion facilitators rather than active proponents of values. The students' success in these exercises is based not so much on the depth and scope of their moral sensibilities, but on how well they spin an argument. They might as well be debating whether to steer a ship northeast or southeast when the motor is broken and nobody is repairing it. What is missing between character formation (the ability to commit and guide oneself) and the development of moral reasoning is the *internalization* of (i.e., making part of oneself) commitments to a set of substantive values, to be achieved through moral *education.*

Whose Values?

The challenge "Whose values will you teach?" can be readily answered by starting with the myriad values we all share. (Many of these are shared not only in one community or by Americans, but much more widely.) Nobody considers it moral to abuse children, rape, steal (not to mention commit murder), be disrespectful of others, discriminate, and so on.

At this point someone is sure to ask, "What are you going to teach about abortion?" The pro-choice, pro-life debate is an exception that does not disprove the rule. Some values, a small subset of the total in well-functioning communities, are contested. These exceptions can be dealt with either by letting the students learn about both sides of the issue or by openly omitting them. Moreover, these issues are helpful in showing the pain of moral conflicts and the merit of genuine consensus building, a consensus we do have on most values.

Sure, say the opponents, but people agree only on vague generalities, which amount almost to banalities. They argue: When you come down to specifics, disagreements will dominate, and then whose specifics will you teach? Reverend Charles Fink of Northport, New York, who participated in an effort to form a value curriculum, writes:

> Let Mr. Castelli [former director of church-state issues for People for the American Way], Norman Lear . . . and I sit on a committee to flesh out a program for teaching values in the public schools. Yes, we will all resonate to words like honesty, truthfulness, responsibility, self-respect, respect for others, etc., but when it comes time to apply these civic virtues to concrete cases, I think it will be found that Mr. Lear and I will disagree sharply on what responsibility means in terms of sexual conduct, or what respect for others entails as it relates to abortion and euthanasia, or what self-respect implies when it comes to smoking pot.

Not so fast. Even when it comes to specifics, there is more consensus than at first seems to be the case.

Take the following quite specific conducts education professor William Damon reports we would encounter walking around some schools:

> A counselor is calling a student's home about apparently excused absences, only to find that the parent's letters have been forged. A young boy is in the principal's office for threatening

his teacher with a knife. Three students are separated from their class after hurling racial epithets at a fourth. A girl is complaining that her locker has been broken into and all her belongings stolen. A small group of boys are huddling in a corner, shielding an exchange of money for drug packets. In the playground, two girls grab a third and punch her in the stomach for flirting with the wrong boy.

Not many people would claim that these are morally appropriate behaviors; teaching what is wrong with them could keep a whole beehive of educators busy for years to come.

Or take date rape. Let's assume that we can all agree that students must realize that using force to impose themselves on others is morally unacceptable. In teaching it, we run into a "specific," the belief that surprisingly many young males hold that when a woman says "no" she means "yes," and hence it is all right to proceed despite her protests. An educator should be able to build on the students' value that "real no's" are to be heeded, to show that when a woman says "no," a decent person holds back; and that if he has any doubt about a "yes," he should seek further clarification from her before proceeding. That is, a position on specifics can often be worked out when the basic value commitments are in place, a position that almost everyone will find morally compelling.

The same holds for the value we put on life when it comes to questions such as when to terminate medical treatment. There is broad consensus that we should not terminate people who are conscious or able to regain consciousness. There is a strong and widening consensus that we should not continue medical services to people who are brain dead, with no chance of returning to human life. Many also agree that we should allow people to refuse what are called heroic measures (such as resuscitating their hearts when they fail), but fewer agree that it is all right for them to refuse feeding—again, a rather specific, worked-out consensus. Sure, some specific questions are contested, but there is more than enough here for anyone to teach the high value that our society puts on individual life.

Or take the value of truth telling. No one argues that lying wantonly is commendable. And we all realize that there is room for "white" lies, those that are clearly aimed at helping the person to whom we lie. For instance, it is better not to discourage a patient who is about to be wheeled into surgery by reviewing all the dangers involved, unless the patient clearly indicates a desire to be retold the anticipated risks.

It may be further argued that it is debatable whether or not one should lie for national security purposes. But this raises the more general question of how you deal with a situation in which two values come into conflict, a matter that students most assuredly need to be taught. This issue, however, does not detract from the fact that there is no ethical justification for the government to lie unless it has demonstrable, compelling reasons, and even then it would be more morally appropriate to refuse to comment than to actively lie.

Deeper, well-trained philosophers and debaters will find disagreements on specifics of these more complicated issues, such as "What if the government truly believes our military bases in country X are endangered, but it is close to an election?" But such unresolved subtleties need not stop us from teaching second-, fourth-, and even tenth-graders that with rare exceptions, truth telling is preferable to lying.

E. J. Dionne, Jr., in his fine book, *Why Americans Hate Politics,* provides another example of how we are often in agreement on the basics and quite a few specifics of moral issues. He shows how in 1991 Congress (which often engages in symbolic, nonissue-oriented debates) thoroughly and openly discussed the moral appropriateness of the use of military force by the United States to stop Saddam Hussein's threat to other countries after Iraqi forces occupied and brutalized Kuwait. Although some members of Congress wanted to wait a bit longer, to see whether or not economic sanctions would work, others wanted to proceed militarily immediately. There was, though, a basic consensus that the use of force was justified not only in abstract hypothetical situations, but under the specific circumstances at hand. The point is not that the majority supported one position or another, but that a specific situation was examined against the criteria of what is a "just war," and most concerned concluded that the imminent Gulf War was a just one. The remaining difference—wait a bit longer versus hit Hussein now—was primarily a matter of policy and strategy, with little bearing on the moral issue of whether force was justified, upon which there was almost universal consensus.

Far from being necessarily controversial, values education may win wide support. The 148 public schools in Baltimore County, Maryland, teach a common core of twenty-four values, ranging from truth and responsibility to due process. A 1991 survey found that 98 percent of the district administrators, 85 percent of the parents, and *75 percent of the students* held that values education was a good idea.

Most important, we need not worry that educators will "brainwash" students who are captive audiences in their classrooms or indoctrinate them with their moral viewpoints. Students are exposed to a large variety of voices, coming to them from television, radio, magazines, porn shops, peers, and many others. That is, there are natural checks and balances built into the social environment. If somewhere one teacher were to advance a moral concept that was outside the community consensus—say, that we must all become vegetarians, pacifists, or Zen Buddhists—the students would have plenty of other sources to draw on to counter such teaching. Indeed, the opposite is true: if typical educators, whose values tend to be well within the community range, refrain from adding their moral voice to the cacophony of voices the students hear anyhow, the students would miss one perspective—and remain exposed only to all the other voices, many of which are less committed to values the community holds dear. It makes little sense to muzzle the educators and let everyone else spout their messages without inhibition.

The School as a Set of Experiences

How do we teach moral values, as opposed to merely building up the capacity for moral reasoning and disputations? How do we build up moral commitments? There is one way that far surpasses all others. The most important social science observation here is that *experiences are more effective teachers than lectures.* This is particularly evident in extracurricular activities, especially sports. True, these can be abused, such as when coaches focus on winning as the only object and neglect to instill learning to play by the rules, teamwork, and camaraderie. "Graduates" of such activities will tend to be people who are aggressive, maladjusted members of the community. However, if coaches, and the messages they impart, are well integrated into the values education of a school, and if parents see the importance of using sports to educate rather than to win, sports can be a most effective way to enhance values education.

Why are extracurricular activities credited with such extraordinary power? Because they generate experiences that are powerful educational tools. Thus, if one team plays as a bunch of individuals and loses because its adversary played as a well-functioning team, the losing players learn—in a way that no pep talk or slide show can—the merit of playing as a team.

The same holds for other activities that take place at school. They provide experiences that tend to have deep educational effects, either positive or negative. Thus the first step toward enhancing the moral educational role of schools is to *increase the awareness and analysis of the school as a set of experiences*. Schools should be seen not as a collection of teachers, pupils, classrooms, and curricula. Instead, examine the parking lots: Are they places in which wild driving takes place and school authorities are not to be seen, or are they places where one learns respect for others' safety, regulated either by faculty or by fellow students? Are the cafeterias places where students belt each other with food and the noise is overwhelming, or are they civilized places where students can conduct meaningful conversations over lunch? Are the corridors areas where muscles and stature are required to avoid being pushed aside by bullies, or are they safe conduits patrolled by faculty or students? Does vandalism go unpunished, are drugs sold openly, and are pupils rewarded or punished according to criteria other than achievement (perhaps because they avoid confrontation, obey without question, or come from affluent or otherwise socially preferred backgrounds)? Or is vandalism held in check and the damage, when vandalism does occur, is corrected by the offending students? Are drug sales dealt with swiftly and severely? Are students treated according to reasonable and understandable criteria?

In some public schools in large cities, the dominant educational issue is maintaining law and order, which is a minimal precondition for creating experiences that may build morality. If students are armed with guns, sell drugs, and harass teachers, these issues command urgent attention—attention that must be accorded before one can turn to the more subtle points of moral education.

In many other schools, including public-suburban and private schools, a variety of Radical Individualist approaches hinder moral education. Here students are often treated as if they are miniature adults with formed judgments and unbounded rights, rather than as persons whose development needs to be nurtured. In such schools class activities and rules are fashioned to please the students' tastes rather than to cultivate and enrich them. Grades are dished out to make students feel better about themselves and boost their self-esteem, rather than to prod them to grow. Homework (a fine way to build up self-discipline because it must be done largely without close supervision) is curtailed in order not to "overburden" the students.

Not all experiences are generated outside the classroom. A powerful example of how one may generate experiences in a classroom is found in Iowa. In April 1968 Jane Elliott, a teacher in Riceville, Iowa, decided that it would be inappropriate to hold a conventional discussion of the plight of black Americans shortly after the assassination of Martin Luther King, Jr. Instead she decided to try to teach discrimination to her third-graders by affecting their experiences. Her students, Elliott felt, understood discrimination in a neutral, distant sense—what she termed "sympathetic indifference"—but they didn't comprehend its true impact.

So Elliott divided her class into two groups by eye color—the blue-eyed students in one group and the brown-eyed in the other. "Today," she said one Friday, "the blue-eyed people will be on the bottom and the brown-eyed people on the top." Elliott continued: "What I mean is that brown-eyed people are better than blue-eyed people. They are cleaner than blue-eyed people. They are more civilized than blue-eyed people. And they are smarter than blue-eyed people." Rules, and Elliott's attitude, were geared specifically to benefit the brown-eyed children.

The experiment's effects were swift and severe. "Long before noon, I was sick," Elliott recalls. "I wished I had never started it. . . . By the lunch hour, there was no need to think before identifying a child as blue- or brown-eyed. I could tell simply by looking at them. The brown-eyed children were happy, alert, having the times of their lives. . . . The blue-eyed children were miserable." In short, the children had learned through *experience* what discrimination is like.

The children were clearly affected by the exercise. Brown-eyed Debbie Anderson said: "I felt mad [on blue-eye-preferred Monday] . . . I felt dirty. And I did not feel as smart as I did on Friday." Student Theodore Perzynski wrote in part: "I do not like discrimination. It makes me sad. I would not like to be angry all my life."

Perhaps one of the most telling anecdotes is a story one of the mothers of Elliott's students told:

> I want you to know that you've made a tremendous difference in our lives since your Discrimination Day exercise. My mother-in-law stays with us a lot, and she frequently uses the word "nigger." The very first time she did it after your lesson, my daughter went up to her and said, "Grandma, we don't use that word in our house, and if you're going to say it, I'm going to leave until you go home." We were delighted. I've been wanting to say that to her for a long, long time. And it worked, too. She's stopped saying it.

Such experiences leave strong and lasting impressions. In 1984 Jane Elliott's class had a reunion. They vividly recalled the lesson. Former student Susan Rolland noted: "I still find myself sometimes, when I see some blacks together and I see how they act, I think, well, that's black. . . . And then later—as I said, I won't even finish the thought before I remember back when I was in that position."

Verla Buls added: "At a softball game a couple of weekends ago. . . . there was this black guy I know. We said, 'Hi,' and we hugged each other, and some people really looked, just like, 'What are you doing with him?' And you just get this burning feeling in you. You just want to let it out and put them through what we went through to find out they're not any different." Other students reported that their career choices were influenced by the discrimination experience. Several chose as a result to join the Peace Corps or work with other cultures overseas.

Ideally, the teachers and principals of each school should at least once every three years engage in an extensive "retreat." Here they would spend a weekend, in some secluded place, drawing on professional facilitators, to examine the experiences their school generates. They would agree to set aside cognitive questions about the curriculum—such as whether to teach new or old math or which method of teaching English is the best—and focus on one question: What experiences do we fashion? (If possible, a social scientist would first interview students on this matter and then make the report available at the retreat.)

Once a school has analyzed itself in terms of the experiences it generates, those experiences need to be compared to the moral and social lessons the school intends to impart. If the lesson imparted and the intentions agreed upon are in conflict, the school should consider changing its way of conducting itself. Changes may need to encompass the way shared spaces are supervised, the role of competitive sports, the criteria for providing grades, and so on—to bring actual experiences in line with those the school believes will prove more educational.

For example, if a school seeks to impart the message that blacks and whites should treat one another respectfully and develop relations across racial lines, lectures on racial harmony alone will not do the trick. The school would do well to examine seating patterns in the cafeteria. If it finds that students are segregating themselves along racial lines, it may wish to meet with students of both races and explore the reason for this self-imposed ghettolike behavior. The school may then work with the students to encourage interracial lunches (twice a week?), one-on-one interracial contacts, group meetings on tolerance, and so on. Whatever the school tries, it should be aware that its actions, and the experiences they generate, go farther in affecting the moral conduct of the students than most lectures and exhortations.

Less Rotation, More Bonding

For teachers to be more than purveyors of information and skills, for them to be able to educate, they must be able to bond more closely with students than they do now in many schools. Such bonding may be encouraged by arranging for less rotation of pupils. Many American high schools are currently organized as if a powerful sociological engineer were intent on minimizing the bonds between students and teachers and seeking to ensure that whatever peer bonds formed would not be classroom-related. These effects stem from the fact that students are reshuffled each time the bell rings, every forty-five minutes or so, while the various subject teachers stay put. As a consequence, students, especially in larger schools, rarely develop bonds as members of a class group, because the class members who come together in one period do not remain together for the next. As a result, peer groups, which often hold much sway over members, especially in moral matters, are not classroom-based and are formed for other, often irrelevant-to-education reasons. Peer groups tend to be formed around other values or occasions, whether it is racing cars or heavy-metal rock music. Although these peer groups don't necessarily have to oppose community and educational values, sociological studies show that they often do. They are rarely mobilized by educators on the side of moral education in typical high-rotation schools.

Another result is that teachers cannot form bonds with their students because they have few opportunities to get to know them. Teachers are typically responsible for a subject and not for a "class"—not for a given group of pupils, say, all those in the eleventh grade, third section. Thus the highly specialized school organization is, in effect, a systematic hindrance to bonding with educators, which is an essential prerequisite for moral education.

High schools should be reorganized to facilitate experience-based moral education. Teachers should be in charge of a particular "class," teaching the same group of youngsters, say, three subjects (especially those rich in value content such as history and literature) or two subjects and civics. The same teacher would also be the class's homeroom teacher, in charge of disciplinary matters. Discipline should be approached by the teacher not as if he or she were a punitive police officer, but as a faculty member whose task it is to use instances of improper conduct to engage in moral education. Schools might also institute a policy whereby such teachers would follow the same students from ninth through twelfth grades.

Such changes, in turn, would necessitate modifications in the ways the teachers themselves are trained, to make them less specialized. Note, though, that many teachers, especially those who teach humanities or liberal arts, are already properly prepared. In any event, without more bonding and contacts that are more encompassing, extensive, and value rich, moral education is unlikely to succeed.

McDonald's Is Not Our Kind of Place

In today's reality you need to look beyond the school itself to examine those factors that hinder or provide opportunities for generating educational experiences that enhance character formation and moral education. Today's high school students spend much time outside the school and within the work environment. It would be shortsighted to ignore the educational effects of this context. As I have stressed, much of the education of children takes the form of experiences; since work has become such an important part of many high school students' lives, it too must be examined in this light: Is it educational?

I regret to report that from this viewpoint, McDonald's (and other companies like it, from Roy Rogers to Dunkin' Donuts) are far from benign creations. McDonald's is bad for your kids. I don't mean the flat patties and the white-flour buns. I mean the jobs it takes to mass-produce these delicacies. About two-thirds of high school juniors and seniors these days have part-time paying jobs, many in fast-food chains, of which McDonald's is the pioneer, trendsetter, and symbol. Such employment would seem to be straight from the pages of the Founding Fathers' moral education manual on how to bring up self-reliant, work-ethic-driven youngsters. From lemonade stands to newspaper routes, it is a long-standing tradition that American youngsters hold paying jobs. Here, kids learn the fruits of labor and trade and develop the virtue of self-discipline. (Many Europeans have a rather different view of the work ethic: their teenage children are expected to spend their time skiing, improving their tennis or ballet, even honing their manners—not pumping gas.)

Hardee's, Baskin-Robbins, Kentucky Fried Chicken, and the like appear to be nothing more than a vast extension of the lemonade stand. They provide large numbers of steady teen jobs, test the teenagers' stamina, and reward them quite well compared with many other teen jobs. Upon closer examination, however, the McDonald's kind of job is rather uneducational in several ways. Far from providing an opportunity for self-discipline, self-supervision, and self-scheduling, like the old-fashioned paper route, it is highly structured and routinized. True, students still must mobilize themselves to go to work, but once they don their uniforms, their tasks are spelled out in minute detail. The McDonald's Corporation dictates for thousands of local outlets the shape of the coffee cups; the weight, size, shape and color of the patties; the texture of the napkins (if any); how often fresh coffee is to be made (every eight minutes); and so on. There is little room for initiative, creativity, or even elementary rearrangements. Thus, fast-food franchises are breeding grounds for robots working for yesterday's assembly lines and not practice fields for committed workers in tomorrow's high-tech posts.

Some would argue that although these jobs are rather unsuitable for college-bound, middle-class youngsters, they are "ideal" for unemployed, lower-class, "nonacademic" minority youngsters. Indeed, minorities are highly represented in these jobs (over 22 percent of employees in eating establishments are black or Hispanic). In fact, food-service employment of minorities is growing rapidly—from 1980 to 1986, it increased at twice the rate of total industry growth. Although it is true that these workplaces provide income and even some training to such low-skilled youngsters, they also tend to perpetuate their disadvantaged status. Such jobs provide no career incentives and few marketable skills, and they can undermine school attendance and involvement.

The hours are long. Often the stores close late, and after closing workers must tally and clean up. There is no way that such amounts of work will not interfere with schoolwork, especially homework. Fifty-eight percent of the seniors at Walt Whitman High School in Montgomery County, an affluent area in Maryland, acknowledge that their jobs interfere with their schoolwork.

One study did find merit in jobs at McDonald's and similar places. The study reported that this work experience teaches teamwork and working under supervision. That may be true, but it must be noted, however, that such learning is not automatically educational or wholesome. For example, much of the supervision in fast-food places leans toward teaching the wrong kinds of compliance (blind obedience or being pissed off with the world, as the supervisors often are). Also, such compliance helps very little to develop the ability to form quality-of-work circles, in which employees and supervisors together seek to improve operations.

Supervision is often both tight and woefully inappropriate. In the days before industrialization and capitalism, the young were initiated into the world of work in close personal relations such as between a master (adult) craftsman and an apprentice. Even when a young person worked for someone other than his parents, he lived in the master's or farmer's home and was integrated into his family; he was not part of a teen horde.

Today, fast-food chains and other such places of work (record shops, bowling alleys) keep costs down by having teens supervise teens, often with no adult on the premises. There is no mature adult figure to identify with, to emulate, or to provide a role model or mature moral guidance. The work culture varies from one store to another: some places are tightly run shops (must keep the cash registers ringing); in other places the employees may "party," only to be interrupted by the intrusion of customers. Rarely is there a "master" to learn from; rarely is there much worth learning. Indeed, far from being places where solid work values are being transmitted, these are places where all too often teen values dominate. Typically, when one of my sons was dishing out ice cream for Baskin Robbins in upper Manhattan, his fellow teen workers considered him a sucker for not helping himself to the till. Most of them believed they were entitled to a self-awarded "severance pay" of fifty dollars on their last day on the job.

The money raises additional issues. The lemonade stand and paper route money was your allowance. Apprentices, to the extent that they generated a significant flow of income, contributed most, if not all, of it to their parents' household.

Today's teen pay may be low by adult standards, but it is often substantial. Especially among the middle class, it is largely or wholly spent by the teens. That is, the youngsters live free at home and are allowed to keep considerable amounts of money. Where this money goes is not quite clear. Some use it to support themselves, especially among the poor. Some middle-class youngsters set money aside to help pay for college or save it for a major purchase, like a car. But large amounts seem to pay for an early introduction into trite elements of American consumerism: trendy clothes, trinkets, and whatever else is the fast-moving teen craze.

One may say that this is only fair and square: the youngsters are just being good American consumers, working and spending their money on what turns them on. At least, a cynic might add, the money isn't going to buy illicit drugs and booze. On the other hand, an educator might bemoan that these young, as-yet-unformed individuals are driven to buy objects of no intrinsic educational, cultural, or social merit. They learn early and quickly the dubious merit of keeping up with ever-changing mass-merchandising fads.

Moreover, many teens find the instant reward of money, and the youth status symbols it buys, much more alluring than credits earned in algebra, American history, or French. No wonder quite a few would rather skip school, and certainly homework, to work longer hours at a Burger King.

• It would be better if corporations that employ teens would, in cooperation with schools, define what is the proper amount of gainful work (not more than x hours per school week), determine how late kids may be employed on school nights (not later than 9:00 P.M.), and insist on proper supervision.

• Schools might provide credit for jobs if those jobs meet their educational criteria.

• Schools should be consulted by corporations on matters such as the nature of the supervision and on-the-job training setups.

• School representatives should be allowed to inspect the students' places of employment.

• School counselors should guide the students to those places of work that are willing to pay attention to educational elements of these jobs.

• Parents should encourage their children to seek jobs at places that are proper work settings and insist that fast-food chains and other franchises either shape up or else find it harder to employ their kids.

• Parents should agree with their children, the young workers, that a significant share of teen earnings be dedicated to the family or saved for mutually acceptable items.

• Above all, parents should look at teen employment not as automatically educational, but as an activity, like sports, that may be turned into an educational opportunity or could just as easily be abused. It is here that youngsters must learn to balance the quest for income with the need to pursue endeavors that do not pay off instantly.

A Year of National Service

A year of national service after high school could be the capstone of a student's educational experiences. More and more policy makers are supporting the idea of a year spent serving the country, interrupting the "lockstep" march from grade to grade and into and through college (or directly into the adult world of full-time work). It is a major way to build up the moral tenor and sense of social responsibility among the young. Although the suggested programs vary in detail, many favor a year of voluntary service that could be completed in places such as the armed forces, the Peace Corps, VISTA, or the Conservation Corps. Some would make it the senior year of high school; I prefer for it to follow high school, providing a year between school and college or between school and work for those who are not college-bound.

The merits of a year of national service range from primarily pragmatic to the more encompassing matter of character building. To begin with the pragmatic: In 1991, while the overall unemployment rate was 6.7 percent, the rate for twenty- to twenty-four-year-olds was 10.8 percent, and that for sixteen- to nineteen-year-olds was 18.6 percent. Unemployment is an especially demoralizing experience for many young people. It also undermines the rest of society, because young unemployed persons make up a sizable part of the criminal population. A year of national service would remove many unemployed youths from the streets; it would provide them, often for the first time, with legitimate and meaningful work; and it would help protect them from being enticed into crime. Above all, such service would provide a way to develop the character of those who serve, aside from whatever skills they might acquire. Indeed, much of the potential impact of national service lies in psychic development, in enhancing the individual's self-respect, sense of worth, and outlook on the future.

More important, national service would also provide a strong antidote to the ego-centered mentality as youth serve shared needs. An important criterion for including a particular service in the program should be its usefulness to the community. This could encompass myriad possibilities, from improving the environment and beautifying the land to tutoring youngsters having difficulty in school or helping the infirm in nursing homes. At the same time, forms of service that infringe on the rights of others would be excluded; for example, volunteers would not be given responsibilities that would, in effect, take away jobs by providing a pool of cheap labor.

Finally, a year of national service could serve as an important community builder because it would act as a grand sociological mixer. At present, America provides few opportunities for shared experience and for developing shared values and bonds among people from different racial, class, and regional backgrounds. One of the major reasons for the low consensus-building capacity of American society is that schools are locally run. They do not subscribe to a common national curriculum, and they transmit different sets of regional, racial, or class values. A year of national service, especially if it was designed to enable people from different geographical and sociological backgrounds to work and live together, could be an effective way for boys and girls, whites and nonwhites, people from parochial and public schools, north and south, the city and the country, to come together constructively while working together at a common task.

A 1989 poll found that many young people who have participated in community service have positive feelings about their experiences. Fifty-seven percent of the respondents said it felt good to help someone, while 40 percent called it a good learning experience. Only 1 percent stated that they didn't like giving up their free time, and only 2 percent felt they hadn't gotten anything out of their volunteer experience.

What is missing are opportunities to serve. Forty-two percent of the students said no one had asked them to help or showed them how; 45 percent said that the fact that there was no parental encouragement to perform community service was a strong reason for their not being more involved.

The costs of a full program are formidable. If every American who reaches eighteen were to participate—a very farfetched assumption—it would cost an estimated $33 billion a year (at least $11,000 per person times three million people). True, one must deduct from this figure such items as salaries for young people who would be serving in the armed forces anyway; savings on welfare and unemployment benefits that would not be paid to those in national service; and "savings" from a reduction in crime, police work, and jail sentences. Even so, the program has a multibillion-dollar net price tag.

However, national service could become competitive with other national priorities if the social and economic dividends proved substantial. By encouraging and developing the virtues of hard work, responsibility and cooperation—to name a few—national service would help the nation in its efforts to restore a climate of basic civility and improve economic productivity. For instance, national service would probably provide young people with greater maturity and skills than they would normally have upon entering college or vocational training. Then, as students, they would gain more from their education, benefitting themselves and the community.

In Conclusion

To state the obvious, that the first duty of schools is education, turns out not to be self-evident. First, there is a strong tendency to equate education with teaching—transmitting skills and knowledge—which it is not. Second, there is a lack of understanding of the ways character formation enable effective teaching and allows for moral education. Character formation is equally essential if we are to graduate young adults who can be upstanding members of the community and employees able to hold their own in today's competitive world.

The single most important factor that affects education from within the schools is neither the curriculum nor the teaching style, at least not as these terms are normally used, but the experiences the school generates. In many American schools, perhaps as many as one-half, these experiences do not support sound character formation or moral education.

Many factors combine to account for the weakened condition of many American schools, but the self-centered mentality is probably easiest to reverse. It is almost certainly a good place to start the reconstruction of the schools as *educational* institutions if they are to become places where *self*-discipline is evolved. Otherwise schools will not only fail their graduates, they will also be unable to serve as a major foundation of the moral infrastructure of our communities.

4 ♦ Back to We

The Loss of Traditional Community

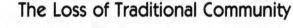

I T'S hard to believe now, but for a long time the loss of community was considered to be liberating. Societies were believed to progress from closely knit, "primitive," or rural villages to unrestrictive, "modern," or urban societies. The former were depicted as based on kinship and loyalty in an age in which both were suspect; the latter, however, were seen as based on reason (or "rationality") in an era in which reason's power to illuminate was admired with little attention paid to the deep shadows it casts. The two types of social relations have often been labeled with the terms supplied by a German sociologist, Ferdinand Tönnies. One is gemeinschaft, the German term for community, and the other is gesellschaft, the German word for society, which he used to refer to people who have rather few bonds, like people in a crowd or a mass society.

Far from decrying the loss of community, this sanguine approach to the rise of modernity depicted small towns and villages as backward places that confined behavior. American writers such as Sinclair Lewis and John O'Hara satirized small towns as insular, claustrophobic places, inhabited by petty, mean-spirited people. They were depicted as the opposite of "big cities," whose atmosphere was said to set people free. Anonymity would allow each person to pursue what he or she wished rather than what the community dictated. It was further argued that relations in the gesellschaft would be based not on preexisting, "ascribed" social bonds, such as between cousins, but on contractual relations, freely negotiated among autonomous individuals.

Other major forms of progress were believed to accompany the movement from a world of villages to one of cities. Magic, superstition, alchemy, and religion—"backward beliefs"—would be replaced by bright, shining science and technology. There would be no more villagers willing to sell their wares only to their own kind and not to outsiders—a phenomenon anthropologists have often noted. Old-fashioned values and a sense of obligation were expected to yield to logic and calculation. Social bonds dominating all relations (you did not charge interest on a loan to members of your community because such a charge was considered indecent usury) were pushed aside to make room for a free market, with prices and interest rates set according to market logic. By the same token, the network of reciprocal obligations and care that is at the heart of communities would give way to individual rights protected by the state. The impersonal right to social services and welfare payments, for instance, would replace any reliance on members of one's family, tribe, or ethnic benevolent association.

The sun, moon, and stars of the new universe would be individuals, not the community. In a typical case, the U.S. Supreme Court ruled that the Sierra Club had no legal standing to argue for the preservation of parkland as a community resource. Rather, if the Sierra Club wished to show standing, it would have to demonstrate that particular individuals were harmed.

Throughout twentieth-century America, as the transition to gesellschaft evolved, even its champions realized that it was not the unmitigated blessing they had expected. Although it was true that those who moved from villages and small towns into urban centers often shed tight social relations and strong community bonds, the result for many was isolation, lack of caring for one another, and exposure to rowdiness and crime.

Criminologists report that young farmhands in rural America in the early nineteenth century did not always work on their parents' land. However, when they were sent to work outside their home they usually lived with other farmers and were integrated into their family life. In this way they were placed in a community context that sustained the moral voice, reinforced the values of their upbringing, and promoted socially constructive behavior. It was only when these farmhands went to work in factories in cities—and were housed on their own in barracks without established social networks, elders, and values—that rowdy and criminal behavior, alcoholism, and prostitution became common. Even in those early days attempts to correct these proclivities were made not by returning these young people to their families and villages, but by trying to generate Communitarian elements in the cities. Among the best analysts of these developments is James Q. Wilson, a leading political scientist. He notes that associations such as the Young Men's Christian Association (YMCA), temperance societies, and the Children's Aid Society sought to provide a socially appropriate, morality-sustaining context for young people.

Other experiences paralleled those of the factory hands. The migration to the American West, for example, is usually thought of as a time when individuals were free to venture forth and carve out a life of their own in the Great Plains. Actually, many people traveled in caravans and settled as communities, although each family claimed its own plot of land. Mutual assistance in such rough terrain was an absolute requirement. Mining towns and trading posts, however, in which rampant individualism often did prevail, were places of much chicanery. People who had mined gold often lost their stakes to unscrupulous traders; those who owned land were driven off it with little compensation by railroad companies, among others. Fly-by-night banks frequently welshed on notes that they themselves had issued. An unfettered market, one without a community context, turned out to lack the essential moral underpinnings that trade requires, and not just by sound social relations.

In many ways these frontier settlements—with their washed-out social bonds, loose morals, and unbridled greed—were the forerunners of Wall Street in the 1980s. The Street became a "den of thieves," thick with knaves who held that anything went as long as you made millions more than the next guy. Moreover, the mood of self-centered "making it" of the me generation spilled over into large segments of society. It was celebrated by the White House and many in Congress, who saw in an unfettered pursuit of self-interest the social force that revitalizes economies and societies. By the end of the eighties even some of the proponents of me-ism felt that the pursuit of greed had run amok.

By the early nineties the waning of community, which had long concerned sociologists, became more pronounced and drew more attention. As writer Jonathan Rowe put it: "It was common to think about the community as we used to think about air and water. It is there. It takes care of itself, and it can and will absorb whatever we unleash into it." Now it became evident that the social environment needed fostering just as nature did. Responding to the new cues, George Bush evoked the image of a "kinder, gentler" society as a central theme for his first presidential campaign in 1988. The time was right to return to community and the moral order it harbored. Bill Clinton made the spirit of community a theme of his 1992 campaign.

The prolonged recession of 1991–1992 and the generally low and slowing growth of the American economy worked against this new concern with we-ness. Interracial and interethnic tensions rose considerably, not only between blacks and whites, but also between blacks and Hispanics and among various segments of the community and Asian-Americans. This is one more reason why the United States will have to work its way to a stronger, growing, more competitive economy: interracial and ethnic peace are much easier to maintain in a rising than in a stagnant economy. However, it does not mean that community rebuilding has to be deferred until the economy is shored up. It does indicate that enhancing we-ness will require greater commitment and effort from both the government and the people, if community rebuilding is to take place in a sluggish economy.

The New Community

Does this mean that we all have to move back to live in small towns and villages in order to ensure the social foundations of morality, to rebuild and shore up we-ness? Can one not bring up decent young people in the city? Isn't it possible to have a modern society, which requires a high concentration of labor and a great deal of geographic mobility—and still sustain a web of social bonds, a Communitarian nexus? There is more than one sociological answer to these queries.

First, many cities have sustained (or reclaimed) some elements of community. Herbert Gans, a Columbia University sociologist, observed that within cities there were what he called "urban villages." He found communities where, generally speaking, "neighbors were friendly and quick to say hello to each other," where the various ethnic groups, transients, and bohemians "could live together side by side without much difficulty." Gans further noted that "for most West Enders [in Boston] . . . life in the area resembled that found in the village or small town, and even in the suburb." Even in large metropolises, such as New York City, there are neighborhoods in which many people know their neighbors, their shopkeepers, and their local leaders. They are likely to meet one another in neighborhood bars, bowling alleys, and places of worship. They watch out for each other's safety and children. They act in concert to protect their parks and bus stops. They form political clubs and are a force in local politics. (Jim Sleeper's *Closest of Strangers* provides a fine description of these New York City communities.)

In some instances members of one ethnic group live comfortably next to one another, as in New York City's Chinatown and Miami's Little Havana. In other cities ethnic groups are more geographically dispersed but sustain ethnic-community bonds around such institutions as churches and synagogues, social clubs, and private schools. In recent decades a measure of return to community has benefited from the revival of loyalty to ethnic groups. While the sons and daughters of immigrants, the so-called second generation, often sought to assimilate, to become Americanized to the point that their distinct backgrounds were lost in a new identity, *their* children, the third generation and onward, often seek to reestablish their ethnic identity and bonds.

How does one reconcile the two sociological pictures—the James Q. Wilson concept of the city as gesellschaft, with little community or moral base, and the Herbert Gans image of gemeinschaft, of urban villages? The answer, first of all, is that both exist side by side. Between the urban villages, in row houses and high rises, you find large pockets of people who do not know their next-door neighbors, with whom they may have shared a floor, corridors, and elevators for a generation. Elderly people especially, who have no social bonds at work and are largely abandoned by their families, often lead rather isolated lives. In 1950 14.4 percent of those sixty-five years of age and older lived alone; by 1990 the percentage stood at nearly 31 percent.

Also, to some extent a welcome return to small-town life of sorts has been occurring in modern America. Although not all suburbs, which attracted millions of city dwellers, make for viable communities, as a rule the movement to the suburbs has enhanced the Communitarian nexus.

In addition, postmodern technology helps. More people are again able to work at home or nearby, and a high concentration of labor is less and less necessary, in contrast with the industrial age. People can use their computers and modems at home to do a good part of their office work, from processing insurance claims to trading worldwide in commodities, stocks, and bonds. Architects can design buildings and engineers monitor faraway power networks from their places of residence.

It used to be widely observed that Americans, unlike Europeans, move around so much that they are hard-pressed to put down real community roots. On average, it is said, the whole country moves about once every five years. These figures, however, may be a bit obsolete. For various reasons, in recent years Americans seem to move somewhat less often. One explanation is a growing desire to maintain the bonds of friendship and local social roots of their children, spouses, and themselves. In effect there is little reason to believe that the economy will suffer if this trend continues, and it may actually benefit from less shuttling around of people. Surely the Communitarian nexus will benefit.

Finally, there are new, nongeographic, communities made up of people who do not live near one another. Their foundations may not be as stable and deep-rooted as residential communities, but they fulfill many of the social and moral functions of traditional communities. Work-based and professional communities are among the most common of these. That is, people who work together in a steel mill or a high-tech firm such as Lotus or Microsoft often develop work-related friendships and community webs; groups of co-workers hang around together, help one another, play and party together, and go on joint outings. As they learn to know and care for one another, they also form and reinforce moral expectations.

Other communities are found in some law firms, on many

campuses (although one community may not encompass everyone on campus), among physicians at the same hospital or with the same specialty in a town, and among some labor union members.

Some critics have attacked these communities as being artificially constructed, because they lack geographical definition or because they are merely social networks, without a residential concentration. Ray Oldenburg, author of *The Great Good Place,* decries the new definitions of community that encompass co-workers and even radio call-in show audiences. "Can we really create a satisfactory community apart from geography?" he asks. "My answer is 'no.' " But people who work every day in the same place spend more hours together and in closer proximity than people who live on the same village street. Most important, these nongeographic communities often provide at least some elements of the Communitarian nexus, and hence they tend to have the moral infrastructure we consider essential for a civil and humane society.

In short, our society is neither without community nor sufficiently Communitarian; it is neither gemeinschaft nor gesellschaft, but a mixture of the two sociological conditions. America does not need a simple return to gemeinschaft, to the traditional community. Modern economic prerequisites preclude such a shift, but even if it were possible, such backpedaling would be undesirable because traditional communities have been too constraining and authoritarian. Such traditional communities were usually homogeneous. What we need now are communities that balance both diversity and unity. As John W. Gardner has noted: "To prevent the wholeness from smothering diversity, there must be a philosophy of pluralism, an open climate for dissent, and an opportunity for subcommunities to retain their identity and share in the setting of larger group goals." Thus, we need to strengthen the communitarian elements in the urban and suburban centers, to provide the social bonds that sustain the moral voice, but at the same time avoid tight networks that suppress pluralism and dissent. James Pinkerton, who served in the Bush White House, speaks eloquently about a new paradigm focused around what he calls a "new gemeinschaft." It would be, he says, neither oppressive nor hierarchical. In short, we need new communities in which people have choices and readily accommodate divergent *sub*communities but still maintain common bonds.

What Can We Do?

To strengthen the Communitarian nexus requires four measures, each of which deserves some discussion: changing orientation, changing the "habits of the heart"; working out conflicts between career needs and community bonds; redesigning our physical environment to render it more community-friendly; and fostering volunteer endeavors that do not trivialize and squander our commitments to the commons.

Investing in the Communitarian Nexus

We constantly, whether we are conscious of it or not, choose how to invest our psychic energy, allocate our time, and invest our resources. Some who are under the spell of modernity, and who try to live up to the image of gesellschaft, choose to invest ever more of themselves in the pursuit of "making it": to gain a raise or a promotion, to advance their careers or profits one more notch, then another. To the extent that these efforts become their dominant pursuit, one to which all others are subordinated, "making it" becomes a self-defeating endeavor because it is inherently Sisyphean in nature. There is no point of satiation. It is an intrinsically *unsat*isfying activity. Like other addictions and obsessions, the more one takes in, the more one requires—and the less one enjoys the process. Regardless of how much you earn or gain, there are always higher salaries and ranks to aspire to, always some Joneses ahead of you in the race. When financier Michael Milken was making $550 million a year, more than some nations, he cheated to make some more.

Social science findings leave no doubt that genuine inner satisfaction cannot be attained in this way. As a matter of fact, people whose incomes are higher are not happier than those whose incomes are lower. As Diane Swanbrow, who summarized the relevant data, observes: "Although poverty clearly makes people miserable, studies consistently show that having more than enough money to meet your needs doesn't guarantee more happiness." She also notes that as the real income of Americans rose dramatically from 1946 to 1978, Americans reported no increase in happiness. Indeed, the proportion of those who reported that they were happy with their fate and those who were discontented did not change.

Also, there is little difference in personal contentment among countries, regardless of their socioeconomic conditions, according to a cross-national study by political scientists Ronald Inglehart and opinion researcher Jacques-René Rabier. For example, the United States and Great Britain were neck and neck in satisfaction scores (7.57 vs. 7.52), despite the fact that the average income in the United States was twice that of Britain when the study was conducted. Moreover, Northern Ireland and Ireland, both with rather low GNPs per capita, ranked higher in satisfaction scores (at 7.77 and 7.76) than either the United States or Britain. Japan ranked second to last in satisfaction scores in the Inglehart and Rabier study, "beaten" only by Greece, with a *much* lower per capita GNP.

Further, R. A. Easterlin, in a review of other data from nineteen countries, concluded that "richer countries are not typically happier than poorer ones. . . . By and large, the evidence indicates no relation—positive or negative—between happiness and national income." In short, once your elementary needs are sated, chasing money won't make you more content.

People are better off when they combine their self-advancement with investment in their community. The observations made earlier about children and spouses hold for relatives, friends, and neighbors: people who have several significant others with whom they have meaningful, stable, affective relationships—especially when they share a sense of we-ness with one or more groups of people—are psychologically much better off than those who do not.

There are many well-known ways to develop, cultivate, and nourish these relationships. Popular self-help books for singles are full of advice that applies to couples as well: join a church group, do some volunteer work, go fishing or bowling together with other couples. Preparing dinners for guests has become less popular as many people work full days outside the home, but Communitarian meals (in which all participants contribute a dish) are growing in social acceptance. These are all small steps that, at least potentially, enhance not merely one-on-one relations but we-ness as well.

The problem is not listing ways to enhance the Communitarian nexus, but to make the commitment to connect and sustain the effort, despite some initial awkwardness. Community facilitators may be a modern necessity. Here I do not mean quick-buck dating services that often exploit the lonely, but individuals who organize social activities in which interpersonal and social bonds can be initiated. These may range from church choirs to weekend outings, from groups that discuss books to groups that organize charity events.

The best social events do not merely develop social bonds, but also serve a Communitarian purpose, from organizing neighborhood crime watches to running soup kitchens. Groups that focus directly on the social relations themselves, like parties for singles aimed at fishing for dates, are often less socially constructive; more effective groups are those where members focus on bettering others and allow social networks to evolve as a by-product. Even investment clubs and bridge groups seem to do better than most meet-a-mate pot lucks.

True, some of these social activities can be fairly shallow; this is especially the case when get-togethers are limited in scope, intensity, and regularity. Thus a onetime evening of folk dancing at the local church is not nearly as socially constructive as a folk dance group that meets every week. Even the best book club is not as involving as an Alcoholics Anonymous chapter. (The same holds for many organizations that follow the AA pattern, from groups that help people cope with cancer to those that support those who have children or spouses who are addicted.) Centers for senior citizens are particularly effective because beyond fostering one-on-one relations, they often encompass group activities and provide a continual, often daily, community space.

It is sociologically naive to sit back and wait for new communities to spring up. It is often necessary, and there is nothing artificial or otherwise improper, in recruiting or training organizers and facilitators of we-ness. (One way this is done, for instance by the Montgomery County Volunteer and Community Service Center, is to provide an office that trains volunteers and helps them find opportunities for service as well as occasions to get together with other volunteers to exchange experiences, to recognize achievements, and—to socialize.) Sure, some group leaders may be tedious, overbearing, or a bit pompous. But such human frailties are far from unknown among leaders of natural communities. When all is said and done, the more individuals dedicate themselves to fostering a Communitarian nexus, the more their fellow persons will join in and bring about the revival of communities where they are waning.

Harmonizing Careers and the Communitarian Nexus

Under the spell of the curse of either/or that befuddles much of our thinking, many young people view their alternatives as either a career of self-centered aggrandizement ("making a million before you are thirty") or a life of social service and self-sacrifice. Joining a religious order provided a dedicated and ascetic existence in earlier times; more recently, joining the Peace Corps provided an outlet for such altruistic aspirations.

The sociological fact, though, is that one's interests in finding a career and serving the community can be fused in many ways, avoiding the two extremes of a life of self-aggrandizement and one of self-sacrifice. Former president Jimmy Càrter, unlike several other ex-presidents, provides a fine role model that shows one can earn a decent living without being consumed by attempts to swell one's bankroll. He does not sell his time to the highest bidder, or help Japanese corporations promote their wares, or spend his retirement days playing golf. He set up a center to study many key international problems; helped negotiate peace in Ethiopia; and built housing for the poor in several cities, without starving, although he must do without stretch limos and his wife without tiaras and designer dresses. As a result, Carter is now widely recognized as our best former president and basks in the appreciation of many Americans. He must feel at the end of the day the special glow of an inner affirmation of having done right and good.

For the rest of us, nursing, teaching, and social work all provide careers that are reasonably rewarding in the traditional sense of a career and, at the same time (if carried out with dedication), often contribute directly to the community. A physician does not have to choose between tucking tummies and lifting breasts in Beverly Hills and family medicine in the Gobi Desert. There are many medical pursuits, such as emergency medicine, in which a doctor can lead a rewarding life that is also of service.

Similarly, lawyers' choices range beyond specializing in fanning conflicts between spouses (and turning them into protracted divorce proceedings that run up the legal bills) and spending their lives as public defenders. Lawyers who spend much of their lives *resolving* conflicts between clients will find themselves socially constructive and still able to pay the rent.

When gesellschaft was considered all the rage, when modernity reigned, it was considered good corporate policy to move managers around frequently. As a consequence, social bonds of all kinds—of the extended family, friendships on and off the job, relations with neighbors, and those of young people in schools—were disrupted regularly to serve real or imaginary corporate and career needs. Moving as often as once every three years was far from unknown. In recent years, however, it has become evident that many companies may do quite well, and perhaps even better, if their employees are moved around less often, allowing them to cultivate rather than uproot their Communitarian roots.

In general, there is a need for corporations to become not only more family-friendly, but also more community-friendly. I do not mean merely to contribute to the local Red Cross, children's museum, and chamber music society, but to examine their policies from a community standpoint. Moving corporate headquarters to another town fifty miles away may lower a corporation's office-space costs, but it will also severely disrupt the social bonds of many employees. And the savings in costs may well be less than the losses due to a decline in morale and increases in tardiness, absenteeism, and resentment that such disruptions often engender.

Closing plants that are the mainstay of a community sometimes cannot be avoided, but such closings should not be undertaken capriciously or abruptly. Affected communities should be accorded an opportunity to help the corporation solve its economic problems or to find buyers for the plant (including its workers), if it is to be sold rather than transferred. At least the employees should be afforded some time (and, if at all possible, financial help) to assist them and their community to adapt. Even those who are opposed to government controls as a rule may see merit in new laws that slow plant closings by corporations that are grossly insensitive to community needs.

Communitarian Design, Architecture, and Planning

To make our physical environment more community-friendly, our homes, places of work, streets, and public spaces—whole developments, suburbs, and even whole cities—need to be designed to enhance the Communitarian nexus. Although paying attention

to the effects of architecture and city planning on the Communitarian nexus is hardly a new idea, it is a consideration often given
short shrift. An era dedicated to a return to we-ness would value
and promote design that is pro-community.

A systematic study of the numerous ways to proceed is a major
topic for future Communitarian studies. Here are some places to
start, places others have been and more need to turn:

On a small scale: *Provide people shared space to mingle.* It does not
require a grand social science study to note that when chairs are
placed in the empty spaces in many public buildings next to the
elevators, people are often found there "visiting." The same holds
true for other places to sit, from park benches to lounges in public
libraries. Sure, there are some sterile places (such as the huge, wind-
swept plazas among the high-rise buildings in downtown Minneapolis) in which probably no set of benches could foster sociability.
These are the exceptions, however, that do not disprove the rule.

Sandboxes and playgrounds don't work just for kids. Some of
my best friends are those I met when I watched over my sons' play
in the sandboxes of Riverside Drive in New York City. The streets
adjacent to Riverside Drive, which had no strips of park to accommodate such play areas, had much less social life.

Even high-rise buildings can be made more community-
friendly. Just having in-house services, such as self-service laun-
dries and barber shops, offers residents some places to get to
know one another and to "hang out." Some have in-house restaurants, in which tenants (and outsiders) can eat. Community
swimming pools, tennis courts, and such simple sports facilities as
basketball hoops or volleyball nets are socially constructive. If
you set aside rooms to play cards, dominoes, and chess, more
often than not they fill up, demonstrating the unstated need for
social connectedness.

On a larger scale: *Plan developments in ways that enhance* rather
than hinder *the sociological mix that sustains a community.* For instance,
earmarking a proportion of a building's units for senior citizens, by
providing small units with small kitchens and by enhancing safety
devices, will ensure the presence and comfort of elders. They, in
turn, provide a group of adults who are on the premises during the
workday and when children come home and make it easier for
families that wish to attend to their parents to be able to maintain

their extended families rather than institutionalize elders prematurely in remote nursing homes.

Whole developments are now being designed around courtyards, rather than buildings set row upon row. Public and social spaces are set aside for the role that traditional plazas served. An old chocolate factory in San Francisco (Ghirardelli Square) and a railroad station in Washington, D.C. (Union Station), have been converted into bustling social spaces, in which people interact merrily, safely, and in constructive ways. Numerous shopping malls are opened early to allow senior citizens safe and heated (or air-conditioned) spaces to walk. Pedestrian pockets, in which automobiles are banned and people can stroll and promenade and visit with one another, are springing up in many urban centers.

Thirty years ago a student of urban planning, Jane Jacobs, recommended that buildings be integrated into the street. She argued that windows be kept low and face the street, so that mothers would be able to prepare dinner and keep a watchful eye on their children. By the same token, the streets would be safer and encourage people to hang around together. Similarly, she pointed out that short blocks, with corners dedicated to shops, favor sociability. Wide pavements encourage children to play in front of their houses. Vest-pocket parks and gardens are more community-friendly than grand ones or those designed for decoration and effect. In London, for example, one often finds sets of buildings that together form a pleasant enclosed space used for a garden. Those who live on the block have keys to the garden gates and can send their children to play in the shared safe area.

Extreme attempts to be community-friendly are found in totally planned towns such as Reston, Virginia; Columbia, Maryland; Roosevelt Island, New York; and Irvine, California. Here, schools, libraries, bike paths, and social spaces have all been carefully located to enhance community. Not all of these arrangements are successful. Some, in fact, are excessively regimented and costly. Others presume that people will give up the use of their cars.

Recently several designers of what are called "new villages" have called attention to the fact that existing zoning regulations reflect the days when workplaces were smoky, ugly factories that were kept out of suburbs. Now these designers see a need to integrate residential units with workplaces, interspersed with shops.

This reorganization is said to allow people to walk, within a quarter of a mile, to most places they need to be. It would reduce the use of cars and enhance the formation of social webs—the basis of community.

These ideas may leave some wrinkles to be worked out. Having carried groceries for one-fourth of a mile, I would prefer in my old age to have them delivered if I am to give up the use of my car. But surely they indicate directions that are to be explored if the design of space is to support a community rather than be a hindrance.

Communitarian Action: Making It Count

So much has been written about Tocqueville's America, the land of voluntary associations and activities, that the notion that Americans are much more active Communitarians than Europeans has become a sociological cliché. Indeed, in America there are many tens of thousands of associations that promote block parties, baby-sitting pools, lodges, and clubs. One is tempted to bless them, saying, "May they grow, flourish, and multiply," and let them be. However, for them to sustain the gemeinschaft elements in a society that tends toward gesellschaft, it is essential that Communitarian activities not be trivialized.

We must learn to distinguish between activities that provide at least a reasonable modicum of opportunity to serve the commons and those that provide all too facile a way to discharge our obligation to the commons. True, for busy homemakers with a full-time paying job and a houseful of children, making some cookies for the PTA might be all they can do. Usually, though, the community must ask people for greater and more consequential contributions.

Peter Drucker, one of our leading pundits, made a strong case that in the nineties we will need to rely even more on voluntary efforts than in the past. He expects that attempts by governments to provide for numerous social needs will continue to suffer both a shortage of funds and what seems to be a congenital inability to provide services that match in quality those that voluntary associations regularly render.

It will not do simply to urge people to turn off lights to help conserve energy or require New Yorkers to request a glass of water in restaurants (rather than being routinely served one) to save water. Plugging the leak in one of New York City's many old water mains would save more water and electricity than such "public services." It might be argued that the purpose of such measures is public education, to sensitize people to the need to conserve. However, phony devices are not educational. Most of the public realizes that the benefits of these measures are slight at best (and phony at worst), which adds to their alienation from public authorities and community causes. Public education should endeavor to find ways to highlight genuine steps the public can undertake that are truly helpful.

Trivialization is particularly likely once politicians try to use American Communitarian inclinations to avoid having to make major public commitments. President Bush's 1988 election slogan of seeking a gentler and kinder society was quite welcome and timely, following eight years of unabashed celebration of conspicuous consumption and greed. However, when his rhetoric yielded largely to the "thousand points of light" program, it became something of a joke, even among many of his supporters. The "points" are too often awarded for activities that entail rather little service, such as some visits to a nursing home by a few members of the community. Commendable, to be sure, but hardly worthy of presidential honors.

I have long supported a year of national service for young Americans. As a result I have attended more than my share of meetings on the subject, and I am still a member of a national secretariat that promotes national service. In these meetings I have noticed a curious development. Every few years someone comes forward and suggests activities that are to qualify as "national service" that are less taxing and less of service than those previously suggested—such as going downtown from comfortable suburban homes to assist in public libraries for a few hours. (Some would even reward such "national service" with college fellowships.) As I see it, it does not serve us well to squander our Communitarian approbations. The term *national service* is best reserved for those who make a significant contribution of time or effort.

Serious community endeavors that deserve our appreciation are illustrated by the following two prime examples, chosen from the scores that could be given.

Nearly half of the nation's 486,000 emergency medical technicians (EMTs) are unpaid volunteers. Volunteer EMTs do virtually everything professionals do: they monitor the victim's vital signs, provide an initial diagnosis, stop bleeding, transport the victim to a hospital, or call for emergency helicopter evacuation. Volunteers have completed an extensive training program (sometimes taking as long as 120 hours) and are usually trained to perform CPR (cardiopulmonary resuscitation) and administer first aid. EMT volunteers must be willing to see other persons suffer greatly, even die, and cope with the resulting trauma; they must be willing to risk themselves to pull people out of fires or overturned cars. Many towns and villages still have only voluntary ambulance crews and EMTs.

Similarly, the Seattle CPR program highlights what community service is all about. To appreciate its importance, you must take into account that medical studies show that victims of heart failure will have a much stronger chance for survival if they are resuscitated in the field. Indeed, the main result of having to wait for an ambulance crew for medical service to be initiated is often a dehumanizing and costly death. In contrast, victims who received CPR from citizens, without waiting for an ambulance, are *twice* as likely to recover as those who had to wait for professional care.

Given these facts, if you must have a heart failure, try to have it in Seattle. Unlike the residents of most cities, as many as 40 percent of those suffering out-of-hospital heart failure in Seattle have their resuscitations begun by bystanders, *before* they are moved to a hospital. By 1988 Medic II, which trains citizens to perform CPR, had certified more than four hundred thousand Seattle-area residents. Between them, the good citizens of Seattle have already saved hundred of lives and sustain many others on a much more meaningful level.

These are but two examples of how dedicated individual effort benefits the community. Staffing telephone hot lines for those who are suicidal or runaways, running kitchens and clinics for the homeless, shelters for battered women, being a PAL to a child from a disadvantaged background—these are among many genuine community services.

In Conclusion

The nineties are going to be difficult economic times. Beyond the usual ups and downs, we face an economy whose growth rate has been slowing down for decades and that has accumulated mountains of debt that it used largely to enhance consumption rather than investment—in short, an economy that will not return quickly to a high-growth pathway. In this context it will be even more important for members of communities to reach out and help one another and those of less endowed communities.

Even if the American economy performs much better than it has since the early seventies, there is a need to restore stronger social bonds, not merely friend to friend but among groups of people, the Communitarian nexus.

Each community—whether residential, work-related, monoethnic, or "integrated"—needs to work out its own agenda, depending on local circumstances and needs. However, some guidelines are clear. Communities need more people who dedicate more of their time and energy and resources—more of themselves—to the commons. Young people and those who change jobs or retrain will do best if they seek to combine their career with pursuits that are supportive of the community. And the physical environment needs to be designed to be much more community-friendly. A special role in this return to community is to be played by institutions, our next stop.

5 ♦ Rebuilding Community Institutions

Institutions as Common Cores

UST as American society since the fifties has been cannibalizing families and is now saddled with the dire moral and social consequences of their diminished capacity, so society has cannibalized communities, with similar antisocial consequences. In effect, the two often go hand in hand. As both parents commute to work in the big city, leaving the children without the educational presence of an adult, they abandon the streets, public spaces (from bus stops to parks), and neighborhoods as well. Local governments must now hire police to patrol largely empty suburbs during the day, and there are fewer hands than before to serve the community. More and more people have been gobbled up by the economy—which is taxed to pay for hired hands to accomplish what people used to do as volunteers. Where we had ethnic groups taking care of new immigrants (which some still do), we now have a U.S. Refugee Resettlement Agency and a plethora of government-run welfare agencies. Where once we had families attending to their elderly, now we see families otherwise occupied and many of the elderly institutionalized in nursing homes (which are often heavily subsidized by the government, while in-community care is not). And so it goes.

A return to family, which we argue is needed in its own right, will also help us shore up Communitarian institutions. Thus, if more people work at home, there will be more hands for crime watches during the day. If people value children more, they will be more likely to find the time and energy to create (and pay for) public parks and help ensure their safety. If neighbors are more available to help one another, including new immigrants and people who are temporarily down on their luck, the pressure on public institutions will be alleviated.

Institutions as a Mainstay of Communities

Institutions, from local schools to community policing, from local churches to museums, are important for communities above and beyond the services they provide. Communities congeal around such institutions. And when these institutions of several commu-

Cartoon by John Overmyer. Reprinted with permission of John Overmyer.

nities are "consolidated" in the name of greater efficiency, communities are often undermined.

Take, for instance, local schools. They are frequently more than a place to which parents send their children. The buildings, and the sports teams, are a source of identity for the community. Schools offer shelter during natural disasters and places to hold town hall meetings, dances, and band concerts. When bean counters decide that it is more efficient to consolidate the schools of several communities, many communities lose their unifying institution. It may be true that from a narrow accounting viewpoint, it saves money to mesh several small local schools into one regional school. However, if the loss of community—and the social cost resulting from such a loss—is included in the calculations, keeping open many of these schools may well turn out to be justified.

The same holds for other institutions, ranging from small local churches and synagogues to social (such as senior citizen) centers, even neighborhood grocery stores. (A black community on the South Side of Chicago declined further when it lost its local shops to impersonal and remote shopping malls.)

We need not overstate the case. There are instances in which consolidation is quite justified, and communities do decline for other reasons. Communitarians should not favor keeping all institutions open whatever the cost. They should advocate, however, an *encompassing* analysis that takes into account the moral and social, as well as financial, consequences of consolidation. As a result, to reiterate, in many cases it will make sense to retain core community institutions.

Simply closing core institutions is not the only way communities are diminished. It is widely recognized that communities provide the social base of the mediating institutions, that stand between the individual and the state, protecting the individual from excessive encroachment by the state. For these mediating institutions to be able to discharge this important function, they themselves need to be shielded from the government. Such protection is high on the agenda of the Communitarian movement.

The following admittedly extreme example of the way in which some government agencies rob communities of their functions, and diminish them in the process, will have to stand for the many that could be provided. In the South Bronx, an area known for its lack of social fabric, a resident, Carlos A. Padilla, volunteered to clear a stinking, rat-infested lot next to his children's school that was knee deep in litter. The school had appealed for help to the local government but had been given the runaround and was finally informed that no action could be taken because the lot was private. So Padilla and fifteen co-workers spent a weekend clearing the lot, stuffing bags and loading a truck that Padilla had rented. As *The New York Times* reports:

> Despite the nature of the work, the weekend clean-up effort took on an almost festive air. The owner of a nearby bodega offered the workers free refreshments. Fire fighters from the local station came by and suggested that the crew use their larger garbage drums. The priest from the nearby St. Luke's School came out and blessed everyone in sight. To see a community so often plagued by apathy and neglect responding in a positive way, taking care of problems on its own, was uplifting for everyone.

All was fine—until officers of the New York City Sanitation Department police stopped the truck with drawn guns, arrested Padilla, and confiscated his truck for illegal hauling of garbage. It took several rounds in the courts—and lawyers' fees and time missed from work—to free Padilla and his vehicle.

We need to move in the opposite direction: to encourage actual and potential communities to take at least a stab at their own problems. Each city should have a civilian review board whose duty it would be to review the city's procedures to check whether they enhance or hinder the Communitarian nexus. The board would work with the city council to change procedures that lead to people like Padilla being hauled off to jail instead of being honored on the steps of City Hall.

A Case in Point: Community Policing

In quite a few instances it actually makes sense to try to reconstruct core institutions in order to rebuild communities. The movement toward community policing is a case in point. (Among the others are efforts to restore dilapidated housing rather than allowing in the bulldozers of urban renewal, and opening and operating community mental health centers to reduce the need to place patients in massive faraway state mental hospitals—or leave them to roam the streets.)

Community policing has been introduced in Madison, Wisconsin, is being tried in New York City, and was imported by the new police commissioner from Philadelphia to Los Angeles after the 1992 riots. When we cut through the broad rhetoric used by some enthusiastic advocates of community policing, we find at the core a simple and interesting idea. Rather than have police patrol neighborhoods in cars, have them patrol the streets on foot. Insist that police officers know the people on their beats and develop trusting relations with them, which is virtually impossible if they zoom by in their cars.

A typical incident is reported by Robert Trojanowicz, an expert on community policing, whose father was a cop in Bay City, Michigan. One time, the father exercised what some bystanders considered undue force in subduing an unruly patron in a bar. In the following days, as he patrolled his beat, townspeople stopped by to chat with him about the incident. He was able to explain why he had used force, add an apology of sorts for possibly having been carried away, and mention the frustrations of his job. Because he had established close relations with the people of the community, they accepted both his explanation and apology. As a result he was able to continue to be an effective cop. People continued to feel free to talk to him, and he was able to know whom on "his" street he could ignore and whom he had to keep an eye on.

Walking the streets turns the police from an alien, almost occupying force that is unfamiliar with the turf (and therefore suspect) into an integral part of the community. (Critics sneer at this kind of "unprofessional" police work. "What do you mean, go and stretch out your hand and say hello to people on the block? What kind of police work is that? What about fighting criminals?")

For the same basic reasons, community policing reduces the need for extensive formal police review mechanisms, in which citizens submit written complaints that lead to investigations and hearings. Grievances are typically expressed and resolved directly. And with a shift to community policing, there is often greater decentralization of command and greater flexibility, allowing for some differences in applying citywide policies to each locality.

It is not my purpose here to provide a full evaluation of this approach. Surely, like most innovations, it has its down side. For instance, the approach may be more open to corruption than a professional police force, which has fewer close ties to one neighborhood. My purpose is to show that if one takes into account the community-building merits of an institution, and broadens the definition of efficiency to include such Communitarian goals, creative approaches such as community policing may gain more favor.

The jury is still out on the question of whether institutions such as community policing can shore up communities by themselves or whether community rebuilding needs also to be advanced by other means. Can community policing, for instance, work in those parts of Los Angeles in which there is precious little community? In some ways this is an academic question. Even if community policing could work well on its own, community shoring up is of such import that we should draw on all available sources and let them strengthen one another as they combine to restore community. It is like asking whether in restoring a building you must be more concerned with the foundations or the steel framework. It is unwise to neglect either.

Enhancing Public Safety, the Communitarian Way

There are ways to enhance public safety, the most elementary requirement of community life, and rebuild the Communitarian nexus without relying on specific institutions, such as local schools or the police. People can work directly with one another. Crime watches, in which people undertake to watch out for one another's safety and property, and citizen patrols, in which people volunteer to patrol their neighborhood, if properly carried out, are activities that contribute to a community need and build community bonds among the participants. In such programs residents notify one another when neighbors are going to be away, and citizens on foot and in cars patrol their communities. For example, in Fairfax, Virginia, two-person patrols watch the neighborhood with CB radios. The Beat Keepers in Los Angeles use a more confrontational (and dangerous) tactic of harassing drug sellers. Groups such as the Orange Caps in Washington, D.C., and the Guardian Angels in New York City are known for their organized, anticrime patrols.

At the same time, crime watch itself needs watching. We must ensure that it is used to protect neighborhoods rather than to chase out people of different social or racial backgrounds or to pry into personal affairs.

Bringing government closer to the people has much merit. For example, a program instituted in Brooklyn, New York, in September 1991, is designed to decentralize the borough's court system and make it more responsive to its citizens. The new Brooklyn Community Prosecution Program divides the borough into five judicial zones based on precinct and community boundaries. Each area controls its own case assignment and management, although the program itself operates out of the central courthouse. Prosecutors can now learn about the neighborhood they serve, the problems the residents face, the crimes that are generally committed in the area, and the police officers who work there.

Sentencing nonviolent offenders (such as people convicted of mail theft or fraud) to community service is an effective way of preventing repetition of criminal behavior. The costs to the public, though, are much lower, and there are the benefits of the community service, from picking up litter to raking leaves.

Public humiliation is a surprisingly effective and low-cost way of deterring criminals and expressing the moral order of a community. Some jurisdictions publish the names of "Johns" who are caught frequenting prostitutes. Lincoln County, Oregon, will plea-bargain with a criminal only if he first places an advertisement in a local newspaper to apologize for his crime. This practice is limited to nonviolent criminals, such as some burglars and thieves. The ad includes a snapshot of the miscreant and is paid for by the offender. Judges in Sarasota, Florida, and in Midwest City, Oklahoma, have required people caught driving while under the influence to display an easy-to-see sticker on their cars that declares: "Convicted of Drunken Driving."

When I mention public shaming to some of my social science colleagues, their first reaction is a mixture of horror and disbelief. Such punishment is judged to be degrading and a violation of a person's right to privacy. But if one grants that convicted criminals ought to be punished, what is the alternative? Nobody denies that incarceration is a very poor way of dealing with criminals, especially first offenders. Rehabilitation in existing jails is rare; homosexual rapes, drug abuse, and crime are common. People are cut off from their families, which makes their successful return to the community even more difficult than it already is. Imprisonment costs are high—higher, in effect, than attending many colleges. Jails and prisons are overcrowded, and judges are refusing to lock up many offenders because the living conditions are considered inhumane. In contrast, public humiliation is swift, involves no socializing with other criminals, is very low in cost, and allows reintegration of the offender into the community he or she has not left in the first place.

Some people respond that such penalties remind them of the stars that Jews were made to wear in Nazi Germany. The horrible injustice in those insignia, however, was that they were imposed on innocent people, on the basis of creed. Public shaming, as discussed here, would be limited to first-time offenders (not hardened criminals) and would serve to underscore society's disapproval of the *crime* committed rather than of the people themselves. Temporarily marking those convicted in open court, after due process, seems a legitimate and community-building device.

Political Participation Broadly Defined

The notion that the Communitarian action par excellence is political participation is age old. (William F. Buckley put it about as strongly as one can when he referred to the act of voting as a "civic sacrament.") It is common to romanticize the Greek *polis* as a place in which all free people participated in public life, which is equated with political life. The implication is that the best community action is one long, nonstop town hall meeting. Although few members of most communities find public life that compelling, an important way to build community is to ensure that there are numerous occasions for active participation of the members in its governance.

This is achieved not only, or even primarily, by voting once every few years to determine who will sit on the town's council. Participating in the governance of one of the many institutions of the community—schools, hospitals, libraries—is also to participate in public life. So is worrying about the local dump, organizing the annual Fourth of July parade, or manning the welcome wagon to greet new members.

These activities have in common what has become fashionable to call *empowerment*—that is, enabling people to participate openly and directly in making the decisions that govern their lives. What this actually means is best illustrated by a discussion of the way our schools are run. In every school in which I ever studied or visited as a parent (and as a father of five, this constitutes quite a list), I found that parents' involvement was not quite welcomed. Parents are often nominally invited to participate, but most principals and teachers actually feel that parents, especially the active ones, are meddlesome. Teachers tend to believe that they know what is best for the children. Parental participation, as they see it, is pushing the schools in "unprofessional" directions.

As I see it, teachers and principals ought to find ways to share with parents their convictions and to win them over—or allow parents to change the direction of the school. (By this I mean they should be responsive not to each parent's agenda, but to the wisdom that arises from a consensus of parents' groups, after they have been fully briefed about the school's circumstances and have dialogued with one another.) Schools need to involve parents much more, both in order for the schools to be able to discharge their duties (which requires active parental backing) and because empowering parents is a way of building community.

Many volumes have been written on the ways to empower people and enhance community activities (including books about some of the difficulties that such approaches entail). My purpose here is not to add to this abundant literature, but to flag some of the central methods we can use once we set our minds on community building, on returning to we-ness: increase our investment in community; seek to harmonize career with community involvement; make the spaces in which we live more community-friendly; pursue meaningful rather than trivial community service; and lay claims on others to be similarly involved in, and dedicated to, community. Our ultimate purpose is to provide an opportunity for deep human satisfaction, the kind found only when we are engaged with one another, and to strengthen the community as a moral infrastructure, the most important morality-enhancing factor other than individual conscience.

Personal Responsibility, Self-Help, and Social Justice

Community service is a fine thing, say the liberals, but it is far from enough. What America requires, they say, is massive "reallocation" (a code word for taking from the haves and giving to the have-nots) within each community and, above all, among them: take from the rich and give to the poor. Above all, liberals balk at the suggestion that people ought to take responsibility for their own lives and that communities should be the first to take care of their own.

In his book *The Content of Our Character,* Shelby Steele, a black writer, argues that blacks ought to stop complaining and cease placing demands on white society. They should give up the mind-set of the helpless victim and instead take responsibility for their future, learn to help themselves. Steele is particularly critical of calling poor blacks the true blacks. This, he points out, suggests that those who make it into the middle class are somehow less black. L. Douglas Wilder, the first black to be elected governor of Virginia, takes a similar position. He pointedly observed that black Americans must face the long hard road of making it on their own.

Some black critics, such as Roger Wilkins of George Mason University and Ronald Walters of Howard University, argue that Steele, Wilder, and their intellectual associates disregard what they call the repressiveness of the social structure. The socioeconomic conditions of blacks, they argue, even today are significantly affected by pervasive discrimination that is built into American society. As a result, they maintain, it is much harder for black Americans to make progress than for whites. And minorities in general ought to demand that the social structure be changed, as a major way to open the doors for their advancement. Finally, they say, advancing as a group, by means of such collective acts as protest demonstrations, provides a psychological lift that is badly needed by individual blacks. Indeed, they point out, other groups—Jews, Asian-Americans, Irish, Italians—help and sustain their own. Blacks should do no less.

William Julius Wilson, a black sociologist at the University of Chicago, points here to the curse of either/or, the distorting effects of intellectual polarization. As he sees it, there is a need to call on

black people not to wallow in self-pity and to blame "the System."
At the same time, there is no denying that structural factors still
inhibit minorities, and that changes in these factors would ease the
advancement of minorities in American society.

A Communitarian position on social justice (for *all* groups)
includes the following elements: First, *people have a moral responsibility to help themselves as best as they can.* At first it may seem heart-
less to ask, say, disabled people, older people who have lost their
jobs, and minority young people who have suffered discrimination
to participate actively in improving their lot. There is a valid sense
that we owe them, that they are entitled to our help. But the laying
of a claim to participate actively in advancing their lives on those
who are disadvantaged in one form or another—rather than to lie
back and wait to be compensated, lifted, and preferred—is based,
first of all, on a concept of human dignity. There is, as conservatives keep reminding us, something deeply degrading about being
dependent on others. It is respectful of human dignity to encourage
people to control their fate the best they can—under the circumstances. For some, taking responsibility for themselves may mean
only tying their own shoelaces or learning to feed themselves again
following a stroke. For still others, it may mean admitting illiteracy
and learning how to read. For others, it could mean continuing to
look for a job following several rejections. But people should not be
exempt from responsibility for themselves—for their own good.

Communities, reacting against the explosion of claims and the
very widespread sense of entitlement (even among people who are
quite well off), are less likely to be motivated by guilt and more
likely to honor their obligations to people who do their best on their
own. In the long run people are reluctant to help those who lie back
and wait to be rescued or demand to be paid reparations because
they were discriminated against in the past.

The second line of responsibility lies with those closest to the person,
including kin, friends, neighbors, and other community members.
They are next in line because they know best what the genuine
needs are (they are much less likely to be cheated than are welfare
bureaucrats) and are able to tailor the help to what is required.
Thus, when the government provides meals on wheels, everybody
either eats the same meals or must choose from a limited menu. But
when neighbors take turns bringing food to a sick or needy person,

they can take into account personal tastes. When a friend or neighbor provides counsel, it is likely to be based on more personalized knowledge than that of many overworked social workers. One reason many homeless people prefer the streets over government-run shelters is that they tend to be cavernous hangars with a strict regimen, in which everyone has to be in bed by a certain time, lights are turned down on cue, and so on. When neighbors take in a new immigrant or a child whose parents are ill, they tailor their assistance to the specific person. Moreover, in close relations with one's community, *reciprocity* is most sustainable. I refer not to the cold-blooded calculations that economists presume drive human exchanges, but to the open-ended mutual support among neighbors.

Some time ago I was driving home in snow that had snarled Washington, D.C., and was forced to abandon my car and hitch a ride with someone whose car had four-wheel drive. When I finally arrived at my home in Bethesda, Maryland, neighbors were standing in my kitchen—crying. I found out that my wife had been in a serious car accident. My young son had been taken to an emergency room with her. Two of my neighbors offered to drive me to the emergency room, despite the icy roads (we did spin out of control on the way), and others simply stated that they were going to stay in my place to wait for my other sons to arrive. My wife did not survive the accident, and in the weeks that followed, my neighbors took care of me. They brought over food; one couple spent the entire evening with me, although it was one of two evenings their son was home from college. Another dedicated his only day off from work to go to the car wreck and retrieve some documents, a task I could not face. They called on me frequently for weeks on end.

I know, as clearly as one can ever tell about human motivations, that they did not calculate how much I had done for them in the past or would do for them in a future moment of need. It was quite evident that they did what they could to help out of a sense of compassion. True, there is, quite properly, in any relationship or community some *vague* sense of appropriate reciprocity, of the need to contribute to a climate of mutuality. But basically people help one another and sustain the spirit of community because they sense it is the right thing to do.

For the same reasons, *as a rule every community ought to be expected to do the best it can to take care of its own.* Society, as a community of communities, should encourage the moral expectation that attending to welfare is the responsibility of the local community. We follow this rule already when there is a fire. The local fire company is the first one to be called in; only if it cannot handle the blaze are companies from other communities mobilized. Likewise whether the problem is mounting garbage, crime, drug abuse, or any of the well-known host of social problems that beset us, the first social responsibility lies with those who share a community.

The saying, though, is to be taken in full measure: Charity—and, more broadly, social responsibility—ought to begin, but not end, at home. Indeed, one of the gravest dangers in rebuilding communities is that they will tend to become insular and indifferent to the fate of outsiders. Each community must be expected to reach out to members of other communities that are less well endowed and hence less able to deal with their own problems. The ways are almost endless, from sending food, blankets, and volunteers when a neighboring community is overwhelmed, housing "refugees" from a hurricane or earthquake, to sharing equipment such as snow plows.

Last but not least, *societies (which are nothing but communities of communities) must help those communities whose ability to help their members is severely limited.* Thus, if the Federal Reserve System causes a recession by jacking up interest rates in order to cool off inflation and thus slows down the economy, the effects hit some communities harder than others. If, as a result, major employers in some towns shut down their plants, it is futile and unfair to expect that only the members of those towns should bear the full brunt of resulting dislocations, which were caused by the federal government to benefit the nationwide economy. *Social justice is an inter-community issue, not only an intracommunity matter.* Providing federal unemployment insurance, which is partially funded by taxes that are paid by all Americans, is here fully justified. The same holds for compensation that is being paid to Japanese-Americans who were unduly detained during World War II and for opportunities for programs that assist the poor to catch up and compete on an equal footing, such as Head Start. There is room and need for "realloca-tion" among communities, but this is not the only or the first place that Communitarians should turn. We start with our responsibility to ourselves and to members of our community; we expand the reach of our moral claims and duties from there.

America as a Community of Communities; on the Limits of Multiculturalism

Communitarians must concern themselves with the danger that a community may become self-centered and turn against others. Such errant communities undermine the bonds that tie various communities into more encompassing supracommunities (citywide or national). And such divisive communities work against the evolution of still more encompassing regional or cross-national communities, such as the attempts to develop a United States of Europe.

In recent years the danger that local and ethnic conflicts may shred national societies, even turn them into killing fields of civil war, has been far from theoretical. Violent intercommunity strife has engulfed such diverse places as India, Somalia, the former Soviet Union, Ethiopia, and Yugoslavia. In the United States, Los Angeles, 1992, a loud warning bell rang: interracial tensions are rising. What the proper relations should be among communities, and between them and the overarching American society, is debated on two major levels: what we should teach the younger generation about these questions in colleges and schools and what kind of society we are preparing for them. In effect, a discussion of the first question (the debate over multicultural curricula) provides a good way to enter the second complex and controversial question—the future composition of America. Should we aspire to a melting pot, a multiracial and ethnic conglomerate, or pluralism-with-unity?

America in the Classroom: Divisiveness in Curricula

The fact that various racial and ethnic groups constitute parts of one supracommunity is no longer taken for granted in American schools and colleges. As Ellen K. Coughlin, a writer for the *Chronicle of Higher Education,* reports: "The issue [of multiculturalism] raises a series of key questions about how American history should be conceived: Is the story of America that of a common culture or of many different, perhaps irreconcilable ones?"

The debate often focuses on what is called "multiculturalism," specifically on what is to be taught about our cultural heritage. Unfortunately the debate has been unnecessarily polarized in the worst tradition of the curse of either/or. Coughlin notes, "The public debate over multiculturalism is sometimes portrayed in rather stark terms—pitting charges of 'Eurocentrism' against countercharges of 'ethnic separatism.' "

Rita McWilliams, a television producer, called in the winter of 1992 to ask whether I would participate in a public television show dealing with multiculturalism. The other participant was going to be Ronald Walters, a black political scientist from Howard University. As Rita and I discussed the subject, I explained that if by multiculturalism one means that young Americans should learn more about the many backgrounds of those who together make up America, it would enrich us all. If one means by multiculturalism, however, that there would be no shared heroes or values, that there would be no recognition of one shared core—especially democracy, mutual respect, and individual rights, which had very little support in traditions other than the European one—it might destroy our unity and thus our society. Rita McWilliams was interested in my ideas, but then added somewhat uneasily: "But you *do* disagree with him?" I said that Ron is a person I respect a great deal and had over to my home, but we do differ on *some* of these matters.

During the show that followed, Ron and I had a fine dialogue, agreeing on some issues, clarifying some others, and differing on still others. When the show was over and the moderator, Morton Kondracke, and I were taking off our makeup in the men's room, I could see that Mort was clearly peeved. "You should have disagreed more with one another," he exclaimed. "We should have put Pat Buchanan on the show!" When the show was aired, the dialogue between Ron and myself was cut by half, and the first half of the show was dedicated to a one-sided critique of multiculturalism by Daniel Boorstin.

I and many of my colleagues often find ourselves under similar pressures: "If you are not part of the solution, you are part of the problem." We are left with the clear message that if we wish our views to be aired, we must be more polarizing and confrontational.

Specifically, we are under pressure to view American values and cultures as either a single, undifferentiated entity (the culture of "white male Europeans")—or as a hodgepodge of unrelated clusters, one for each ethnic group, like the animals on Noah's Ark. A Communitarian points to a third alternative that allows us to keep a set of shared values while providing full opportunities for the constituent ethnic and racial communities to honor their particular heritages as important, indeed enriching, subcultures.

In the multicultural debate, there are on the one hand those who demand that the works taught in high school and college classrooms be drawn from the cultural heritage of those being taught. That is, minorities should be exposed to their traditions rather than to "European" or "Western" tomes (such as those by Plato, Shakespeare, and the authors of the *Federalist Papers*). Black students should be taught the works of black authors, such as Richard Wright, Langston Hughes, Gayle Jones, and John Oliver Killens. Women should read the works of female authors, such as Charlotte Perkins Gilman's *Women and Economics*, Simone de Beauvoir's *The Second Sex,* and so on.

As Lewis H. Lapham put it in *Harper's*:

> Were I to believe what I read in the papers, I would find it easy to think that I no longer can identify myself simply as an American. The noun apparently means nothing unless it is dressed up with at least one modifying adjective. As a plain American I have neither voice nor authentic proofs of existence. I acquire presence only as an old American, a female American, a white American, a rich American, a black American, a gay American, a poor American, a Native American, a dead American. The subordination of the noun to the adjective makes a mockery of both the American premise and the democratic spirit.

The same one-sided proponents of multiculturalism maintain that the idea of a core curriculum—one shared, centrally agreed-upon body of knowledge—should be abandoned and replaced by a cafeteria of offerings from a variety of cultural and historical origins, one to each taste, without any particular commitment, some "soul," some Chinese, Cajun, Tex-Mex, Italian, and so on. Once ethnic-racial nourishment is served up in schools, it is all too often spiced with the condiments of "superiority" of the particular culture that has been offered, over all others. And quite a few of them are steeped in hate, as American history is depicted as one of oppression and conquest and very little else.

Albert Shanker, president of the American Federation of Teachers, argues that

> new multiculturalists want to go to the . . . extreme of putting down everything American. For them, "Americanize" is a dirty word. They want to present this country as a place where only bad things have happened to people who are not white Europeans. Instead of teaching children that they all share a civic culture to which every group has contributed, they want to make kids believe that the common culture is a sham and that the true identity and true self-interest lie in the fact they belong to different cultures.

On the other side of the unnecessary conflict, a group of largely white, largely male traditionalists in the humanities lined up and formed the National Association of Scholars. Their purpose is to champion one core curriculum. They challenged the materials advanced by various other groups as poor in literary quality (did not stand the test of times), ideologically driven and studded with bogus historical claims (such as a statement that many of history's great figures, from Aristotle to Beethoven, had black origins or simply were black). They heaped scorn on the notion that curricula should be geared to the psychic needs (building self-esteem) of students. The association argues that "the idea that students will be discouraged by not encountering more works by members of their own race, sex, or ethnic group, even were it substantiated, would not justify adding inferior works. Such paternalism conveys a message opposite to the one desired." They state that they are more than content, even proud, to teach the works of dead white men, such as Plato and Shakespeare, although they will and do include the works of others if they meet "generally applicable intellectual and aesthetic standards."

If you move beyond these polarizing positions, you discern *a fertile middle ground*. You soon realize that to the extent that multiculturalism suggests that the curricula in American schools and colleges should be enriched, so that students learn more about cultures other than their own, especially the cultural origins of various American minorities and women, the suggestion has much merit. These subcultures are of obvious interest and value to members of these groups. (Why should an Asian-American learn in core courses only about the history of Europe and only from books by Europeans?) Moreover, educated people—whatever their origins—ought to be conversant with the main works and seminal ideas of other civilizations, especially those many of his or her fellow Americans consider part of their heritage, such as African traditions and Hispanic culture.

At the same time, one notes that teaching materials are used not only to communicate knowledge, but also to transmit the core values of a society. It is desirable that students acquire a rudimentary knowledge of not only the Old Testament and New Testament but also the Koran and Confucius' proverbs. But the works of Locke and Kant, the *Federalist Papers,* the Constitution, and other core documents of American democracy should not be treated as coequals with *Mein Kampf, Das Kapital,* and other ideological tracts that served to legitimate tyrannical political systems. The merits of our institutions and the failings of dictatorships should be presented without hesitation or apology.

To avoid a misunderstanding: I am certainly not suggesting that the writings tyrants have used to justify their regimes of oppression and terror should be suppressed, or that students should be prevented from reading them. But I do suggest that teachers should not be expected to present them as neutral alternatives, as if historical records and human experiences teach us nothing about the great virtues of the democratic political system of our society and communities—yes, our ways—and the oppression caused by other political systems.

The details are matters for curricula committees, boards of education, parents and students, to work out. The guidelines for a Communitarian teaching on the subject at hand stand out: cultural enrichment is welcome; cultural superiority is not. Cultural diversity is enriching; attack on the core values undermines the framework in which the pieces are to be placed, undermines the shared values that help keep us together as a community of communities.

People of Color, Melting Pot, or Pluralism-with-Unity?

The main issue is not one of curriculum, although what is taught provides a convenient prism to illuminate deeper and more complex issues that American society faces as it strives to maintain itself as a supracommunity. The main question is: Should we forgo the notion of one society and allow it to be replaced by a conglomerate of tribes of various colors? And if we seek to maintain a measure of national unity, is the only or best way to achieve this goal by melting away the subcultures?

The notion that America should give up its core and recognize that it has become a society of "people of color," a rainbow society, has both political and demographic sources. The term was introduced by Jesse Jackson during his 1984 presidential campaign. Seeking to build a political base beyond his black constituency, Jackson appealed to various minorities, labor unions, farmers, and environmentalists to follow him to a new America, one in which people of all backgrounds would be socially and culturally equal. He never elaborated on what such a society would look like or what its core values would be. (When I repeatedly asked his close adviser, Ron Walters, this question, he refrained from answering, even when I somewhat teasingly inquired whether he and Jesse recognized white as a color.) In recent years, though, the term *people of color* is often used to signify the notion that America will become, or ought to become, a pastiche of various racial and ethnic groups, each with its own culture, rather than one homogeneous nation.

Another source is a report sponsored by the Labor Department that describes the composition of the American labor force by the year 2000 (which is only a few years away). The report was said to show that soon the majority of workers would be members of minorities. Demographic projections that deal with the total American population, and not just those in the labor force, have been subjected to a similar interpretation.

Another voice trumpeting the new multicultural America can be heard in Martha Farnsworth Riche's article in the prestigious scientific journal *American Demographics*. The article's title, "We're All Minorities Now," well summarizes its thesis. The article states that "the United States is undergoing a new demographic transition: it is becoming a multicultural society. During the 1990s, it will shift from a society dominated by whites and rooted in Western culture to a world society characterized by three large racial and ethnic minorities." It adds that only a few of the immigrants currently flowing into the United States are white, and that new immigrants and blacks and Hispanics tend to have more children than whites. Most important, "we have left the time when the nonwhite, non-Western part of our population could be expected to assimilate to the dominant majority." On the contrary, it is time for whites to do some assimilating into the new rainbow society.

Others have carried the argument further. June Jordan, in an article in *The Progressive* entitled "Diversity or Death," puts her views succinctly: "Opposition to diversity is opposition to life itself." Little wonder some Americans of European ancestry have begun to organize as a minority, anxious to maintain their rights in the brave new world.

Actually, the Labor Department-sponsored report, *Workforce 2000,* only shows that 20 percent of the net *new* entrants into the labor force between the years 1989 and 2000 will be nonwhites, and that 22 percent will be immigrants. Forty-two percent will be native white women, and only 15 percent of the net new entrants will be native white males. To conclude from this and similar projections that white males will become a minority is like saying that if one adds a bit of Scotch to a watery drink, there will be little water left in the glass. As a matter of fact, according to the U.S. Bureau of the Census, the proportion of blacks in the United States will by the year 2000 rise only to 13.1 percent from 12.1 percent in 1989. Hispanics will reach 9.4 percent (up from 8 percent in the same period). Other racial groups, mainly Asian, will increase to 4 percent from 3.4 percent. All together, members of these groups will amount to 26.5 percent—an important, sizable population—but only about one out of every four Americans.

In addition, there is no reason to believe that members of various minorities are ready to array themselves against white men in some kind of grand new alliance, the dream of a handful of left-leaning radicals. On the contrary, there are important differences within each group and among them—between Hispanics and blacks, for instance, not to mention between those two groups and Asian-Americans. The instances in which different minority groups have supported opposing candidates for public office are numerous, and there are almost no occasions in which they have coalesced to support the same candidate or to endorse the same set of "minority" values. Similarly, competition and conflict over jobs, housing, and trade are common among blacks and Hispanics and Asians from New York City to fishing ports of the Florida Panhandle to Los Angeles.

And within each ethnic group there are significant moral, social, and political differences. For example, only a minority of women consider themselves feminists. Some women support some feminist positions but oppose others. Some are staunch conservatives (such as the followers of such leaders as Phyllis Schlafly and many who are outspoken advocates of a conservative, pro-life agenda). Similarly, there are now important black intellectuals, politicians, and voters who are conservative and/or Republican, including Alan Keyes, Shelby Steele, Thomas Sowell, and Michael L. Williams. Actually, it is rather racist to assume that people who share a particular skin color will favor one political position, while those of another pigmentation will take the opposite view. In short, the rainbow society is not within sight. Should it be?

Out Goes the Melting Pot

If one takes the notion of a rainbow society as a criticism of America as a melting pot, it is a useful metaphor. The view of American culture as a melting pot does imply that new Americans and their children are to abandon their heritages and subcultures and become homogenized Americans, without distinct traits or culture. It does favor what James Bryce in *The American Commonwealth* saw as "the amazing solvent power which American institutions, habits, and ideas exercise upon newcomers of all races . . . quickly dissolving and assimilating the foreign bodies that are poured into her mass."

In the same vein, Shelby Steele argues in *The Content of Our Character* that black Americans should seek advancement not as members of a race, but as individual Americans. ("There will be no end to despair and no lasting solution to any of our problems until we rely on individual effort within the American mainstream—rather than collective action against the mainstream—as our means of advancement.") Others have written about Americans forgoing their hyphen—that which connects them to their various backgrounds and ethnic groups, such as Irish-Americans, Polish-Americans, and so on. Woodrow Wilson told his fellow Americans that "you cannot become thorough Americans if you think of yourselves in groups. America does not consist of groups. A man who thinks of himself as belonging to a particular national group in America has not yet become an American." In short, the expectation was for one people, one culture, a single nation without internal differentiation along group lines.

Although two generations ago there was a widespread acceptance of the melting pot idea, Communitarians can now readily recognize that the melting pot is *unnecessarily homogenizing*. There is no reason to expect or to welcome, let alone to use the moral voice to foster, the idea that all Americans should learn to favor one cuisine (hamburgers, French fries, and a Coke? roast beef, mashed potatoes, and green peas?), one form of folk dancing (square?), one kind of music (rap?), and so on. On the contrary, the variety of heritages, subcultures, and communities can readily be embraced as enriching American society. As Diane Ravitch, an assistant secretary of education for research and improvement, put it, multiculturalism should expand the understanding of American culture into a rich and more varied tapestry. In short, it is possible to accommodate cultural differences up to a point within a framework of unity; our choices are not limited either to melting away differences or to breaking American society into a bunch of squabbling nationalities.

Pluralism-Within-Unity

Unfortunately, from a Communitarian viewpoint, some concepts of multiculturalism do not favor maintaining one overarching community, in which various subcultures will find a legitimate place. I speak not of the constituent communities—neighborhoods, ethnic groups, and so on—but of the community of communities, of the American society. Without a firm sense of one supracommunity, there is considerable danger that the constituent communities will turn on one another. Indeed, *the more one favors strengthening communities*, a core of the Communitarian agenda, *the more one must concern oneself with ensuring that they see themselves as parts of a more encompassing whole*, rather than as fully independent and antagonistic.

From this perspective, the concept of "people of color" is not completely helpful; it carries within itself two implications that go way beyond enriching American society and allowing ethnic and racial communities to maintain ties to their origins. These ideas challenge American society as a community of communities, as one that provides a set of overarching and nestling values and bonds.

One relatively moderate version of the concept suggests that there will be many separate Americas—a black nation, a Hispanic hemisphere, a Native American country, and so on, without over-arching bonds or values. This concept of *unbounded* pluralism threatens to balkanize America, to turn it, as Arthur M. Schlesinger, Jr., writes in his *The Disuniting of America,* into a bunch of warring tribes. The nation would break up into groups without a shared vision, without a commitment that all share a common fate—that is, without shared perspectives that are essential to work out major differences among the constituent communities. As reported by Paul Berman, who has collected writings on the subject:

> The educational emphasis on ethnic distinctions and the sus-
> picion of American democratic institutions are going to wear
> down the bonds that hold the country together. And sooner
> or later, according to these accusations, problems that are poli-
> tical and social, not just educational, will come of all of this,
> and the United States will break up into a swarm of warring
> Croatias and Serbias.

It is basically this notion of putting group loyalties and identities above the commons that sent Yugoslavia into civil war in 1991, that endangers Canadian society, and that threatens Indian society and many others. Americans need only to think back to the horrors of the Civil War to realize that confrontations on basic values between antagonistic communities are cruel and devastating. Civil societies seek to resolve differences without internal wars—by drawing on shared values.

A less moderate version of the people-of-color notion springs from the premise that if there must be a set of overarching values that bind the parts into one society, they need not be Western or European.

The attitude toward language allows you to gauge where people stand on this issue. Melting pot advocates assume that everybody will learn English and forget their language of origin, as indeed was often the case in the past. Some moderate "people of color" suggest that everybody is entitled to their own language, say, blacks to "black English," and are indifferent to the ways that different groups will communicate with one another. As the black leader Bayard Rustin noted a long time ago: "[T]he concept of bilingual teaching is all too often being advocated as a means of creating a separatist, alternative culture in which the speaking of English does not play a pivotal role."

Extremists go one step farther: they argue that we live in a Hispanic hemisphere, and hence we should all learn Spanish. English is a second language of those who may wish to learn it. In contrast, Communitarian proponents of pluralism-within-unity urge that everybody learn English while maintaining or regaining a knowledge of Hebrew, Italian, Japanese, or whatever as part of their subculture.

The Core Values

Beyond language, there is the even more important matter of a set of shared core values, especially the commitment to democracy, the Bill of Rights, and mutual respect among the subgroups. Constituent communities can follow their own subsets of values without endangering the body society, as long as they accept these shared values. They provide the frame of unity to contain the "plurals" from falling out.

Fortunately, far from following a few radical leaders, most members of American minority groups strongly favor core American values, despite their European origin. For example, a 1992 survey found that although most Americans (79 percent) favor "fair treatment for all, without prejudice or discrimination," the proportion of blacks and Hispanics is even higher (86 percent and 85 percent, respectively). Similarly, a poll of New York residents shows that the vast majority of respondents considered teaching "the common heritage and values that we share as Americans" to be "very important." Again, minorities endorse this position even more than whites: 70 percent of whites compared with 88 percent of Hispanics and 89 percent of blacks. This is surprising only to the extremists. After all, the first and foremost beneficiaries of the Constitution, the democratic process, and mutual tolerance are vulnerable groups, especially minorities.

Last but not least, note that these shared values are not found, or are poorly grounded, in other cultures. For example, few black women would like to be treated the way fundamentalist Islamic countries treat women. In some of those states, women are forced to wear veils, are not allowed to drive cars, and are generally subordinated to men's whims. The rights of criminal offenders are not held in high regard. Under strict Islamic law, or *sharia,* a thief's limbs are to be amputated. A woman who commits adultery is to be stoned to death, and those who drink alcohol are subject to flogging.

Minorities do not fare much better. According to Islam, there are three main religious categories: Muslims, People of the Book (mainly Jews and Christians), and unbelievers. People of the Book are entitled to some respect, though they are not allowed to hold positions of authority over Muslims. As for unbelievers, as Abdullahi A. An-Na'im puts it, Islamic law "does not contemplate their permanent residence. . . . Unbelievers are to be killed on sight unless they are granted temporary . . . safe conduct."

Habib C. Malik, a professor of philosophy at Catholic University of America, notes: "In all Arab countries except Lebanon, Christian Arabs were long ago reduced by the Islamic government to second-class . . . status." Such a classification "continues in all countries to mean severe limitations in the domain of personal, political, and religious freedom, particularly in the freedom of expression." The way the Kurds have been treated by various governments in Iraq is well known.

There are more moderate versions of Islam, and some versions—especially those practiced by some blacks in the United States—are much more tolerant. However, the fundamental religion provides no sound, firm foundation for individual rights, tolerance, or democracy.

Asian cultures are similarly far from hospitable to individual rights, liberties, and mutual tolerance. Japan is often correctly pointed to as a place where community and society hold great power over people. But what is missing is the other component: a firm anchoring of individual rights. *Japan: 2000,* a report prepared for the CIA by the executive assistant to the president of Rochester

Institute of Technology, with the help of eight respected scholars and area experts, concludes:

> The role of women in Japanese society is definitely inferior and destined to remain so; there is no place in their culture for a female in a relationship superior to the male. Those women who enter the workplace are relegated to jobs as elevator starters, door openers, tea servers and, by cultural tradition and modern definition, are inferior to men.

The study overstates the case. There are now some women in management positions in Japan. But they are rather few and seem to be there largely due to the influence of Western ideals. Still, the Bank of Tokyo, reported to be one of Japan's more progressive employers, even today requires women to obtain their husband's approval to work overseas, and unmarried women must get their parents' approval.

Of Japan's population of 120 million, only 850,000 are non-Japanese. Still, they are rather poorly tolerated. Koreans, who make up Japan's largest minority, are rarely hired by major corporations. Most Koreans use Japanese aliases and hide their origins in an attempt to avoid Japanese prejudice and discrimination. And then there are the burakumin, the Japanese "untouchables," who are still stigmatized because of their ancestors' caste occupations as butchers, undertakers, and other jobs that were considered unclean or involved the killing of animals.

Some Asian scholars have recently found some support in Confucius for human rights and democracy. Professor Jonathan Chaves, an expert on Asia, finds that these scholars use ambiguous passages of Confucian thought in order to incorporate Western ideals without actually admitting that they are Western, and are intellectually suspect.

In short, those committed to democracy, individual rights, and mutual respect will find little comfort in other major cultural traditions.

In Conclusion

To rebuild communities, we must draw on community institutions. These may vary from those that are based on individual citizens banding together, say, in a neighborhood crime watch to those provided by communities as a group, for instance public schools. The more opportunities we provide of both kinds to allow people to apply their civic commitment, the more powerful it will grow to be, and the more the moral and social order will be carried by the community rather than the state.

The focus on rebuilding community is sometimes challenged by those who are concerned with social justice. There is no necessary contradiction between these two concerns. Communitarians hold that all people, no matter how disadvantaged or handicapped, should take some responsibility for themselves. For the sake of their own dignity, it should be expected of them to do for themselves the best that they can, however limited the results of such endeavors.

Second, communities should be the first places that people who require help turn to. Friends, neighbors, those closest, are the most naturally able to assist. However, Communitarians recognize that some communities are more richly endowed than others, and they see a clear need for wealthier communities to help those that are disadvantaged.

Finally, Communitarians are concerned with maintaining a supracommunity, a community of communities—*the* American society. The notion that a coalition of nonwhites and women will take over America and impose its values—values that are different from those gained from "dead white males"—is a cross between overblown campaign rhetoric and radical fantasy. There is no coming together of the various groups; there is no coalition of minorities or minorities and women. Moreover, if one coalition were to be formed on core values, evidence shows that most would favor those that prevail today.

The supracommunity can be well sustained and readily accommodate subgroup differences—as long as these do not threaten a limited set of core values and shared bonds. There can be debate about where exactly the boundaries lie between shared elements and those of subgroupings. Some, for instance, point to Switzerland to suggest that a shared language is not essential. But a commitment to core American ideals—democratic political institutions, the legal concepts of the Constitution and its Bill of Rights, and the notion of social and religious tolerance—are the linchpins that maintain the American society, protect minority members, and undergird individual rights.

PART
II

Too Many Rights, Too Few Responsibilities

PART

II

Too Many Rights,
Too Few
Responsibilities

6 ♦ New Responsibilities: Public Safety and Public Health

Authoritarian Voices

THE growing despair over the inability of American public authorities to deal effectively with violent crime, gang warfare, drug abuse, and AIDS has already caused Authoritarian voices to be raised. At first, only isolated voices called for contaminating illegal drugs to make users "wretchedly ill"; arming all citizens (because, as one syndicated columnist put it, "when everybody owned a gun there was less crime"); quarantining HIV carriers; and suspending the Constitution until the war against drugs is won. Recently, even some authority figures have picked up on such extremist calls. The police superintendent of Chicago, LeRoy Martin, suggested that the United States emulate the Chinese penal system, in which drug dealers are shot. State district judge Michael McSpadden of Houston said he favored castrating violent criminals. The appeal of former Ku Klux Klan grand wizard David Duke to 39 percent of Louisiana's voters in the 1991 governor's race, and to financial contributors from all over the United States, is a troubling sign of the spread of utter frustration in growing segments of the public.

True, so far these Authoritarian recommendations and voices have not amounted to much (although if you were on the receiving end of their nightsticks, you might think otherwise). The main danger is that *unless we fashion reasonable, carefully calibrated measures to enhance public safety and public health, these voices will gain in following.* We should not underestimate the frustrations among many who must live behind triple-locked doors and barred windows; who fear to venture into most parks and many streets after dark; and who, in quite a few places, can't walk the streets safely even in broad daylight. In areas frequented by drug dealers, there are Americans who sleep on the floor to dodge bullets, who live in constant fear of violence, especially if they are old, young, female, or otherwise vulnerable. In other realms of life, many also fear intimacy, blood transfusions, or even a visit to the dentist. Children carry guns to school because they fear preteen gunslingers, finding no effective protection by school or public authorities. Being mugged on the way to school—for lunch money or a bus pass—is all too common in some parts. Although some of these fears are exaggerated, most are, to a considerable extent, quite realistic. Little wonder people are all too anxious to find effective measures that will reestablish a reasonable degree of public safety and public health.

It is here that Radical Individualists unwittingly play into the hands of the Authoritarians. By adhering to an absolutist, uncompromising line that focuses on the rights of individuals and pays no heed to the needs of the community, they help set the stage for a major right-wing, Authoritarian backlash.

Suspicion of Any and All Government Authority

Radical Individualists basically treat every authority as at least potentially Authoritarian. They hinder the development of legitimate, democratically controlled, essential public authorities. Gene Guerrero, an ACLU representative, cites Justice Brandeis in testimony he presented in opposition to drug testing:

> Experience should teach us to be most on guard to protect liberty when the Government's purposes are beneficent. Men born to freedom are naturally alert to repel invasions of their liberty by evil-minded rulers. The greatest dangers to liberty lurk in insidious encounters by men of zeal, well-meaning but without understanding.

If this philosophy is applied to a functioning democratic government—if you play on the fear that the government *may* exceed its powers to a point that it will turn Authoritarian—then you reach all kinds of untenable conclusions, including a stubborn refusal to reinterpret constitutional rights to meet compelling social need. You end up perceiving constitutional rights not as a basis for sound government policies, but as a way to hobble most, if not all, government actions.

The generalized mistrust of public authorities, however benign their purpose and appropriate their service, is reflected in a 1991 book, *Visions of Liberty,* by Ira Glasser, the executive director of the ACLU. He writes, "In one century, it [government power] comes in the form of a British soldier; in another, a careworker or a federally funded clinic. Encroaching power wears many disguises." As I see it, we must guard against welfare cheats and excessive bureaucratization of welfare, but we must be able to tell the difference between a British (or other) occupying force and social workers' well-intended attempts to help the most vulnerable members of the community. We must be able to distinguish between illegitimate autocrats and duly elected and responsive public servants discharging their legitimate duties.

The lengths to which we can be driven by suspicion of any and all authorities is highlighted by the ACLU's opposition, despite a significant increase in the number of children who are kidnapped, to *voluntary* fingerprinting of children by some schools. Such fingerprinting makes it possible for children who are found years later to be reunited with their parents and to prove that they are not the kidnappers' children. It also facilitates the notification of parents when bodies are found—parents who might otherwise look in vain for their missing children for years on end, long after they had been buried in some pauper's grave.

Why is the ACLU opposed to the voluntary fingerprinting of children? Because of the "possibility" that the government might gain access to the fingerprints and misuse them. The policy paper, entitled "Children's Rights," warns:

Among the dangers posed by fingerprinting are the possibility of access by government agencies to fingerprinting records and dissemination of records without the child's consent and without a warrant, either by consent of the child's parents or by subpoena.

Furthermore, the ACLU's institutionalized paranoia leads it to believe that "fingerprinting tends to condition children and society to accept without protest unnecessary personal data collection and other invasions of privacy." This is a piece of sociological rubbish, akin to claiming that the issuance of driver licenses, or responding to the census, "conditions" people to tell all to anybody who asks.

This and other such Radical Individualist positions—the libertarian ethos—lead to a paralysis of public authorities that has grave human and moral consequences. *If we do not act because we fear that somehow, someday, an innocent law may lead to tyranny, we may well set forth conditions that raise social stress to a level that serves those who call for "strong" government.* What is needed is a lean, well-contained government—rather than to assume that no government act can be sanitized.

Some argue that the dogmatic, extremist positions of the ACLU and other Radical Individualists are useful because they provide a political counterbalance to other equally extremist positions against individual rights. Maybe so. However, extremity in the defense of virtue *is* a vice. Actions taken by Radical Individualists do cause harm, because they often block (and in other instances tie up in the courts for years) programs that respond to compelling social needs.

New Approaches

Communitarians suggest a series of measures that would significantly enhance public safety and public health, without endangering basic individual rights and constitutional protections. Often these modifications entail no more than limited reinterpretations of legal traditions—for instance, of what constitutes *reasonable* search and seizure, which, of course, the Constitution allows. Such reinterpretations have been taking place continuously over the past two hundred years. There are those who openly admit that the courts, especially the United States Supreme Court, treat the Constitution as a living document that may be modified to respond to the changing times and changes in our moral values. Others argue that the

Constitution is to be treated as a sacred text that is unalterable. The latter group of legal scholars does its adjusting of the Constitution by interpreting what they see as the Founding Fathers' intent. In either case, we are not irrevocably bound by what was written two hundred years ago. Otherwise, we would still treat each black person as three-fifths of a human being, deny women's rights, and find no explicit reference to the concept of privacy.

Note that the *Miranda* rule (the requirement that police must read you your rights), which is now considered by many a major foundation of our liberties, was not part of the American legal legacy until 1966. Indeed, in comparison, the modifications that Communitarians seek are rather modest in scope. In short, what Communitarians favor is akin to opening a window to allow air into a stuffy room—not breaking out a wall with a sledgehammer.

If we modify our concept of rights, will we start down the proverbial "slippery slope"? That is, it is said that if we make small adjustments, which are sound in themselves, we will lose our grip on our liberties and end up on our collective rear ends on the low end of a hill. The answer, we shall see, lies in making notches on that slope so that we can advance ourselves as a society without slipping down into authoritarianism.

How can this be achieved? My main proposal is that we agree with one another that we shall make a contribution to public safety and public health by accepting some measures that do encumber us to some extent but allow significant benefits to the community. For example, we will agree to halt for a minute and a half at a sobriety checkpoint (which is the length of an average stop) to help deter murderous drunk drivers. Why would anybody oppose such a measure?

An examination of the debate over the introduction of airport screening gates allows us to cast light on what constitutes a reasonable versus unreasonable solution.

"Suspicionless Searches": The Case of Airport Screening

Between 1969 and 1972, the traveling public experienced a rash of skyjackings. There were at least 115 incidents, including 24 terrorist bomb explosions aboard aircraft that killed a total of 256 people. Enhancing security was widely debated, but little action was taken. On November 10, 1972, three escaped convicts hijacked a plane out of Birmingham, Alabama. The hijacking lasted twenty-nine hours, during which the plane made nine stops and was flown to two foreign countries. The hijackers asked for ransom money, they threatened first to crash the plane into an atomic plant and then to shoot all the passengers, until they were finally arrested by the Cubans. The incident prodded the United States into instituting a new security system. On December 5, 1972, U.S. airports were given sixty days to place checkpoints in boarding and reboarding areas. On January 5, 1973, it became mandatory for all passengers to be searched electronically and for their carry-on luggage to be searched as well.

The benefits of these screening gates has been quite substantial. During the first year of implementation, in which 165 million U.S. travelers passed through the new gates, more than 2,000 guns and 3,500 pounds of explosives were discovered. The number of hijackings in the United States fell from twenty-nine in 1972 to two in 1973. During the first ten years of the program, about 25,000 firearms were detected and confiscated, and more than 10,000 related arrests were made.

Millions of Americans and their baggage pass each day through screening gates at airports and at the entrances of many public buildings, from the halls of Congress to those of many courts. They often entail a minor delay. Americans have shown that they are quite willing to accept these delays as their contribution to enhancing safety, to deterring terrorists and skyjackers, and to stopping in their tracks those who would plant bombs in Congress and in the courts.

Americans also seem to prefer screening gates to the previous strategy, in which the authorities used "profiles" to single out individuals who seemed suspicious. These often resulted in discrimination against minorities or members of the counterculture.

The introduction of screening gates is a good example of the type of new measures that Communitarians favor. They entail a small contribution by each of us, typically a minor inconvenience, and provide a major benefit for all of us. Likewise, sobriety checkpoints enable us to drive more safely, and drug testing allows us to travel more safely on mass transit, airplanes, and school buses.

To frame these measures as suspicionless searches makes them sound like the tentacles of a police state. Actually they are carefully crafted, limited opportunities for community service.

When screening gates were introduced, the ACLU immediately opposed them. As they saw it, a major constitutional principle was at stake. The American Constitution basically assumes, fairly and justly, that the government should not persecute groups but only go after a particular individual—*if* specific, demonstrable suspicion exists. Thus it might be true that, statistically speaking, young people commit more violent crimes than older ones, but nobody suggests detaining, or even searching, all those who are twenty-five years or younger and out on the street after midnight. (Curfews imposed on minors are also opposed by Radical Individualists, precisely because they are applied to a whole group or category of people.) Public authorities must show that they have specific reasons to suspect that a youth has committed a crime (say, a police officer sees him running from the scene) or is about to commit one (an officer observes a person lurking with a gun in a dark alley next to a money machine), before they may detain or search that person.

Normally, such evidence must be brought before an independent authority, usually a judge, to determine if it is sufficient to search a home or person, and a warrant must be obtained. The law recognizes that when this is impractical, public authorities may proceed on their own, as long as after the fact they can show that they had sufficient individualized suspicion to detain or search the person or enter a house (such as the presence of weapons). On the other hand, if it turns out that the police stopped all those who were driving big Cadillacs on Interstate 95 (which is frequented by drug dealers), who were carefully observing the speed limit (which drug dealers carrying loads are known to do), and they caught a dealer, the conviction might well be thrown out of court. That is because the police pursued a category of people, not an individual suspect.

The ACLU bases its opposition to screening gates, and to other such measures, on this constitutional tradition. According to the ACLU, "although the circumstance of an airport search may justify a departure from the warrant requirement, it does not justify ignoring the constitutional insistence on probable cause. The current practice of searching the persons and belongings of *all* individuals, simply because they wish to board an airplane, is completely inconsistent with these Fourth Amendment principles." These are called "suspicionless searches."

But after the rash of skyjacking and sabotage by terrorists, a new approach was tried. It was not practical to wait to establish "reasonable suspicion" before searching someone about to board an airplane. Courts had already established in other areas that short delays in travel were reasonable (in other words, allowable under the Constitution) if there were no other encumbering steps (for example, demanding identification papers). Moreover, the public has shown an almost complete acceptance of the new approach of screening gates. They became an instance in which we *did* accept as legitimate "suspicionless searches" of *groups* of people *because the intrusion was small and the public gain was considerable.* (If airport safety entailed long delays or involved strip searches, or if skyjacking wasn't in fact curtailed, screening gates would be rejected by the courts, by the public, and by Communitarians.)

Still, the ACLU maintained its institutionalized paranoia:

> Perhaps the most troublesome aspect of the airport search question is the readiness with which most people, civil libertarians included, have accepted and indeed welcome such procedures. It reflects a disturbing tendency to accept any measure, such as routine searches in public places, which are supposedly devised to protect our safety.

Other Reasonable Searches and Contributions

Sobriety Checkpoints

Drunk drivers cause a lot of mayhem. In the last decade some 250,000 Americans lost their lives in alcohol-related crashes, which translates into a fatality every twenty-two minutes. In addition, about 500,000 people are injured each year. Alcohol-related deaths are the number one killer of fifteen- to twenty-four-year-olds. Two out of every five people in the United States will be involved in an alcohol-related crash during their lifetime.

Ideally, the moral voice of the community would suffice to discourage people from drinking to excess and, above all, from driving drunk. This is happening to some extent, as evidenced by the fact that more Americans than a decade ago consider heavy drinking uncouth. Also, the notion of a designated driver seems to be catching on in some parts. And efforts are made to treat the problem through public education and raising the moral voice of the community through such campaigns as "Friends don't let friends drive drunk." But these changes are insufficient.

As a result, sobriety checkpoints are being introduced. Thirty-eight states have adopted the practice (twenty-eight conduct checkpoints at least once a month), as well as the District of Columbia, Puerto Rico, the Virgin Islands, and many other democracies (including Great Britain and Australia).*

A study of checkpoints in New Jersey found that they reduced by 10 to 15 percent nighttime single-vehicle crashes, and that the program's impact was greater and more sustainable than those of alternative treatments. A study in New South Wales, Australia, where checkpoints are often used, found that alcohol-related crashes decreased approximately 30 percent and that this improvement was sustained for at least five years.

Aside from plucking drunk drivers off the road, sobriety checkpoints heighten public awareness of the risk of being arrested while driving drunk—that is, they have a deterrent effect. A study of a Canadian program found that the arrest of drunk drivers was less effective in reducing alcohol-related crashes than the publicity surrounding the very existence of checkpoints. Another study found that 85 percent of those who served alcohol in bars in Charlottesville, Virginia, reported hearing customers discussing checkpoints; many patrons said that they were drinking less and/or selecting designated drivers.

Twenty-nine states have also initiated policies in which police officers may seize a driver's license, if the driver refuses to take an alcohol test or fails one. Under California's law, which is typical of these efforts, the driver is then given a temporary license that is valid for forty-five days, during which time the revocation can be challenged. If the driver is not successful, the license expires. First-

---

* State supreme courts in Idaho, Louisiana, Rhode Island, and Washington have found the checkpoints to violate the state's constitution. States that impose legal or administrative impediments are New Hampshire, Oklahoma, Oregon, and Utah. States that have decided not to initiate them include Alaska, Arkansas, and North Dakota.

time offenders must wait four months before applying for a new license; each subsequent suspension is for a year. In California, more than three hundred thousand licenses were removed from drivers on the spot during the first year of the law, and alcohol-related traffic accidents dropped 8.5 percent during the first six months.

Courts have carefully circumscribed these searches to make them reasonable. Sobriety checkpoints must be announced in advance to give drivers fair warning. They must be set up so as not to cause major traffic delays. They may not be extensive events (on average each stop lasts ninety seconds). Checkpoints must be clearly marked and otherwise conducted safely, so that cars will not stop suddenly and endanger others behind them.

Public opinion polls show that Americans favor these sobriety checkpoints by a wide margin. Close to 90 percent of those responding stated that they favored these measures. Even those who reported that they are likely to drink and drive favor the checkpoints. One writer captured the sentiments of many. Anthony Kimbrough, the editor of the *Daily Herald* in Columbia, Tennessee, wrote:

> Stop my car. Take 30 seconds, maybe even a full minute, of my time to make sure I'm not driving while drunk. I will not feel like you have violated my Fourth Amendment protections against intrusive searches. I will not feel like you have made an unreasonable police search. . . . Instead, I will feel just a little bit safer about driving on the highway.

Still the Radical Individualists focus only on one issue: according to their definition of rights, such limited and circumscribed searches will turn us into nothing less than a police state. States the Michigan ACLU:

> When the U.S. Supreme Court abdicates its historic role and defers completely to the judgment of the police, allowing police to stop, detain and interrogate people who are suspected of no wrongdoing whatsoever, we have gone a long way down the road toward a police state.

This is more than mere rhetoric. The ACLU has filed suits in state courts and is one of the main reasons that the introduction of sobriety checkpoints was delayed in many states and why they are still not in place in twelve others. Communitarians may well act to support sobriety checkpoints, as long as they remain carefully circumscribed.

Drug Checkpoints

Since airport screening gates are nearly universally accepted, and sobriety checkpoints are in place in thirty-eight states, drug checkpoints would seem a logical extension of the same new approach, another acceptable technique to become available to police. But look at what happened in Inkster, Michigan. In this "poverty-stricken" suburb of Detroit, the streets had been turned into an open-air drug market. Residents were afraid to walk the streets, especially after dark. Many slept on the floor to be out of the reach of stray bullets. Children could not play outside late in the day. Various attempts to oust the drug dealers had failed.

After being himself asked to purchase an illegal drug, the local sheriff, Robert Ficano, came up with an idea. In September 1989, following a public announcement, he set up a checkpoint on a main thoroughfare that led to the drug market area. The officers did not search the cars that were stopped but asked only that drivers show their license, registration, and proof of insurance. This was sufficient to drive away both the dealers and their customers, who were not keen on revealing their identities. The drug market had vanished, until a libertarian, former Inkster mayor Edward Bivens, Jr., challenged the checkpoint in court, asserting that it was unconstitutional search and seizure and reminiscent of Nazi Germany. He argued that the Constitution does not permit the police to stop a driver without the "showing of an individualized, articulate suspicion that the particular motorist was involved in some criminal activity."

A Communitarian may well hold that it would be best if people just refrained from using illegal drugs and succeeded in encouraging others to find meaning, solace, and profits elsewhere. But as long as we choose to control certain substances, and people require a law to help them to implement this community consensus, carefully circumscribed drug checkpoints seem a reasonable way to proceed.

The intrusion is minimal, the public gain significant, and the line is clearly drawn: only cars are stopped and only in public spaces. Homes are not invaded. Drivers and their cars are not searched without a warrant. People are asked to produce only those items of identification that they are already required to carry.

Special Community Service

Beyond the measures already cited that we may all accept as part of our civic duty, special groups are to be asked to make additional contributions to the well-being of the community. We already ask presidential appointees to the Supreme Court and high government positions to submit to FBI background screenings that most citizens would consider a tremendous invasion of their privacy. We ask elected officials to disclose their income, while most Americans would not dream of doing so. And we ask people working for the CIA and the National Security Agency and quite a few others to keep mum about details of their work—a gag that most Americans would consider unthinkable.

The common thread is that public service requires these concessions, and that in all cases those who enter such employment are notified of the requirements before they sign up. (If new requirements are introduced, and the employees find them unacceptable, they should be given plenty of time, say, a year, to find another job.) The same logic now applies when we ask, as a community, that train engineers, police officers, school bus drivers, and pilots be subjected to drug tests.

You guessed it: drug tests are opposed by the Radical Individualists on the usual grounds. (They also argue that performance testing, in which people's ability to carry out a task is examined, would be reasonable. However, such tests are not fully developed and are unlikely to be able to detect the erratic effects of mind-altering drugs such as PCP. That is, a pilot may pass a performance test and still go berserk while flying; only a drug test would reveal that he or she consumed such a drug.)

Other measures are clearly beyond the pale. Detaining people without a trial (say, because they are HIV carriers), searching homes without a warrant, planting listening devices in homes—measures that constitute serious intrusions and violations of individual rights—are unacceptable.

How can we be sure that once we introduce measures most of us would agree are reasonable, we do not slide down a slippery slope of ever more intrusive measures, toward a police state? And how can we systematically distinguish between what is a proper call on citizens, given the pressure of social problems, and what imposes improper demands?

The Slippery Slope

Probably the most common argument against any adjustments in the balance between individual rights and social responsibilities is a vastly overused piece of sociology: the notion that once one seeks to modify a tradition, it crumbles. This argument is often used by Orthodox Jews who oppose any changes in Jewish practice (such as seating men and women together in the synagogue) and, as well, in the Catholic tradition (as can be seen in the opposition to conducting mass in the vernacular). The opponents of change draw on various analogies, especially that old chestnut the slippery slope. Or we hear about the danger of allowing the camel's nose into the tent, lest all of it will follow, and about the risk of allowing in the thin edge of a wedge, which then might be used to pry open gates that ought to have been kept under seal. All of these clichéd images evoke the fear that if we allow some limited, harmless, or even beneficial measures, they will lead us willy-nilly—without opportunities to examine and, above all, stop—to some dire consequences.

Harvard professor Frederick Schauer describes the slippery slope as "a particular act, seemingly innocuous when taken in isolation [that] may yet lead to a future host of similar but increasingly pernicious events." He goes on to point out that "implicit in the 'Where do your draw the line?' argument is the assertion that there is no precise, natural line between the instant case and the danger case—that acting in the instant case will leave us with no logical stopping point short of the danger case."

Referring to the "dangers" of antismoking legislation, Barry Glassner, a fellow sociologist, takes the plunge:

[I]f this pattern continues, we'll have a homogenized population in which everybody will be within recommended weight

ranges, and nobody will smoke anymore, and nobody will
drink and everybody will work out.

According to various estimates, from one-third to two-thirds of
the homeless are mental patients who were dumped onto the streets.
This occurred after liberal reformers argued that large-scale state
mental hospitals, which were dreadful, should be replaced by nice
community centers. The trouble was that the patients were kicked
out of state hospitals before many community centers—of any
kind—were ready. For numerous homeless people, these centers
are still unavailable.

Among the suggestions that are now under consideration is to
recommit many of the mental patients on the streets into the large-
scale state mental hospitals. A less extreme measure is to require
them to be treated as outpatients. Many of the mental patients could
function much more effectively if someone saw to it that they took
their medications regularly—either family members or practitio-
ners in community clinics. In many states, however, this requires a
change in the statutes, away from the Radical Individualist assumption that persons who are not endangering others or themselves
cannot be treated for their own sake or ours. However, when such
rules are discussed, opponents fear that they might lead us to in-
carcerate people against their will: today, mental patients; tomorrow, dissenters.

Another case in point: The ACLU opposes screening gates not
only because it believes that they violate the Fourth Amendment,
but also because of what the ACLU fears they may lead to:

> Regrettably, we live in dangerous times. If the danger posed in
> one situation is thought to justify unconstitutional, emergency
> measures, where can the line be drawn? Today it is airports,
> tomorrow it may be banks or city streets.

The fear of slippery slopes is not *wholly* without foundation.
Once taboos are broken by a community tolerating a modification
of its ethical code, it is not easy to stop. Those who challenged the
traditional vows of fidelity in marriage often found it difficult to
sustain their marital contracts and frequently ended up with no
stable relationship at all. And "reform" in Judaism was followed

(although it may well have occurred anyhow) by a massive flight from religious commitment. However, it is also evident that each time we individually or as a community negotiate a step on the top of what are potentially slippery slopes, we do *not* necessarily end up at the bottom.

Not every young woman who allows herself to be kissed before marriage ends up a hooker, and not everyone who experiments with marijuana ends up a crackhead. Similarly, sexual education, introduced in many schools, has not led, as Authoritarians feared, to new heights of promiscuity, orgies, let alone to the destruction of American society. That is, societies can reset their moral codes without necessarily losing their grip. And, to reiterate, sliding down the slippery slope is not necessarily the result of an avalanche set off by bad precedents; it may well be the consequence of not attending to true needs of the community and thus in effect paving the way to Authoritarian voices and leaders.

Notching Principles

We can notch the slope, formulate principles that allow us to stop, before we reach a danger point. These principles are, of necessity, introduced one by one. However, when it comes to actually fashioning public policies, the guidelines must be applied jointly. That is, policies that qualify by the first measure are still to be examined to establish whether or not they meet the second and third criteria and so on.

First Criterion: Clear and Present Danger

No adjustments should be attempted unless there is a clear and present danger—a verifiable and sizable social problem or need. Unfortunately, in a media-ized society, prophets of doom often alarm wide audiences. There are frequent calls on policy makers and citizens alike to tighten their belts and modify their life-styles, as well as calls to suspend or violate basic rights in order to combat some imagined or anticipated scourge. For example, in the mid-seventies, Americans were told that they would soon be forced out of their cars and onto mass transit because the United States was running out of oil. More recently we were warned that America must introduce central planning or industrial policy in order to compete with the Japanese.

In the early nineties alarmists became exercised about the danger of killer bees invading the United States from Mexico. As a matter of fact, there have been no reports of American deaths due to killer bees, although thirty-eight Mexicans are said to have died from their stings in the late 1980s and early 1990s, about eight a year. Although every life is valuable, societies should articulate new civic duties and social responsibilities only when they face more serious challenges. Thus it is impractical and unjustifiable to demand, by force of law, that every American wear long sleeves and long pants, roll up their car windows, and screen their doors and windows to ward off the killer bees. To reiterate: So far, the danger of these bees in the United States is quite theoretical. The same measures that now look preposterous and contain uncalled-for diminutions of our freedoms would become quite reasonable if Americans were attacked by swarms of bees and began to keel over by the thousands—and no other effective measures would be available to save their lives.

It seems best to act more humbly, refraining from grand changes that involve major economic and human costs and even small diminutions of liberties—until there is a clear and present danger. Nuclear weapons, handguns, AIDS, and crack are examples of clear and present threats. The evidence that they endanger large numbers of lives, if not our societal existence, is incontestable. The threat of global warming may be approaching but in my opinion has not yet reached a level that (as these lines are written in 1992) justifies the kinds of measures that several alarmists advocate.

Other measures are justified because of an especially direct link between the cause and effect. If someone points a machine gun at a person's head, we have a right to take away the other's "property," even wrestle him or her to the ground, even if only one life is at stake. The danger is clear and present. At the same time, we would condemn, indeed penalize, the same conduct if one had only a suspicion that a person might use his or her fists.

A specific case may help illustrate the issue at hand. The U.S. Department of Transportation maintained, after several train wrecks, that there was enough of a problem to warrant an adjustment of rights and responsibilities, to allow testing of train engineers for drugs and alcohol. Radical Individualists opposed the policy for the usual reasons: only individualized, case-by-case evidence of "probable cause" constitutes proper grounds. However, in April 1991 the Ninth Circuit Court of Appeals upheld the U.S. Department of Transportation regulations that authorized truck and bus companies to drug test their employees at random. (The suit was initiated by labor groups claiming that the regulations infringed on the Fourth Amendment and violate privacy.) The Ninth Circuit Court had earlier upheld as constitutional the FAA policy of random drug testing of airline employees.

What was the problem the test seeks to address? Between 1975 and 1984, drugs or alcohol were "directly affecting" causes in 48 train accidents, accounting for 37 fatalities and 80 injuries. Of 179 railroad accidents in 1987, the engineers in 39 of the cases tested positive for drugs. In one crash alone in January 1987, 16 people died and over 170 were injured when an Amtrak train was struck by a Conrail train. Investigators found traces of marijuana in the Conrail engineer's blood and urine.

On August 28, 1991, a New York City subway motorman was speeding, and his train derailed while switching from the express to the local track. The resulting crash killed five passengers and injured more than two hundred others. Hours after the crash, the motorman's blood-alcohol level was twice the legal limit. After this accident the local transit workers union dropped its opposition to random testing, not only for drugs but for alcohol as well.

According to a 1979 study, 23 percent of railroad operating employees were "problem drinkers," many of whom got drunk on the job. True, there are no simple numbers or criteria that tell you that 23 percent is "too much." However, when nearly one out of four of the staff is involved, and when they *directly* have in their hands the life and death of others (unlike the National Weather Bureau staff, which was also to be tested!), you may agree that random testing for drugs and alcohol is justified. This high-risk group includes train engineers, airline pilots, school bus drivers, police officers, and fire fighters.

We can also establish a clear and present danger in the case of handguns. Nine thousand people were murdered with handguns in the United States in 1988; another fourteen thousand were killed in handgun accidents. In contrast, Great Britain had seven handgun murders, while Canada had eight. And we may also see a clear and present danger in AIDS. The AIDS epidemic spread to more than two hundred thousand reported cases by 1992, only twenty-six months after reaching the one-hundred-thousand-case milestone. It took eight years for this first figure to be reached. The number of reported cases is expected to rise by another one hundred thousand in less than two years.

Once the community—if it is a local or national one—establishes that there is a clear and present danger, the policies devised to cope with it must be examined by the other criteria. Here Communitarians can readily agree with Radical Individualists: it does not suffice to point to a serious threat to justify modifying the balance between rights and responsibilities.

Second Criterion: There Is No Alternative Way to Proceed

Assume we already agree as a community that, say, smoking constitutes a clear and present danger. (More than 300,000 people in the United States die from smoking annually.) Moreover, assume we conclude that the link between smoking and ill health is sufficiently tight for smoking to be considered a direct cause of illness and death and hence justified an adjustment according to the first criterion, that smoking is a clear and present danger.

Moreover, additional moral justification for public action comes from ethicists: they point out that even if one accepts the Radical Individualist notion that people ought to be free to choose their purchases, even if self-injurious, smoking harms others. Secondhand smoke (which nonsmokers inhale) accounts for an estimated 2,400 cases of lung cancer per year. Others die from fires that smokers start. In addition, ethicists point out, the preferences of the young are not formed yet. You cannot rely on them to act in line with their self-interest; they have not yet learned what it is. Finally, ethicists see justification for public action in that people reveal that their true preference is to stop smoking. The fact that 90 percent of smokers have tried to quit is a signal for help. (It would be different if we sought to impose, say, Buddhism on Americans, who show precious little indication that this is what they prefer on or below the surface.)

Nevertheless, it still does not follow that an adjustment of rights and responsibilities is justified. *We ought first to look for ways that do not require any reinterpretation of the Constitution.* Drawing on this second criterion, we are likely to conclude that raising taxes on cigarettes is more justified than prohibiting cigarette advertising, as has been suggested. One reason is that raising taxes seems much more efficient than curbing ads. A 10 percent increase in the price of cigarettes as a result of higher taxes is reported to cause a 12 percent decrease in the purchase of cigarettes. In contrast, curbing ads is unlikely to cause much difference. Although some young people may be convinced by advertisements to pick up smoking, it is widely agreed that the main effect of advertisements is to shift people from one brand to another. Hence, a ban on ads would mainly keep people smoking what they have been smoking, rather than cause them to stop.

Second, and more to our point, *curbing ads raises constitutional issues involving the freedom of speech, while raising taxes raises no such issues.* Hence, even if curbing ads proved to be somewhat more efficient, raising taxes would still be preferable, as long as one could show that cigarette advertisements were not significantly more influential than price. In short, because we want to preserve respect for the law, we should not seek to modify it wantonly. It is best to try other ways first, although the law should not be treated as immutable.

Third Criterion: Adjustments Should Be as Limited as Possible

Once it is established that there is no effective alternative to adjusting the balance between individual rights and social responsibilities (for example, because we seek to prevent the harm of secondhand smoke and avoid health care costs imposed on society by smoking), *we must look for options that are the least intrusive.*

An examination of the debate over *Miranda* provides a good example of how one may find ways to trim rather than to slash. In recent years *Miranda* has come under criticism as excessively favorable to criminals. The extent to which *Miranda* actually hobbles the police and prosecutors is a much debated subject, which is still unresolved. Also, it is difficult to determine readily whether recent court rulings have already sharply or only moderately affected the reach of *Miranda*. Most observers would agree that since the mid-eighties the balance has tilted somewhat toward diminished rights for criminals and a bit more toward enhancing the public safety. Our concern here is to illustrate what a reasonable intermediate position looks like, rather than settling many attendant intricacies.

At one extreme is the Radical Individualist position that no changes may be made whatsoever in *Miranda,* as if this legal measure, which did not take effect until 1966, was part of the Bill of Rights or carried the endorsement of the Founding Fathers. On the other hand, Authoritarians argue that *Miranda,* in toto, is but one of those many rights that accord criminals greater constitutional protection than is accorded to their victims. Indeed, former attorney general Edwin Meese wanted to do away with reading *Miranda* rights altogether. He believed that "it provides incentives for criminals not to talk" and "only helps guilty defendants." The Office of Legal Policy of the U.S. Attorney General under the Reagan administration issued a position paper that called for a wholesale overturning of *Miranda.* Here, as in many other matters, social wisdom and justice may well lie in third, intermediate positions, which balance individual rights with social needs.

Some intermediate positions have already been advanced. In 1985 the Supreme Court reviewed a case in which a suspect confessed to a crime before he was read his *Miranda* rights. He was later apprised of his rights and then confessed again. The Court unanimously agreed that the first confession could not be used as evidence, even though it had been given voluntarily, but it ruled six to three that the unsolicited admission of guilt did not taint the second confession, and hence it was allowed to stand.

In a similar decision, the Supreme Court ruled in 1987 that the police are not required to "Mirandize" a suspect for each crime that he or she is suspected of. Justice Lewis Powell explained that *Miranda* specifically requires that "the police inform a suspect that he has the right to remain silent and that *anything* he says may be used against him."

In the same vein, Communitarians may wish to examine closely an intermediate position that caused much controversy. It calls for allowing to stand evidence collected by the police even if the law was violated in a limited technical manner, as long as there is no indication of bad faith.

A case in point: In 1984 a police officer believed that in a given house a murderer had left the instrument of his crime. Since it was a Sunday afternoon and the local court was closed, the officer called on a judge at his home. The officer presented the judge with an application for a search warrant accompanied by an affidavit showing sufficient reason for the request (as required by the Fourth Amendment). The judge fully agreed that the "probable cause" needed for a legal search was present and indicated his approval on a form, as is routinely done. The officer conducted a search and indeed found the murder instrument. However, when the perpetrator was brought before the court, the defense argued that there was no legal warrant—because the judge by mistake had filled out the form inappropriately. (It referred to drug paraphernalia rather than a murder instrument, but the police confined their search to the items indicated in the police affidavit.) The lower court wanted to let the killer walk, but the Supreme Court ruled that the incriminating evidence gathered by the police should not be excluded on the basis of the judge's technical mistake because the officers relied on the warrant in good faith. A clause to cover such cases was included in the 1992 anticrime bill agreed upon by both Democrats and Republicans but adamantly opposed by Radical Individualists led by the ACLU. It was dropped from the final version of the bill.

The debate over the rights of students provides another example of reasonable, intermediate positions. Many observers agree that both substantive rights of students in public schools and their due process rights have been pushed to a point that makes it difficult for public schools to function. Linda Bruin, legal counsel for the Michigan Association of School Boards, writes: "Following the split decision in *Goss* v. *Lopez* . . . which struck down an Ohio statute permitting student suspensions from school without a hearing, educators expressed fears that they no longer would be able to discipline students efficiently."*

The president of the American Federation of Teachers, Albert Shanker, states:

> A whole series of legal decision defining students' rights have made it all but impossible to get rid of the few kids who can

---

* The subject is complicated by the fact that procedures vary from state to state. Some schools have already developed intermediate procedures that others have not yet examined, let alone embraced.

change a school into a holding tank. The decisions were made for what looked like the best possible reasons: Concern with fairness and due process for students and the lack of any alternative. When judges asked themselves whether disruptive students would be better off in the streets or in the school, the answer was usually in school. But no matter how well meaning, these decisions have played havoc with our schools.

In the end, he notes, "teachers have to assume the role of warden."

What is an intermediate position between according students full-fledged due process rights (in effect deterring teachers and principals from suspending them) and declaring them fair game to any capricious school authority? It seems reasonable that students who are subject to suspension and expulsion should be granted due process—to the extent that they be notified of the nature of their misconduct and given an opportunity to respond, and that both actions occur before expulsion takes place. However, schools need not guarantee students a right to counsel or to call and cross-examine witnesses. This would unduly hamper the schools' ability to maintain an educational environment. Moreover, it is in the interest of education that schools be approached as small communities rather than as adversarial environments in which full-court procedures would be appropriate. Several state courts have already begun modifying school policies in this far-from-novel direction.

The search for intermediary positions may also take into account the substance of the issues. Thus, although we may deem it appropriate for students who face expulsion from a school (especially if they can show racial or religious discrimination) to draw on their rights to due process, we might readily agree that "due process," in the legal sense, need not be followed when they want to protest a grade they've received on an exam.

A fine example of notching is found in a new antiloitering proposal by citizen groups in Alexandria, Virginia, one that was challenged by Radical Individualists but upheld by the courts. The regulation allows the police to arrest those who are "loitering for purposes of engaging in an unlawful drug transaction." Unlike old loitering laws, which were used by the police to harass minorities, the new antiloitering statutes are designed to prevent such violations by articulating *seven* conditions that must be met before an arrest can be made. The person must be on the street in a drug-trafficking area for more than fifteen minutes, during which time he or she must have more than one face-to-face contact that lasts less than two minutes and be involved in acts during which an object is transferred, and so on.

The ACLU's main objection to these antiloitering statutes is that innocent activities could be misconstrued as illegal. For instance, the ACLU argues, the new Alexandria statute used as one of its criteria that the person suspected of being a drug dealer put concealed objects into another person's pocket. (If the police could see that the packages contained illegal drugs, the whole issue might well be moot. Under this condition the police would have sufficient cause to act, which is, of course, the reason that dealers wrap their wares.) The ACLU maintains that this condition sets a dangerous precedent: among those who stand on street corners and put concealed objects into the pockets of others, the ACLU suggests, might be lawyers handing out business cards.

A Menu of Low-Intrusive Measures

Before we discuss the last criterion for evaluating measures to enhance public safety and public health, I want first to put before the reader a list of measures that I find acceptable and those that seem hard to swallow. Aside from illustrating the important criteria, the measures themselves seem of interest for those concerned about community and public life. Several of these measures are already being tried throughout the nation, while others are merely being discussed.

Among those that deserve such consideration are *curfews*. These have been introduced in several cities, such as Atlanta, Newark, and Detroit. While the details vary, the purpose is to keep young people, usually under the age of eighteen, off the street late at night to prevent them from participating in drug running and becoming involved in violence among drug dealers. The responsibility of families is stressed. They are expected to ensure that the youngsters are home by 11:00 P.M. on weekdays and midnight on weekends. Those who travel through town, or are on the way to or from political or religious activities, are exempt. In some cities families are notified the first time their youngsters violate the curfew; the second time the kids are held in police stations, sometimes all night, until their parents or guardians are located. It might be preferable to fine the parents rather than hold the kids in police stations. In either case curfews do not seem excessively intrusive if they keep children away from drug dealers and other criminals and enhance the responsibility of parents.

More controversial is the introduction of a *national identification card,* or an upgraded Social Security card, one that is much more counterfeit proof. Such ID cards are in use in many democratic countries. They are helpful in preventing people convicted in one state, say, of child abuse, from opening child care facilities in other states; they also help to locate criminals and curb illegal immigration. The very wide use of Social Security numbers, which has resulted in no harm, prepares the ground for a national ID card. Indeed, even liberals such as Robert Kuttner have advocated their use, although many Radical Individualists oppose them. Suggestions to introduce such cards do tap more deeply into Americans' fear of big government than many other measures. And there are kinks that must be worked out, especially in ensuring that the information used in issuing the cards is kept current (for instance, that they are canceled once a person dies). Finally, attention should be given to various suggestions to combine the national ID card with some other card, such as a national driver's license and/or voter registration card.

The *use of dogs* to sniff out bombs or drugs is another police technique that deserves at least additional examination. At first it may evoke in many minds the specter of threatening pit bulls, the snarling dogs that were used to threaten civil rights marchers in the South or even of Nazis patrolling the fences of concentration camps. On second and more careful thought, one may still reject their use altogether or conclude that much depends on the small print. To use dogs to check unopened luggage, say, for bombs in airports, without the owners being present (and hence without their being threatened), seems quite reasonable. Using dogs to check school lockers, assuming that the students are not present and hence are not threatened, may well make us a bit more uncomfortable, at least as long as we consider these lockers to be private spaces. If dogs are used to screen travelers on public buses, we may react rather differently to a poodle that kneels next to a person carrying, for example, explosives, compared with a Doberman that grasps at the throat of the same person. The point here is not which dog uses are "constitutional" or might be legitimate, but the fact that details of the measures suggested, and how they are to be applied, may deeply affect our judgment of their appropriateness.

In the same vein, it seems worthwhile to assume that whenever a bleeding person is brought into an emergency room unable to consent (assumimg that he or she is unconscious), the person's *blood will be tested for HIV* to protect the health care personnel and other patients. At the same time, health care personnel who carry HIV, if they are engaged in invasive procedures, should be required to disclose their condition to their patients or transfer to other branches of medicine (such as consulting).

Of particular merit is the guideline suggested by the Centers for Disease Control that would require hospitals to strongly encourage all those whose blood is being tested anyhow to allow it also to be tested for HIV. Such testing is efficient and often finds carriers unaware of their dangerous illness.

To reiterate, this recommendation, opposed by various Radical Individualists, is for patients to be encouraged—not required—to allow such a test. It would not be done without their consent.

Gay people object to this line of argument because they feel that those found to be HIV carriers would be subject to intense and pervasive discrimination. They argue that it is the responsibility of others to take standard precautions rather than wait for people to be tested.

It seems to me that, first of all, HIV carriers are not to be identified with gay people; there are numerous carriers who are intravenous drug users and some who were infected as a result of blood transfusions, especially before blood was screened for HIV. Second, I fully agree that we should do more to prevent discrimination against gay people, whether or not they agree to be tested; civil rights are theirs, without requiring any particular performance.

Third, if such HIV tests are routinely to be made, we must ensure that confidentiality is observed. And I have no trouble at all agreeing that everyone should act responsibly and engage only in safe sex, if at all.

But when all is said and done, the community—faced as it is with a massive and tragic loss of life, including many young and talented people—is entitled to encourage likely HIV carriers to agree to be tested. This will make it easier for them to spare others and to motivate those who are informed (by the carrier) that their contact is a carrier—to be extra sure not to exchange needles, to engage only in safer sex, and to take other precautions.

Not all measures that deserve our attention are punitive or preventive; some allow people to reach out and help others and the community. Nearly twenty-four thousand Americans are awaiting organs for transplantation. Therefore it seems proper to require hospitals to ask all people who check in if they wish to donate their organs in the event that they die. (They need these days to face their mortality anyhow, because hospitals are already required to ask if they wish to make a living will.) Those who do not indicate an objection, and whose families do not file a counterindication, *should be assumed to be willing to donate* their organs if they die. This measure would greatly enhance the quality of life of many thousands each year and is the Communitarian thing to do.

When outbreaks of food poisoning occur, health authorities are allowed broad powers to confiscate food and even to shut down establishments, to prevent people from taking ill. Likewise, the *summary revocation of the driver's licenses* of drunks at sobriety checkpoints seems in line with other measures and not excessively intrusive. Evicting a family from public housing, however, because someone dealt drugs in the unit seems improper. Unlike food that spreads poison and the drunk driver on the road, there is no present danger here. There is time to hold a hearing. And we know that there are numerous instances in which the person who lived in the apartment, say, an elderly widow, had no knowledge or control over a relative who was dealing. Similarly, suggestions to use nuisance laws to *revoke the licenses of problem bars* (for example, those that are hangouts for drug dealers) is called for only if there is evidence that the owners were aware of the situation and did not try to deal with it by alerting the police or systematically discouraging such customers.

New principles need to be developed for dealing with mental patients. Currently they are treated as if they were in full command of their faculties, unless they are endangering others or themselves. As a result, a large number of mental patients are refused treatment (through deinstitutionalization) or are refusing treatment. We may draw upon a person's expressed wishes when he or she was well (before mental illness set in, say, for an elderly person), or while he or she is in command of his or her faculties (say, a schizophrenic patient who is on medication), about the ways we may treat him or her when ill. This may lead to some reinstitutionalization (at more suitable institutions than the state provided in the past) and families being allowed to provide medication to adult patients as if they were minors. We have been too laid back in this area.

In short, far from yielding to demands to gun down all private airplanes and speedboats that approach the U.S. border unidentified, breaking down doors of people's homes at midnight to search for drugs, and other such drastic, authoritarian measures, we advocate introducing steps that are minimally intrusive, in both legal and practical terms. Introduction of more of these measures, and others like them, is both overdue and legitimate.

Criterion Four: Opportunities to Minimize, Avoid, or Treat Side Effects

A final check of policies against the suggested notching principles is that the policies should minimize their deleterious offshoots. For example, to the extent that HIV testing and contact tracing are introduced, we must take into account that they can lead to a person losing his or her job, housing, and health insurance if confidentiality is not maintained. Hence any introduction of such a program (if it is deemed justified) should be accompanied by a thorough review of control of access to lists of names of those tested; a review of procedures used in contacting sexual partners; professional education programs on the need for confidentiality; and penalties for unauthorized disclosure and for those who discriminate against AIDS patients or HIV carriers. If the community seeks to benefit from encouraging HIV testing and contact tracing, it should intensify its efforts to protect those who are tested and who disclose their contacts.

Similarly, if "good faith evidence" is allowed to stand in the courts, we need to worry about the effects on police personnel. If a police officer makes an honest mistake and finds out that the courts will nevertheless allow the evidence to be used against the defendant, we cannot let the matter rest there. Authorities should note in the personnel file of the police officer involved that he or she made the mistake. In this way the officer will be put on notice that if the mistake is repeated, we will be much less likely to accept that it was a good faith error. And officers ought to be informed that reprimands will follow repeated mistakes, especially if they are of the same basic kind.

Crime and Social Justice

When various civic groups discuss new measures that public authorities may be allowed to use to help combat crime, liberals often argue that these will serve, at best, to curb crime, not to prevent it. It is suggested that the best way to fight crime is to ensure that everybody has a well-paying job, is treated with dignity and not discriminated against, and is not alienated from society. Although these are worthy goals in their own right, the question of what causes crime is a surprisingly complex one. One of the best authorities on the subject, James Q. Wilson, dedicated more than six hundred pages to the issue in his book *Crime and Human Nature*. Still, no easy conclusions emerged. I cite here, very briefly, major findings that are relevant to our Communitarian approach.

First, while vulnerable members of the society, those who truly cannot help themselves, ought to be helped, and while social justice should be advanced—these and other social goals should be advanced because they are good in themselves, not because they are likely to reduce crime significantly. The fact is that crime is more rampant in the United States than in many countries where the average income per capita is much lower (including Portugal, Chile, Spain, Indonesia, and Kenya). Crime has *risen* in the United States as income has *risen* (crime has increased three- to fourfold since the fifties). And there are many law-abiding citizens among the poor and quite a few lawbreakers among those who are well off.

Second, the level of crime is deeply affected by the total community fabric. It is not enough for families to be strong, or schools to be fine educational institutions, and so on. To minimize crime, all of these elements must reinforce one another. Thus, in those parts of the country (and the world) where families are strong, schools teach moral values, communities are well intact, and values command respect. In Utah, for instance, crime is much lower than in places where these factors are absent. The national violent crime rate in 1990 was 730 per 100,000; in Utah it was 284. In the first part of this book we saw what works in situations such as Utah is that families, schools, and communities—all the factors that go into making the moral infrastructure—come together to support moral conduct. In effect, they work not merely or even mainly to fight crime, but to sustain civility and values in general. Prevention of crime is a bonus of a moral and civil society.

Third, even in the most intact communities, some individuals will—because of genetic, chemical, or physiological aberrations or deep-seated psychological distortions—act in an immoral manner. There is a hard core of psychopaths and criminals that the most dedicated parents, the most effective schools, and the most attentive and caring neighborhoods cannot reach. To cope with them, all communities require the hand of public authorities, lest people be subject to serial killers; wilding gangs out to torture, maim, and kill for kicks; child abusers and arsonists. To suggest that these people can be reached by involving them in positive community work, meaningful creative work, or national service is a fairy tale. They are the proper subjects for police. Their legal rights should be fully protected, but otherwise there is no denying that when it comes to hard-core criminals and dangerous mental patients, public authorities are not only essential, but a legitimate, morally appropriate way to protect the public.

7 ♦ Hate Speech: Nonlegal Remedies

A Right To Racial Slurs and Ethnic Insults?—A Satire About Gays at Yale

IN 1986, before some people concerned with racist, sexist, and homophobic speech sought to curb free speech on, of all places, university campuses, Wayne Dick, a student at Yale, displayed a satiric poster. It was entitled "Bestiality Awareness Days (BAD) Week" and was intended to satirize "GLAD Week"—Gay and Lesbian Awareness Days—an annual event at Yale. On the poster, Dick included the thinly veiled names of several gay faculty members and students. One of the students, Pat Santana (referred to in the poster as Professor Pet Satanna), argued that he had been "slandered" by the poster, which he deemed "visual harassment." Dick defended himself by saying that homosexuality is "immoral," and that "although homosexuality might be considered normal now, not all people consider it normal."

After a contentious hearing, Dick was put on probation for two years for harassing and intimidating Santana and other gays and lesbians. His defenders, however, continued to argue that he was well within his right of free speech. The executive director of the Connecticut Civil Liberties Union, William Olds, protested that the student was disciplined "for what appears to be an exercise in free expression." Others noted that Yale's undergraduate regulations read, in part: "Even when some members of the university community fail to meet their social and ethical responsibilities, the paramount obligation of the university is to protect their right to free expression."

Those who favored Dick's punishment, though, argued that one should not wantonly hurt others. An alumna of Yale, Carrie Costello, a founder of the Ad Hoc Committee Against Defamation, explained that "we stand very strongly for free speech, but that does not include the right to harass or intimidate, or the right to slander individuals."

Others countered that once we limit speech because it hurts some people, soon much speech, especially that of dissenting voices, would be banned. This would violate a main idea behind the First Amendment: to protect especially well the right to speech of those who provoke someone else's ire. After all, it is hardly necessary to protect speech that is endearing, evokes wide favor, or is conformist. In the same vein, Yale's president, Benno C. Schmidt, Jr., stated that the university should accord "paramount value" to "freedom of expression, even to expression that is distasteful or silly." Others argued, in effect, "Sticks and stones may break my bones, but words will never harm me"— that people should be mature enough to be able to handle verbal slurs.

In the end, the original decision against Dick was reversed in a rehearing in October 1986. His adviser for the hearing before the Yale College Executive Committee, Professor C. Vann Woodward, called the acquittal a "victory for free speech." And there the matter rested, at Yale.

Other universities faced the same basic question: What is the proper balance between the right to free speech and the need to sustain community? Should our commitment to allow people to speak freely permit those who spout hate to set one group apart from others? How can we respect the right to free speech and at the same time reduce the tension that breaks community into groups seething with hatred for one another?

Regulating Slurs

By 1992 more than 130 American universities had enacted so-called speech codes—codes that define what may or may not be said on campus and how prohibited speech will be punished. Among them are Emory, Trinity, Tufts, the University of Connecticut, the University of Pennsylvania, the University of North Carolina at Chapel Hill, and Stanford.

At the University of Pennsylvania, students may be punished for "behavior, verbal or physical, that stigmatizes or victimizes individuals" and "creates an intimidating or offensive environment." (A Penn professor commented sarcastically: "Penn is a tolerant and diverse community, and if you do not agree with its particular notions of tolerance and diversity, it gladly will reeducate you.") Tufts forbids slurs or insults in classrooms or dormitories but allows them in the student newspaper, on the campus radio station, and in public lectures. The University of Connecticut was much less tolerant: students could have been expelled from class for using "derogatory names, inappropriately directed laughter, inconsiderate jokes, and conspicuous exclusion [of a classmate] from conversation."

At the University of Wisconsin, a student would violate the school's code if "he or she intentionally made demeaning remarks to an individual based on that person's ethnicity, such as name calling, racial slurs, or 'jokes'; and . . . his or her purpose in uttering the remarks was to make the educational environment hostile for the person to whom the demeaning remark was addressed."

These are not idle policies. Two white University of Pennsylvania students were evicted from their dormitory after yelling racial epithets at pledges to a black fraternity. At the University of Michigan, a student was punished for writing a limerick for class that implied that an Olympic athlete was homosexual; he was made to attend a group discussion led by homosexuals and to write an apology that was published in the school newspaper. At Stanford, two students were thrown out of their dormitories and moved into guest housing after defacing a symphony poster; the students had black-faced a picture of Beethoven after African-American students claimed that Beethoven had black ancestors. At Rutgers, a student who posted a note on a friend's door that read "You're a fag" (in retaliation for a note on his door that read "Clayton's a geek") was sentenced to thirty days of janitorial service for violating the school's insult policy. Even after the offender's friend (and "victim") came to his defense, the school rendered its verdict, arguing that a gay student, seeing the note, might be offended.

Tim Usher, a sophomore at Occidental College, was suspended by the school's peer board. Usher had tried to gain entrance to a locked residential hall by knocking on its glass door. When one of the residents called campus security to remove him, he had yelled a sexual epithet at her.

A still harsher fate befell a Brown University junior, Doug Hann, who was expelled after a late-night incident in October 1990. While walking on campus toward a dormitory complex, the intoxicated Hann shouted antiblack statements and uttered the word "nigger." When someone shouted from a window at him to be quiet, he responded: "What are you, a faggot? What are you, a Jew?"

Displaying the wrong kind of magazine, offering a well-meaning compliment, or even excessive staring can get you into trouble on some campuses. At SUNY-Binghamton a student was charged with lewd and indecent behavior for putting *Penthouse* centerfolds on the door of his dormitory room. He was convicted by a student panel, although the school administration later dropped the charges. The school newspaper reported another incident of alleged harassment: someone in the Economics Department commented about a colleague: "She's so smart and pretty, too." At the University of Toronto, Professor Richard Hummel was convicted in 1989 of "prolonged and intense staring" at a university pool. A columnist for *Maclean's* magazine, Barbara Amiel, suggested that the conviction reflected "the utter debasement of the genuinely serious nature of sexual harassment."

If ever there was a slippery slope . . .

Little Community Support

Although these regulations of speech have generated a great deal of attention, one should not overlook the fact that most universities have not embraced them. The overwhelming majority of students, faculty, and citizens, whatever their race or gender, on campus and off, are opposed to these limitations on free speech, according to most public opinion polls.

A 1986 poll of Colorado residents shows that 62 percent disagreed with the statement "It should be against the law for anyone to make public speeches in favor of racism." (Thirty percent agreed.) A 1989 poll of Alabamians shows that a full 87.5 percent agreed with the statement "Even those with unpopular views should have the freedom to publicly express their political feelings." (Only 8.7 percent disagreed.) A 1987 national survey showed that 85 percent of respondents felt that the Constitution did too little or just the right amount to guarantee that people can express "very offensive opinions." Only 10 percent said that it did too much. However, a 1991 poll found that 51 percent of the respondents agreed that the "government should prohibit hateful speech that demeans someone's race, sex, national origin, or religion." (Forty-one percent disagreed, and 8 percent were undecided.) Time will tell if this finding is a fluke or if the sanctity of free speech is beginning to erode.

"Fighting Words": A Notch that Barely Holds

In 1942 the Supreme Court ruled in *Chaplinsky* v. *New Hampshire* that it was permissible to ban words that "by their very utterance inflict injury or tend to incite an immediate breach of the peace." The "fighting words" exception to the freedom of speech constituted a clear attempt to "notch" the First Amendment. That is, the Court attempted to set a standard that would separate prohibited speech from free speech, so that one could ban some forms of speech without endangering all of them. The standard barely holds. Although some lower courts have applied the "fighting words" standard since the 1942 decision, the Supreme Court itself has declined to reapply it.

The difficulty in "notching" the First Amendment is illustrated in the details of the famous 1942 case, the only instance in which the Supreme Court let stand a conviction on the basis that a person had uttered prohibited, "fighting" words. What are the intolerable words that Mr. Chaplinsky spoke? He called organized religion "a racket." Few would consider this epithet particularly offensive these days. Even fewer would disagree that it communicates a political idea, rather than being merely offensive. Protecting the expression of such ideas, however unpopular, is at the core of the freedom of speech under the First Amendment. (The Supreme Court has in effect divided speech into "high value" and "low value" categories. "High value" speech concerns social and political ideas, and the

Court has ruled repeatedly that such speech is what the First Amendment was meant to ensure. Other kinds of speech, especially when they are offensive—not to mention obscene—are deemed to deserve less protection by the courts.)

The same difficulty in finding a defensible line is illustrated by a debate that raged in Harvard Yard after students attempted to prohibit the showing of a Confederate flag because it was offensive to blacks, and others objected to the displaying of a swastika because it was offensive to Jews. The questions raised all focused on the issue of where to draw the line: Would the University also prohibit displaying a flag that others might find offensive, say, a Japanese flag, which would offend survivors of Pearl Harbor? Would Harvard prosecute those who drew a swastika, say, on a building next to a synagogue? What if someone put up a banner with a quote from Hitler's *Mein Kampf* on a synagogue wall (more clearly an expression of "speech" than a mere symbol such as a swastika)?

When St. Paul, Minnesota, tried to ban cross burnings, the constitutionality of the ban was argued before the Supreme Court. Justice Antonin Scalia wondered why the community would ban some racist symbols and not others that some groups might find at least as offensive. He did not have to look far for an example. The ordinance's "definition [of anger, alarm, or resentment] is broad enough to include a Washington Redskins T-shirt, since 'Redskins' is considered a racial epithet by many Native Americans," pointed out a *USA Today* editorial. And the *St. Paul Pioneer Press* wondered: "What if the same ordinance were used to prosecute a rabbi whose Star of David angered Arabs who saw it as a Zionist symbol . . . or an abortion foe whose picture of an aborted fetus alarmed abortion rights advocates?"

In June 1992 the Supreme Court handed down its decision in the St. Paul case, declaring that hate codes were unconstitutional. But the closeness of the margin (five to four) and the justices' arguments reflected deep divisions within the Court. Hate codes are not an issue on which hard and fast rules seem possible.

Although the Court has not abandoned the notion that there is a "well-defined" category of "forbidden" words, it added so many qualifiers to the definition of tabooed expressions that in effect none seem to be legally damnable. An accumulation of rulings suggest that the "fighting words" must constitute an *extremely* (undefined) provocative personal insult. They must cause the average addressee to *immediately* react in violence. ("Average" is usually meant to refer to "the reasonable person." Who the reasonable person is has not been defined.) Such words must also be uttered face-to-face, and the offensive statement must be aimed at a single person and not a group. This seems just a roundabout way of saying that not having found a clear notch, uttering almost anything must be tolerated.

Similarly, after decades of arguing about pornography, what one person considers outright pornography, another may consider a form of art; an attempt to curb such material is then bound to be seen by someone as a limitation on free speech. (Those who define pornography as communication that has "no redeeming social merit" should note that one wit demanded that the U.S. Postal Service stop delivering junk mail to his home because in this person's eyes it had no merit, redeeming or otherwise.)

The Court tried to place another "notch" in the First Amendment. It suggested that if an average person, by applying contemporary community standards, found that a work "taken as a whole appeals to the prurient interest," depicts in a patently offensive way sexual conduct, and lacks social merit—it could be censored. No sooner did the sheriff of Arlington, Virginia, try to apply this standard and ban *Playboy* magazine, however, than the Court ruled that *Playboy* did not meet its criteria. This case is just one illustration of the difficulty the Supreme Court has had in determining what should be classified as obscenity. In fact, numerous Supreme Court justices have expressed frustration with the current obscenity test. For example, Justice William O. Douglas once stated that "anyone who undertakes to examine the Court's decisions . . . which have held particular material obscene or not obscene would find himself in utter bewilderment." Justice John Paul Stevens wants to strike down obscenity laws because the line between obscenity and protected expression is "so intolerably vague that even-handed enforcement of the law is a virtual impossibility."

True, just reading a magazine of child pornography could get one into serious trouble these days under the provisions of the Child Protection Act. It is unclear, though, how the Court will draw a line between a statue of a naked child by an artist and what some may consider child pornography. Until the law is tested more extensively in the courts, it is not certain that even a law that bars only child pornography will hold. The reason is the same: the tabooed area cannot be easily roped off from the artistic, social, and political area that we seek to protect.

In some rather limited areas, taboos on certain speech seem to have taken hold, according to specialists in these matters. For instance, you cannot make a defamatory speech that is intentionally malicious. And we all accept that one cannot shout "Fire!" in a crowded theater when there is none, because it directly endangers the lives of innocent people. But given those few exceptions, it would seem that people who favor a free society must put up here with a very broad, sweeping right—a nearly absolute one. By and large we dare not restrict speech, lest we open the doors to the censors and the Joe McCarthys.

"I'd like to hear less talk about animal rights and more talk about animal responsibilities."

Drawing by Lorenz. Copyright © 1990 by The New Yorker Magazine, Inc.

Treating the Symptoms, Not the Disease

Communitarians like me hold that legal restrictions on free speech are not only very difficult to delineate, but are ineffectual to boot. At best they may curb public expressions of racial, ethnic, and gender hatred, but they do not get at the root causes. The *Los Angeles Times* editorialized: "Speech codes don't attack the racism and other attitudinal baggage that students bring with them to college. Codes suppress the words without exploring and combating the lazy and irrational thinking that spawns prejudice based on ethnicity, religion, or sex." The ACLU's president, Nadine Strossen, similarly argues that speech codes "are doing nothing to stop racism and bigotry. For university administrators, they are a cheap solution to a complex problem."

Those who are concerned about hateful expressions need to seek deeper and more educational remedies. One place to start is to draw a distinction between what you have a right to say and what is civil and Communitarian speech.

This is more or less where the issue was left in recent public debates about speech codes—at a rather unsatisfactory place, from a Communitarian viewpoint. True, the right of free speech has been rather well protected. One may even view the debate about speech codes as a kind of grand social reinoculation, reinforcing in the body politic the antibody against constricting free speech. By arguing vigorously about the issue, the merits of free speech, the values that sustain it were stressed again and again, which is fine as far as it goes. But by and large little was done to deal with the underlying pain and injury to those who are the subjects of verbal abuse that led them to demand curbs on hate speech to begin with. *Speech was attended to, but not community.* If we say that hate is undesirable but we cannot lay a glove on those who instigate it, we are resigning ourselves to a society that will be ever more divided and hostile. There is good reason for concern.

A comprehensive study of universities found that although intolerance was rampant, the universities engaged in "a culture of denial"—either resisting suggestions to deal with the problem or responding with a few ill-conceived, limited countermeasures. Fifty-seven percent of the colleges studied reported that intolerance posed a problem on their campuses. But the majority also reported that they had no programs or limited ones to deal with it.

Franklyn S. Haiman, a Northwestern University professor of communications, concludes in an article in defense of unrestricted speech:

> The roots of group hatreds stretch far beyond the reach of our educational institutions. . . . They are interwoven with problems of economic wealth and poverty, of political power and powerlessness, of psychological insecurity and fear. They will not be solved by writing laws and rules against racist speech.

This basically amounts to saying to minorities who are distressed by streams of verbal abuse, verbal harassment, and psychological hounding: "Tough s——. *It is* good for the First Amendment!" We can do better. We ought to do more.

Communitarian, Nonlegal Remedies

The fact that one has a legal right to say almost anything one wishes does not make it ethically appropriate to spit out whatever comes into one's head. *Rights do not automatically make for rightness.* As Antonin Scalia notes, "There is a perhaps inevitable but nonetheless distressing tendency to equate the existence of a right with the *non*existence of a responsibility. That is to say, if one has a *right* to do something, it is assumed to be *proper* and perhaps even *good* (as opposed to merely *legal*) that he do it."

Scalia argues further that we must realize that a willingness to fight for the complete freedom of speech does not condone hateful speech, but rather that "we are willing to fight and die *for your freedom to be irresponsible and even socially harmful* because the alternative would sweep away too much good speech along with the bad."

William Galston, a leading Communitarian philosopher, writes:

> The language of rights is morally incomplete. To say that "I have a right to do x" is not to conclude that "x is the right thing for me to do." . . . Rights give reasons to others not to

interfere coercively with me in the performance of the protected acts; however, they do not in themselves give me sufficient reason to perform these acts. There is a gap between rights and rightness that cannot be closed without a richer moral vocabulary—one that invokes principles of decency, duty, responsibility, and the common good, among others.

Thus it might be legal to declare "All blacks should go back to Africa" or "It's a shame Hitler did not finish off the Jews." We might even extol the merits of a political system in which people are free to say what they wish to say, however bigoted and hateful their statements are. There is, however, no moral or legal reason to stop members of a community subject to such offensive words—and other members of the community—from freely expressing their disapproval. They, too, have First Amendment rights! If a drunken white man shouts racist expletives on Brown University's campus, charging him with a legal offense or arresting him is not the response of choice; a long line of peers who tell him how despicable they find his utterances is probably a more effective and surely a more legitimate community response. Heed the words of Judge Learned Hand: "I often wonder whether we do not rest our hopes too much upon constitutions, upon laws and upon courts. These are false hopes; believe me, these are false hopes. Liberty lies in the hearts of men and women; when it dies there, no constitution, no law, no court, can save it."

We should inform people who spout prejudice and spread hate that we consider them to be bigoted, uncivilized boors, people whose company we shun. "Sure," we may tell them, "you have a right to say most anything you want, but using this right in certain ways is not morally appropriate or socially acceptable." If enough of us make that clear, they are likely to put their First Amendment rights to better use than insulting others. At least the victims of slurs will know that the community does not share the hate and prejudice expressed by some and that the community *is* offended by them.

Assuming that we will continue to find that the right to free speech is rather difficult to "notch" (and hence conclude that speech codes on campuses and elsewhere are untenable), we should not neglect to treat the hurt of those subject to a stream of insults, a chorus of abuse, founts of taunts. True, a close examination shows that there are some incidents in which those who cry foul seem to be grandstanding. Some agitators stand on the sidelines, lying in wait for some poorly chosen phrase or a tasteless ethnic or sexist joke. They stand by ready to scream racism or sexism and demand more than an apology: the firing of all white males, for example, and reparations for themselves and their followers. And there are those who claim that they are falling apart just because someone called them "Jap" or "queer." Code words and phrases such as "lynching," "Nazi Germany," and "genocide" roll off some people's tongues entirely too easily. The way in which a very serious problem can be extended to absurdity is illustrated by the case of a professor at Penn State who claimed that she was being sexually harassed by Goya's nude *Naked Maja* and had it removed from the classroom. She was strongly supported by the director of the university's affirmative action office.

While the community would do well to ignore these exaggerated and overblown charges, we should not ignore that there are serious incidents in which verbal harassment commands our concern. Imagine the life of Ryan White, a junior high school student who was infected with AIDS from a blood transfusion. His school in Kokomo, Indiana, banned his attendance amid widespread fear among students and parents. Although he won reenrollment in the school, "the boy was taunted at school by other children who wrote obscenities on his locker and shouted insults as he passed in the halls. . . . When his mother, Jeanne White, went to the grocery store, cashiers would throw down her change to avoid touching her hands." White reported that he was falsely accused of biting others and urinating on bathroom walls, and that restaurants would throw away dishes after he used them. The word *fag* was written on his school folders. White finally could not stand life in such a community and was forced to move to another town, Cicero, Indiana.

Nor should we ignore incidents such as the one referred to by a gay leader during a series of conferences on the Bill of Rights. He related how an openly gay student at the University of Kansas had been taunted regularly by other students wearing T-shirts with the slogan "Club Faggots, Not Seals." He had also been subjected to harassing phone calls, in which the callers advocated castration.

Eventually the harassment became unbearable, and the young man dropped out.

Although the problem of intolerance does not present a clear and present danger of the magnitude of a mass murder or a widespread epidemic, it is quite sufficient to command the community's attention. Just to shrug one's shoulders and say "Tough, but the First Amendment requires you to suffer" is an insensitive, legalistic, and wholly inadequate response. As Charles Lawrence, a Stanford University law professor, writes: "There is real harm inflicted by racist speech and . . . this harm is far from trivial."

How To?

The ways to counter hate range from the personal and informal to the organized and institutionalized. Nat Hentoff, a nationally syndicated columnist who frequently writes about civil liberties, illustrates the personal and informal ways in the following report. Four black students were walking on the campus of Arizona State University when they saw a flyer on a dormitory apartment door. It was labeled "Simplified form of a job application. Form for minority applicants." The form requested sources of income and listed among the options to be checked off: "theft, welfare, unemployment." For marital status, the options were "common law, shacked up, other." The form also asked for "number of legitimate children (if any)."

The four women were greatly offended by the bogus form. But they did not call on the university authorities, despite a university code prohibiting such slurs. Instead they knocked on the apartment door and told the person present how they felt about the form. He took it down. The next evening the women organized a meeting with some students in the same dormitory and discussed the matter. They were joined by a supportive professor. Several white people made it clear that they were deeply embarrassed. The session was followed up by more forums, a press conference, and a seminar at the law school. These discussions, in turn, triggered a campuswide debate on the issues at hand. The local newspapers also took note. The article in the campus newspaper included an apology from the person who had put up the form in the first place. The four women said that toward the end they no longer felt like victims but rather "empowered." True, not all such stories have happy endings. And Hentoff closed his account by noting that the campus was in the throes of a new debate: it seems there was a student who liked to put swastikas on his notebooks and the walls of his room. . . . The work of education is never done.

At Emory University, workshops on sexual harassment have been held for students, faculty, and staff who have been accused of making sexist remarks. The participants are first quizzed regarding their notions of what constitutes sexist behavior and harassment. Then they review legal cases about harassment, watch videos that portray it, and participate in role-playing exercises. Robert Ethridge, the assistant vice-president for equal opportunity, explains: "The workshop sessions are eye-opening and enlightening. For some people, the sessions won't change their minds, but for others, being confronted with these issues has a long-term positive benefit." Not everyone is supportive of these programs. The dean for student life at Duke University, Sue Wasiolek, has "a concern about forcing students into mandatory workshops. It bothers me about our society in general that the only way people think they can change behavior is to set up a rule." Educators, however, regularly require students to attend all kinds of classes, from foreign-language courses to math. Why not require them to attend classes that will teach them civility? Afterward, once they have been exposed to the message of a civil community, they are still free to hold on to their viewpoints.

Here's another way of dealing with hate: If a group of Aryans wants to run an ad in a student newspaper (the only one on campus) that claims the Holocaust did not occur, rather than refuse it, the student paper could accompany the ad with an editorial explaining why it is offensive and publish articles by respected historians on the subject. In this way the publication of the ad would turn into an educational event.

Asking students to volunteer or appointing some as student mediators also helps on campuses in which interracial tensions (or some other intergroup tensions) run high. The very fact that people take on a role like that, political scientist Jane Mansbridge points out, changes their behavior. They see themselves as entrusted with the community's values and well-being and often act accordingly. Given some training, they can help defuse verbal conflicts long before they turn into serious confrontations.

There are a whole slew of other educational tools: debates and assemblies, courses on the sources and dynamics of prejudice, and one-on-one and small-group interracial dinners. The use of video-tapes is considered particularly effective. There is, for instance, a video called *Still Burning* that is designed to stimulate discussion about racial prejudice. The video opens with a student's door being defaced with racial slurs and threats from other students; it was produced by the University of Maryland at Baltimore and exists in two versions: one for educators and one for students. A director of the Office of Black Student Affairs on the campus reports that the tape helped greatly in building up support for racial tolerance on her campus. Miami University in Ohio uses an interactive video during its Cultural Awareness Program that features the personal experi-ences of students who have been involved in racial incidents. The video is meant to stimulate discussion among students by present-ing them with questions, such as whether there is a typical black student and how would they react to having a black roommate.

Others report that peer counseling can be quite effective in dealing with sexual harassment. Trained student volunteers work with other students across the campus as peer educators, leading information and discussion sessions. Of course, regular, profes-sional counselors are required, too, but the combination of students and professionals can be positive and productive.

In short, universities are supposed to educate. If faculties cannot reach most students and show them the evils of hatred, prejudice, and discrimination, they need additional training themselves. They ought not to be given the easy way out of their responsibilities by regulating the expression of hate while leaving the hate itself un-scathed. Hate is an ugly and unwholesome human expression all by itself; and it is particularly detrimental to building and sustaining the mutual support and commitment to shared undertakings on which community thrives.

PART
III

The Public
Interest

8 ♦ Communitarian Politics

Built-in Corruption

"CONGRESS is bought!" President Carter exclaimed in exasperation. It was one more day in which Jimmy Carter, presiding in the White House, could not move Congress to enact a policy that was clearly in the interest of the national community. Carter was referring to the special interests that regularly reward members of Congress with lush campaign contributions, fees for speech making (although, as Senator William Proxmire put it, "You can stand there and read the phone book and still be paid"), as well as junkets.

When Representative John Breaux from Louisiana was told about Carter's observation, he retorted in a mock complaint: "I can't be bought; but I can be rented." Some may see in this response only a lame joke. But jokes, psychologists inform us, are revealing. Representative Breaux was saying, in effect, that he could not be owned once and for all; he had to be paid regularly and could be occupied by different parties. Moreover, far from hiding his being affordable, he—like many of those he saw around him—was *unabashed* about it. It's the way much business is conducted, we shall see, in the nation's capital and in quite a few state capitols and town halls.

The subversion of shared, community wide inter-

"Now, don't expect the bribes to start right away—you have to prime the pump with some free samples first."

Cartoon by Baloo. Reprinted with permission of Baloo.

ests is a subject that I approach reluctantly. When I broach this topic in public lectures, I can see how quickly the eyes of my audience glaze over. (Reciting statistics is an even more effective soporific.) One reason is that Americans are preoccupied with individual corruption; most of my fellow citizens are reluctant to heed the pitfalls of a political system that makes corruption *endemic,* infecting almost anybody elected to public office. This preoccupation with the personal is the deeper reason that the press keeps feeding us with an incessant torrent of salacious scandals. (Suzanne Garment, who wrote a book on the subject, said that she stopped counting at four hundred.)

During the 1992 presidential campaign, much was made of the extramarital affairs Governor Bill Clinton was said to have had, and rumors about George Bush's "mistress" were cited. Senator Brock Adams, from the state of Washington, announced that he would not stand for reelection because eight women had accused him of sexual harassment. Before that, Senator Charles Robb was raked over the coals because a former beauty queen, who was not his wife, visited his hotel room. Robb claimed to have merely disrobed to receive a massage. Shortly before that, five other senators were charged with doing favors for Charles Keating, Jr., a major culprit in the savings and loan scandal who made major donations to the senators' campaign coffers.

These reports may well recede in memory by the time these lines see the light of day, as previous scandals have faded by now. But as surely as Tuesday follows Monday, some new ones will take their place. We seem to have an insatiable appetite for news of mischief and wrongdoing by *individual* public figures.

Most Americans even believe, as public opinion polls show, that "all politicians are crooked" and are quite ready to roll up their sleeves "to throw the rascals out." Such a disdain for politicians is, no doubt, behind the current popularity of term limitations, which would allow elected representatives only a limited number of years of service. Americans are reluctant, however, to face up to problems that are entrenched in the political system itself, which is supposed to serve the community at large and so often does not.

In fact, many consider it unpatriotic to criticize "the System." When I wrote in *The New York Times,* after five years of working the corridors of power in Washington (including a year in the White House), that "Washington is corrupt to the core," my patriotism was questioned. A response from John W. Nichols (USNR-Ret) read: "What country are you from??? Cuba? USSR? Bulgaria? You've got a G—D—d nerve. . . . You, sure as hell, are no American Patriot!"

He could not be more in error. I could practice my profession in numerous countries, but I chose to live in this country because of my great respect for its Constitution, institutions, and core values. Although democracy is far from a perfect system, it is clearly the best there is. But there are some serious flaws in the way representatives are now elected, and to ignore these is to allow corruption to fester unchecked. Hence I turn reluctantly to the subject of those who are supposed to represent the community, our elected representatives, who should work for our shared needs but are often captured by special interests. I then turn to what might be done to reclaim politics for the community at large.

Assume for a moment, just for the sake of argument, that I and several other longtime Washington observers (such as Elizabeth Drew, author of *Politics and Money,* Brooks Jackson, author of *Honest Graft,* and William Greider, author of *Who Will Tell the People*) are correct that the problem is the flood of private money into public life. Assume it is sad but true that many members of Congress often vote against the public interest in order to pay off the special interests to which they are indebted. If this is the case, throwing out one bunch of "rascals" or unsavory characters would merely make room for another bunch—which would be just as obligated to formulate policies that please those to whom *they* are indebted. We are often told that what is wrong with us is that too many of us do not vote. If the following analysis is correct, it matters little if we vote or not, until we change the system that typically corrupts whoever is elected.

We tend to overlook the fact that if we tolerate a political system in which most candidates cannot run for office unless they raise hundreds of thousands, if not millions, of dollars every few years, we consent to a system in which only those of unusual strength of character (or possessed of sizable personal fortunes) can withstand the built-in temptations. We consent to a political system in which those elected serve first and foremost the deep pockets, and only on the side the community, to whose interests they are often no longer accountable.

To put it differently, honest politicians do not indulge in free trips to Hawaii or Las Vegas: they pay in full for their tickets to the Super Bowl, and perhaps they even avoid bouncing checks at a congressional bank. But if they want to win elections, they are more or less forced to seek large pools of money, without which it is nearly impossible to finance a campaign. Because nobody grants oodles of money for nothing, elected representatives must pay off special interests, by far the most reliable and easiest source of funds. *In short, America will not have politicians who represent the community rather than special interests, until we fashion a cleaner political system.*

How much money is involved? The costs of being elected are rising all the time. In the 1990 election House candidates spent an average of $262,000 (up from $52,000 in 1974 and $140,000 in 1980), and Senate candidates spent an average of $2.8 million (up from $400,000 in 1974 and $1.1 million in 1980). By 1990 the top spender in the House went through $1.7 million, and the top spender in the Senate, a stunning $18 million. These are huge amounts. Politicians who try to raise these funds from individuals, collecting $25 to $100 a person, end up spending much of their time soliciting money. Meanwhile those who get bucketfuls of money from banks, real estate lobbies, labor unions, the Japanese, and the like are free to dedicate most of their time to campaigning.

To put it bluntly, those of us who care about the future of American democracy must start by not allowing ourselves to be distracted by the "scandal of the week," the most recent titillating revelations about the dalliances or drinking or even junkets of this or that member of Congress, state assembly, or city council. We must learn to disregard press reports about a discount congressional barbershop, free rides on the congressional subway (which provides transportation within Congress only), a well-appointed gym, and members-only subsidized lunches. These are petty larcenies compared to selling legislation to special interests. To focus on those is like fussing about the stained attire of someone who is sinking in a mud hole.

Ask yourself what you would rather have: a member of Congress who gets some free haircuts, plane rides, and vacations but passes legislation that is in the public interest, or one who pays for all of his or her perks to the last penny but sells most legislation to the highest bidder? Wait, you say; what a stupid choice. Can't we find some decent people who can both serve the public and pay for personal expenses from their own pockets? Well, so far we have been able to elect few who do *either*, despite rivers of rhetoric. So we must focus our citizen energy, at least at the outset, where it matters most: stop the selling of legislation to special interests.

Cases in Point

Those who doubt that the political system that is supposed to serve our communities is often compromised should pick any public policy issue at random and examine, in detail, the forces at work. They will find how on numerous occasions policies that were clearly designed to serve the public interest were twisted beyond recognition by the time they were processed by the prevailing political system. They will find that although the details vary from instance to instance, one systemic force consistently mangles our public policies: special-interest groups.

Take the history of Trade Adjustment Assistance (TAA), which was enacted in 1962 to help workers whose jobs had been eliminated by rising imports. Under TAA, workers who could prove that government trade concessions to other countries were a major factor in their unemployment could receive supplementary benefits. From 1962 to 1974 only thirty-five thousand workers qualified. In the following years, Congress, under pressure from labor unions and select industries, introduced a new provision that made workers eligible if they could merely demonstrate that imports had been a "substantial cause" in losing their jobs. Consequently a program that had cost the American taxpayers a paltry $9 million in 1973 consumed $400 million in 1979 and guzzled $1.5 billion by 1981. Moreover, in 1980 most of the aid was flowing not to workers in industries that were shrinking because of imports, but to workers who had been temporarily laid off for any old reason. Not surprisingly, when a recruiter from General Dynamics tried to convince laid-off steelworkers in Ohio to move to a plant in the Northeast, the workers were reluctant: they didn't want to lose their substantial TAA benefits. Thus the TAA program was perverted by special-interest pressure into discouraging labor-force adjustment—the exact opposite of what it was originally intended to do.

The story of the Economic Development Administration (EDA) is remarkably similar. Its original mission was to help areas of the country that were economically depressed by funding public works programs, technical assistance grants, business loans, and loan guarantees. In 1965, when the program began, 12 percent of Americans lived in areas that met the definition of "distressed" and, hence, were entitled to EDA's special help. By 1979 Congress expanded the definition of what is a "distressed" community to a point that *most* of the U.S. population (84.5 percent) could qualify. In 1982 EDA tried to decertify a number of obviously well-off areas—such as Beverly Hills, California. But Congress blocked the move.

By the late eighties paying off special interests had become a rather routine and central part of the work of our legislators. Reporter Brooks Jackson was allowed to follow Tony Coelho, the Democratic master fund-raiser. Jackson concluded that "for Coelho, putting the official machinery of the House of Representatives to work on behalf of a $5,000 donor was not more out of line than giving him fancy luggage tags." Jackson also found that when special interests did not gain their way, they were at least able to block policies that did not serve them well enough to win their endorsement. Coelho was interested in providing housing for the millions of homeless people, considered by many to be the shame of America in the 1980s. However, the AFL-CIO—a major financial backer of Democratic candidates—insisted that the suggested constructions would have to conform to regulations in place since the Depression. Real estate lobbies, which contribute heavily to candidates of both parties, demanded that the housing provide realtors with various tax write-offs and subsidies. By the time they were all through, "the obvious became unthinkable," writes Jackson.

In important instances, innovative policy options are not even considered because it is widely expected that, given our interest-driven political system, they will be readily perverted. For instance, several experts have concluded that an industrial policy, similar to the one used successfully by Japan's Ministry of International Trade and Industry (MITI), ought *not* to be tried in the United States. Both opponents and proponents of an American MITI, a government agency that would promote American competitiveness through strategic planning and public financing, worry that such a policy would fall victim to special interests. Economist George Eads, a former member of the White House Council of Economic Advisors and now a vice-president of General Motors, testified before a congressional subcommittee about creating a national development bank to support new projects—a vital tool of industrial policy. Eads opposed the bank, though he agreed that it was needed, because he feared that the bank would turn into a political pork barrel. Congressional members and special-interest groups, he predicted, would grab hold of the bank and use it to funnel aid to their constituencies, disregarding the need of making the economy more competitive.

The bailout of Social Security and the 1986 Tax Reform Act (both helped along by an unusual bipartisan coalition) provide notable exceptions to the general rule that our legislative system is largely the captive of special interests. Generally—whether the government is dealing with issues such as gun control, textile import quotas, energy taxes, air bags, immigration policies, or health care costs—the nation cannot face a problem and expect that it will be met with a reasonable, workable public policy that is in the public interest.

The National Rifle Association blocks most gun control laws, despite the fact that a majority of Americans strongly favors such laws and feels that they are in the public interest. Textile import levels are set not in line with some established public need, but in response to the pressures exerted by the textile industry and the Amalgamated Clothing and Textile Workers Union. Although since 1973 most experts have strongly endorsed a tax on imports or oil usage as being in the public interest, oil companies and their unwitting allies have blocked its imposition to date. The introduction of air bags into cars, which save many lives each year, was delayed for more than a decade by the automakers, concerned that consumers would not buy some of their more lucrative "option packages" if the price of cars was a bit higher because of the air bags. And so it goes.

Undermining the Opposition

Because three out of four interest groups have no ideological commitments, but are interested only in lining the pockets of their constituents, they sink their hooks into both political parties, making effective opposition often impossible and undermining an essential feature of democratic government. For example, early in the 1992 presidential election campaign, with the economy in a prolonged recession, President Bush was falling rapidly in the polls. One of his particular points of vulnerability was that he and the GOP were considered an ally of the rich and the Democrats more representative of the middle class, which is the class to which most Americans consider themselves to belong. The Democrats suggested a major tax cut for the middle class. The White House more or less matched the offer, taking the wind out of the Democratic sails on this major issue. But the president, in his 1992 budget proposal, offered the Democrats a fight they should not have been able to resist.

Bush repeated his suggestion that the tax on what is called "unearned income," on capital gains, be slashed. The majority of the public perceived this measure as a payoff to the rich. Although some economists favor the tax cut, most agree that it is not in the public interest (especially in the way and under the circumstances in which it was advanced). The Democrats, long exiled from the White House and keen to recapture it, could be expected to make this a major campaign issue. This was hardly possible, though, after a sizable number of Democrats in Congress voted for the tax cut after—you guessed it—they were visited by representatives of Wall Street and others with deep pockets.

Next time you find an opposition party oddly refusing to discharge its duties, under our democratic form of government, check out who is underwriting the opposition. You will soon discover the major reason our political system is hobbled: special interests tie it up in knots.

Unbounded Pluralism

Some political scientists argue that special-interest group representation *adds* to the democratic process. As they see it, each community is made up of groups, each of which has particular interests that it holds dear: farmers and city dwellers; industrialists, workers, and consumers; and so on. The act of satisfying this assemblage of groups, referred to as "pluralism," is a way to serve the community as a whole. As I see it, there are two kinds of pluralism: the kind that is unbounded and unwholesome, and pluralism-within-unity. In the former, each group is out to gain all it can, with little concern for the shared needs of the community. In the latter, groups vie with one another yet voluntarily limit themselves when they impinge on common interests. Our pluralism has been—and there is reason to believe it has become increasingly—mainly of the unbounded kind, severely stressing the political system entrusted with crafting policies in the common interest.

The reasons lie in part in the special nature of American society. We have a larger and less homogeneous society than most other democracies. Unlike other countries, the United States has few community-building institutions that seek to sustain the nation as a community of communities. Our highly fragmented educational system transmits different values in thousands of distinct localities. The very notion of a national curriculum, as adopted in many countries from France to Israel, is considered anathema by most Americans, an extreme intervention by the federal government into local values and traditions. As a result, young Americans grow up with relatively few shared values, mores, symbols, or paradigms that many other communities draw upon to form consensus.

Also, America no longer has a national draft that draws together and mixes people from various backgrounds, similar in sociological purpose to what the frontier used to do. We have no national newspapers, unless you count the rather anemic *USA Today*. Public television has programs such as the "MacNeil/Lehrer NewsHour," but PBS's audience is minuscule. CNN and C-SPAN command sizable national audiences. But ABC, CBS, and NBC have been losing viewers of their national news shows to ever-increasing local coverage. Consequently, many social, economic, cultural, and political differences in the country reach the national capital unaccompanied by a communitywide consensus on the direction we favor as a nation. Such a consensus is required to enable Washington to develop public policies rather than those tailored to special interests.

Moreover, an ideology has developed, supported by some social scientists and intellectuals, that claims there is no such thing as communitywide (or "public") interest, only the give and take of particular interests. The actions of the interest groups are said not to be detrimental; on the contrary, they are part of normal politics through which the "community" benefits by servicing its various constituencies: long live unbounded pluralism.

I disagree with this viewpoint because, first, not all constituencies are served in this way. "In a bidding war, the disadvantaged, which don't have the resources to fight like other interest groups, always lose out," notes David Cohen, a co-director of the Advocacy Institute. At the same time, needs that are represented by those politically powerful, well-underwritten groups are being met. Second, the long-term needs of the community, and those shared needs that have no interest group payoffs, are shortchanged. Among these are investment in the next generation, the education of our children, environmental protection, and basic research (as distinct from applied research), the ultimate source of knowledge, innovation, and competitiveness.

I also reject the suggestion that one cannot tell shared or community interests from particular interests. When Common Cause fights to reduce the power of private money in public life, it is not seeking payoffs for its members; it advances what its members and leaders believe is in the common interest. This sort of cause is quite discernible from, say, an oil company's argument that it should be granted a special tax deduction because oil drilling, it claims, is in the national interest.

The criterion I recommend to one and all is to ask: Who benefits? If the answer is mainly members of the group that is lobbying, then we have the genuine article: a true special-interest group (of which we currently have more than you can shake a stick at). If the main beneficiary is the society at large, then we have found a relatively rare specimen and treasure: a group that serves the public interest. In my judgment, the Sierra Club is such a jewel because its main concern is to conserve the wilderness for us all and not to ensure untrampled ski slopes for its members. So are the neoconservatives, a group of intellectuals who oppose government controls and regulations not just for their handful of sympathizers, but for the whole body politic.

Special-interest groups are often easy to spot. Such industry-based organizations as the National Kraut Packers Association, the Chain Link Fence Manufacturers Institute, and the American Wood-Preservers Association clearly have limited, self-serving agendas. Some groups, however, deliberately obscure the interests they serve. For example, you could not tell from the name "Campaign America" that the organization's true purpose was to reelect a Republican senator. Nor would you be able to tell that the Center for Peace and Freedom lobbies for Star Wars. "Public Advocate" generally favors business deregulation. And behind the label "Free Enterprise PAC," believe it or not, hides an antiabortion group.

Still other political scientists argue that special-interest groups are harmless because they neutralize one another. For instance, while the Business Roundtable favors a lower minimum wage, labor unions push for a higher one, which leaves the legislature free to pursue the public interest. This notion of the way interest groups work could not be farther from the truth.

First of all, not all interest groups are created equal in economic and political power. Compare, for example, the powerful National Rifle Association (NRA) with the weak gun control lobby. For decades the majority of the public has favored various gun control measures, but the NRA was able to block most of them and to dilute and delay the remaining others. Even at a highly emotionally charged moment—after the assassination of a very popular president in broad daylight by a gunman—when Ted Kennedy, the president's brother, introduced a gun control measure, the NRA blocked the legislation. How? The NRA grants large campaign contributions, while the gun control lobby dishes out peanuts. During the 1987-1988 cycle, the contributions of pro-gun political action committees (PACs) totaled $802,906. The antigun PACs contributed only $87,900. The NRA also provided $1.5 million in "independent expenditures" in 1988. Thus the money gauge reads one to twenty-six in favor of guns.

Second, a well-heeled lobby may push Congress from one side, while on the other side is not a balancing counterweight but the unorganized public at large, which is often barely cognizant of what is happening. There are hundreds of such instances, but here's one that illustrates the point. During the 1970s the Federal Trade Commission (FTC) received a large number of complaints from people who purchased used cars. Buyers claimed that dealers had sold them autos that had major defects, and that they had engaged in various chicaneries such as rolling back odometers. In response the FTC drafted guidelines that would require used-car dealers to disclose to buyers all major defects that they were aware of. Given the normal course of democracy, and the fact that there are many hundreds of buyers of used cars for every dealer, one would expect that the suggested guidelines would find wide support in Congress. In effect, the opposite happened. In 1982 Congress vetoed the FTC rule. The reason? The groups that represented the car dealers had followed the matter attentively, lobbied hard, and provided campaign contributions. In fact, 180 of the 216 representatives who supported the veto received a total of almost half a million dollars for the 1980 and 1982 elections from the National Automobile Dealers Association. The buying public remained largely unaware that the FTC's guidelines were shot down.

Unknown even to the careful readers of newspapers, the billboard industry (working under the banner of the Coalition for Property Rights) makes itself felt on Capitol Hill. Before a 1991 vote on legislation to curb billboards, money flowed freely to elected officials. More than $250,000 was granted to House and Senate candidates by industry executives, their spouses, and associates from January to June of 1991 (more than their entire contributions for the 1989-1990 election cycle). Industry-related PACs added $127,000. The antibillboard measure was decisively rejected by the Senate, with a neutered amendment passing sixty to thirty-nine. As a writer for the *National Journal* noted: "The billboard lobby remains a textbook case of a small interest group . . . whose heavy investments in Washington have yielded handsome benefits."

Last, it might be suggested that this line of argumentation is old hat. After all, political observers from David Truman to Theodore Lowi have chronicled the disruptive power of special-interest groups. But this does not mean that the message is any less valid. What is missing is *a wide recognition that special interests are at the core of our systemic problems*, a consensus powerful enough to unlock their grip on our legislators.

I regret to add that the situation in many state capitols and city councils is worse than in Washington, which may be hard to believe. A sixteen-month sting operation conducted in Arizona led to indictments starting in early 1991. In it, a policeman posed as a casino operator interested in trading money for votes. He found seven all-too-willing state legislators. Videotapes of bribes changing hands show legislators making comments, such as Senator Carolyn Walker's: "I like the good life and I'm trying to position myself that I can live the good life and have more money. We all have our prices," Walker added before pocketing some of the more than $25,000 she received during the operation. State Representative Bobby Raymond explained that "there is not an issue in the world that I give a [expletive] about." He added, "My favorite line is 'What's in it for me?' " Apparently not enough. When Raymond found out that a larger payment than his $12,105 had been made to another legislator, he said, "I sold way too cheap."

A similar sting operation in South Carolina in 1989 and 1990 led to the indictments of fourteen current or former legislators, ten of whom have pleaded guilty; four more have been found guilty, and one is awaiting trial. Most of the indictments were for taking bribes from undercover FBI agents in exchange for supporting laws that would legalize gambling on horse and dog racing. Legislation favorable to gambling also played a part in the conviction of a highly placed elected official in West Virginia: The state senate president pleaded guilty to a charge that he extorted $10,000 from a lobbyist. The list of other state legislatures whose members have been caught in illegal acts in recent years includes California, New York, Tennessee, Rhode Island, and Texas, among others.

It's easy to see why the situation is even worse on the state and local level. In many states legislators work only part-time for the public and hence are openly and legally entitled to earn money elsewhere. This sounds innocent enough until you find out (as I did when I served as the staff director of a commission that had been appointed by then-governor Hugh Carey of New York to investigate abuses in nursing homes) that the legislators, many of whom are lawyers, are on retainer to the industries that they are supposed to regulate. The legislative bodies of only eleven states are in session more than one hundred days a year. The mean is seventy-five; it's thirty-two for New Jersey and thirty for Virginia. Nationwide only 11 percent of state legislators work full-time as legislators.

Another problem is that many state legislatures and city councils pass resolutions by voice vote. This means that the vote of each individual representative is not recorded, and hence legislators cannot be held accountable to the voters for supporting a resolution that is favored by a special interest. In short, the system of state legislatures and city councils is even more subject to special interests than Congress is.

New Powers

Most of all, it is *not* business as usual in the government by and for special interests. True, lobbying has always been with us and is constitutionally protected as a means for groups to call attention to their special needs. However, the advantage of special interests, compared to who represents the community's true needs, has increased sharply since the mid-1970s. Following a 1975 Federal Election Commission advisory opinion on the legality of Sun Oil Company's SunPAC, special-interest groups concluded that it was legal to provide large campaign contributions—contributions that obligate politicians to their open-handed benefactors. Since then the number of PACs has grown rapidly. While there were only 608

PACs in 1974, they numbered 2,000 by 1979. By mid-1991 the PAC ranks had swollen to 4,123.

In 1974 PAC contributions made up 17 percent of the average campaign expenditure of a candidate running for the House of Representatives. The proportion rose to 28 percent in 1980 and to 37 percent in the 1988 elections. Because these funds are easier to obtain compared to raising money from individuals, candidates favored by special-interest groups have a much better chance of being reelected than do those that don't get such money.

Moreover, special-interest groups tend to concentrate their money on incumbents. In 1988, 88 percent of all PAC money was funneled to incumbents. Further, *Newsweek* notes what it correctly terms a "disturbing trend in the United States Congress: the use of huge campaign war chests as preemptive weapons to effectively blow away opponents before they reach the starting line." By the end of 1987 the members of Congress had amassed a total of $68 million in campaign war chests.

When one adds the power of money to all the other factors that favor incumbents, it is no wonder that 98 percent of them won reelection in 1986. The reelection rate in 1990 for both the House and Senate was 96 percent. In preceding elections the rate had been "only" about 90 percent. (Special circumstances, such as the check kiting scandal and the faltering economy, led to a much higher turnover in the 1992 election.) Thus, special interests, fortified with PAC money, are undermining the essence of the democratic process. Instead of allowing the electorate to change its representatives, they find it profitable to bet on those already in place—and to keep them there.

I cannot stress enough the importance of this point. It is naive to assume that all democracy requires is regular elections, secret ballot boxes (so that voters cannot be intimidated), and a free press. For democracy to work effectively, those in office—the elected officials—must truly represent the concerns, values, and needs of the people they serve. For representatives to continually reflect the people well, it must be possible to change them when they cease to heed their masters' voice.

What we have had in Congress until recently, and are likely to have in the future, is the extreme opposite: as people's minds and hearts change, representatives are holding on to their offices—as long as they satisfy the special interests. No wonder so many Americans are highly alienated from the political process. They speak, but few listen; they vote, but nothing much ever changes. They see that policies are crafted for interests that are obviously not their own.

Corruption, Second Degree

The same political forces that undermine democracy in the first place also hinder attempts to shore it up. Both of the major parties are deeply implicated; that is, members of both parties accept PAC contributions day in and day out—and on weekends, too. PACs contributed more than $159 million in the 1989-1990 election cycle. Democrats pocketed more than $90 million in 1987-1988, while Republicans stashed away more than $60 million of PAC money. Consequently neither party is willing to bite the hand that feeds it so lavishly, even though a few Democrats and a handful of Republicans have drafted legislation that seeks to stem the rising tide of PAC money. When, in 1992, a bill passed Congress that would have put a ceiling, albeit a very high one, on the funds senators and House members can collect, President Bush vetoed it.

For the same reasons, the public is not informed by congressional hearings about PACs and their ill effects. For example, one main reason the public never found out how the greatest raid in American history on the public till was perpetrated—the $500 billion savings and loan bailout—is that both Democrats and Republicans received hefty campaign contributions and other payoffs from S&Ls. It seems futile, then, to rely on one party or the other to lay bare PAC corruptions or to seriously instigate reforms to curtail their power.

Members of Congress and state legislatures who do advance reform bills soon learn that they can proceed only at their own peril. Senator David Boren (D-OK) is one of the few who occasionally tries. He received an early lesson on the penalties involved. When he was first elected to the Oklahoma State Legislature, he found that it, like many others, did not keep records of how individual legislators voted. In this way a legislator could vote against a bill the community favored (and serve the special interests) and later claim that the bill was defeated by other legislators. Boren suggested legislation that would have enabled the public to find out what was up. As a result, Boren was stripped of a chairpersonship of a sub-committee, removed from the important rules committee, and re-located to a remote office under the roof of the building.

To ensure that their masters will not be frustrated, PACs go be-yond deflecting legislators from their sworn duties; they form lob-bies to ensure that their own businesses will not be interrupted. After President George Bush called in his 1991 State of the Union Address for legislation to eliminate all PACs, about a hundred PACs got to-gether to fight the president's idea. The pack of PACs coordinated their efforts under the auspices of the National Association of Busi-ness PACs, "the broadest groups of interests I have seen at any co-alition meeting since I have been here in Washington," according to one of the participants. Among other measures, the group decided to mount a media campaign, stressing that it is "unfair" to go after PACs, because individual contributions to PACs amount to no more than $61 per person. (This point disregards that PAC managers channel large pools of money unearmarked by the donors.)

The business PACs found an unusual ally in a group of liberal PACs, which also formed a "network" of PACs called PRONET, to head off reforms. Judging from the lack of response to President Bush's appeal, which he himself did not vigorously promote, let it not be said that either group has been wasting its time—or money. And so the system is left unreformed.

In Conclusion

The main reason American democracy is hobbled is that special interests, drawing on deep-pocketed PACs, have gained ever more power since the mid-seventies. Our preoccupation with personal scandals, from extramarital affairs to check kiting, has distracted attention from the fact that the whole political system is twisted: all too often it no longer represents the community at large. Reform is most unlikely to come from those who have grown more depen-dent on PAC money than any welfare mother has become addicted to public handouts. Clearly our salvation will have to come from some other quarter. The public at large, those who care about the whole and not merely the parts, must get back into the act. They must recapture politics for the community. The first step is to sever the link between private pockets and public life, our next subject.

9 ♦ What Is to Be Done?

A Question of New Political Energy

S Sigmund Freud would say, there are no accidents. For every political pathology, as for personal ones, there is an underlying cause. Thus it is no accident that narrow, parochial interests often win in Washington these days, displacing shared community considerations. These victories reflect the new powerful role that special-interest groups have acquired within the American polity. As corporations, labor unions, trade associations, and other economic and social groups penetrate the realm of politics, they overpower the basic democratic precept of "one person, one vote" that aims to make government equally responsive to all members of the community. These interest groups replace the democratic form of government with a government that largely heeds narrow, limited, self-serving groups.

It follows that if you seek to counter this tendency toward domination by special interests by returning the government of the country to all of us, then mere noble intentions, good ideas, and even well-crafted reforms will not do. *There must be a new source of political energy* sufficiently powerful to overcome strong opposition and to propel far-reaching changes in our political system.

But how may such a new political muscle grow? We face here a prize political paradox. Special-interest groups not only often have the upper hand, but they also use it to hold off reform as they seek to perpetuate their special hold on the government. Therefore reformers typically make little headway; they challenge the consequences of government for and by special interests rather than the root causes: the sources of their superiority. In those few instances that reformers do aim at root causes, they soon find that those who favor the status quo are more powerful than the challengers. *For reform to succeed, reformers,* like Archimedes, *must find a point of leverage outside the political world* in order to be able to change it.

Where is the Archimedean point required to give the American polity "back to the people"? What is the source of the political energy needed to propel major reforms? The ultimate protector of the common interest is the public at large. The power of special-interest groups is *not* based on their ability to serve most people most of the time. Their success is based on the fact that most people, most of the time, are politically inactive. This allows groups that often represent only small segments of society to control national and local policies because their efforts go largely unopposed. *Thus the challenge for the politics of change is to find ways to mobilize the great underrepresented majorities.*

Some see the answer in mobilizing public opinion. Indeed, on some occasions the media have been successful in alerting us to the dangers of excessive powers in the hands of particular interests. Once in a while an investigative reporter prepares an article, sometimes even a whole series, on the way this or that lobby has clawed and paid its way through Congress. However, this force is insufficient. The public is preoccupied with many other issues, from health care to crime, from economic well-being to race relations. Typically, rolling back interest groups, changing the way politics are carried out, is lost in the shuffle. The public also tends to mobilize more often on matters of substance (say, protecting the environment) than on matters of process (how representatives win elections).

Furthermore, whatever public concern is aroused over the ways politics need to be recast is often deflected by arguments that massive campaign contributions, the flood of private money into politicans' pockets, are a form of democracy. Typically, Herbert Alexander, in his forthrightly titled book, *The Case for PACs,* asserts that political action committees allow "groups and interests in society to articulate their demands, to coalesce and to oppose government." That is, PACs are favorable to democratic governance. The public is told by Joseph J. Fanelli, the president of the Business-Industry PAC, that "critics lose sight of the constitutional basis of PAC activity. The fundamental expression of First Amendment freedoms through the phrase 'assemble for the redress of grievances' applies to political action committees. PACs, in any segment of society, are nothing more than gatherings of individual citizens exercising their right to assemble." This ignores the fact that PACs are *not* like other groups; in effect, their members rarely, if ever, meet, reason, or vote about the course the PAC follow, how its monies are used, or anything else. They are little more than money bags.

Fanelli also argues that "another key point to reinforce is that PACs do not derive their contributions from corporations. Rather, PAC contributions are derived from individuals—employees, stockholders, and their families. It is well to keep pointing out, too, that all contributions are voluntary." This observation hides the fact that PAC members are not allowed to indicate how their money is to be used by the PAC bosses. Indeed, most times individual contributors are not even told to whom their money flows. We must further stress that nobody is suggesting that groups of citizens should be prohibited from banding together to argue their case. Rather, the issue is whether small groups of well-heeled citizens should be allowed to use their deep pockets to in effect buy legislation—and to twist the arms of elected representatives to serve *them,* while the same representatives shortchange the rest of their constituents, the overwhelming majority.

The defenders of PACs further argue that PACs are innocent committees of citizens who wish to participate in the democratic process by writing a check. If this were true, there would be no reason to object to my all-time favorite solution to PAC plutocracy: allow citizens who make campaign contributions to determine to whom their money will be dedicated, to earmark the politicians who receive their contribution! It would seem elementary that if Jane or John Doe wish to donate money to a candidate they favor, they be allowed to decide who is going to be the beneficiary. *But that is not the way PACs work.* Money is thrown into a collective pot by the executives of a corporation, the members of a labor union, or the members of a trade association. Contributions are *not* earmarked. The *managers* of the PAC then determine whom *they* favor, and channel rivers of money to those whom they wish to support. In short, PACs are run by tight oligarchies of managed money; they are not genuine avenues for public participation.

Most important, public opinion—even if it is aroused by press accounts about politicians in the pocket of special interests—tends to be mercurial; it is quick to rise but has little staying power. Special interests often just wait until the press is bored with their transgressions and turns its attention elsewhere.

A case in point: During an investigation of abuses in nursing homes in New York State, in which I served as a staff director, I found that the evening news (and the morning papers) were saturated with one horrible story after another. Elderly people were tranquilized to control them more easily and were left lying in their own feces. Bedridden patients were not turned over and developed festering bedsores. When their funds had run out, people were left out on porches to catch cold, to hurry them on their way. Nursing home owners used public funds designated for the sick to buy themselves Picassos and Mercedes and so on.

The public was outraged, and the air was filled with angry talk of sweeping reform. During the public furor, the nursing home lobby was uncharacteristically mum. About six months into the scandal, New York City was found to be on the verge of bankruptcy, and something known as the "the New York financial crisis" became topic number one. The nursing home story moved from page one to about page thirty-seven; it disappeared from TV news, and it fell out of sight of the public. Soon the nursing home lobby controlled the legislature as before. A few, chiefly cosmetic, reforms were enacted, but most of the abuses, some of which investigators had found ten years before during a previous wave of moral outrage, continued unabated.

As this case illustrates, in contrast with the public, interest groups have staying power. They occasionally yield a bit to allow for limited reforms, while generally maintaining a choke hold on public policy. In the long run, an aroused public opinion is no match for special interests.

The Import of Social Movements

Historical experience suggests that *social movements are the source of the needed political energy*. We know from the experience of the civil rights, women's, environmental, and neoconservative movements that social movements can succeed in redirecting the nation in significant, deep, and encompassing ways. Social movements are much more effective than mere waves of public opinion because they have a steady core of leaders (rather than being "led" by the media). They draw on strong shared values and molding symbols. They command cadres that mobilize the rank and file to whatever social action is called for. And they apply social techniques such as demonstrations, sit-ins, and boycotts to prod elected officials away from special-interest groups and toward the necessary reforms and service of the community at large.

Social scientists are often asked: "How do you change the moral climate of a community?" The answer that they offer frequently does not satisfy those who raise the question. People look for a wonder drug, a measure that could be readily undertaken and that would provide a simple and, above all, quick cure. Thus they often ask that the president give the country a really good talking-to, "a fireside chat." Such appeals, it is assumed, would suffice to "turn the country around" (an often used phrase). Moreover, many hope that Madison Avenue and the television networks could put together a series of public service announcements ("Just say no!") that would restore our morality.

The fact is that the processes of political reform and social change are complex and slow. They are typically launched by persons who form a new message (such as Luther's theses, Rachel Carson's *Silent Spring,* Betty Friedan's *Feminine Mystique,* and Ralph Nader's *Unsafe at Any Speed*). The message is then disseminated by dramatic events—nailing the theses to the door of the cathedral, creating an environmental Earth Day, or organizing a mass march on Washington. What follows might be called a "multilogue," or a national town hall meeting. In it, millions of citizens—over beers in bowling alleys, at water coolers at work, and over coffee and at cocktail parties—discuss and debate the issues flagged by sit-ins, demonstrations, boycotts, and other such dramatizations. The multilogue is further extended in radio call-in shows, letters to the editor, sermons in churches and synagogues. Gradually a new consensus emerges. In this way we recast our views about the proper relations between whites and blacks, between straight and gay people, between the genders, and toward the environment. More recently, multilogues have dealt with questions such as what we owe the homeless and those not covered by health insurance. These multilogues rarely result in complete agreement, but they do fashion a new consensus among most of us.

By the way, as untidy as the process is, I for one would oppose more top-down, better-regimented appeals or those that draw on leaders' charisma. It is this cumbersome multilogue, which consensus-building requires, that protects our democracy from demagogues. And only if the American people truly participate in the formation of a new moral climate will the moral voice of the community be redirected as public policies change course. If one changes public policy without gaining a moral consensus, we have at best a rather faulty democracy. Often we get reforms that die from lack of public support, as the Prohibition did.

Once we have all these elements in place—a new message, well-established modes of dissemination, and a broad and well-processed consensus—we are ready as a community to push in a sustained manner for the required changes.

A Historical Model

The Progressive movement provides a direct precedent for the political cleanup and reform now needed, particularly because the movement grew out of an era that in several ways resembles our own. At the beginning of the century, large concentrations of wealth and political powers came into being in the United States, following the rapid industrialization of the late nineteenth and early twentieth centuries. The Industrial Revolution was carried forward by new American business plutocrats—among them Jay Gould, Andrew Carnegie, the Rockefellers, Harrimans, and Morgans—who amassed fortunes and monopolized business in many sectors by forming giant conglomerates or "trusts." They used their large concentrations of private power to direct local, state, and federal public policy in a manner that reflected their special interests. The

Senate was frequently called the "Millionaires Club," because the rich often got themselves selected for it, while others used their Senate seats to gain riches. There were numerous reports of bought senatorships, and senators were often plied with favorable loans and offers of stocks at below market rates. Immune to public anger, they prevented tariff reform, blocked election reform, and stopped in their tracks most changes in the monetary system that business opposed.

As abuses became more prevalent and were brought to light by muckraking reporters and public investigations, more and more individuals dedicated themselves to becoming leaders for broad-based reform, known as the Progressive movement. Unlike some of its predecessors, the new movement appealed to all classes, since its focus was on formulating proper rules of the game rather than on serving the interest of one class. The movement's initial successes were in Wisconsin and California, where it succeeded in electing Progressive mayors and governors. It later spread nationwide to play a major role in the elections of presidents Theodore Roosevelt and Woodrow Wilson.

Furthermore, the movement provided the political muscle that pushed through many reforms that brought politics out in the open. Local initiatives and referenda were introduced to allow more direct citizen participation in government. President Roosevelt enforced antitrust laws by prosecuting, among others, J. P. Morgan's Northern Securities railroad monopoly. He also pushed legislation through Congress to prohibit corporate contributions to candidates for federal office.

Prodded by the Progressives, a constitutional amendment was ratified in 1913 that provided for the direct popular election of senators, replacing their election by state legislatures, which were deeply influenced by corporations. State legislatures, in effect, represented industries: "Ohio sent oilmen; Nevada sent silver mine owners; Maine, Michigan, and Oregon sent lumber barons; New York sent bankers. It was in a very real sense the ultimate pork barrel, a legislature of lobbyists," reports historian William Ashworth. Finally, President Woodrow Wilson removed protective tariffs previously imposed at the urging of big business, and he established the Federal Reserve Board to regulate private banking in the public interest.

Although the details are numerous and complex, by seeking to end the intrusion of private power into public policy, the Progressive movement worked in two spheres. It limited the concentration of private economic power and it reduced the influence of special-interest groups on public life. In addition, Progressives promoted political reforms that made the government more responsive to the people.

Historians differ in their regard for the Progressive movement. Some argue that it was too rationalist in its reliance on the civil service and experts in public policies. Others observe that the movement did not progress far enough. The latter point is almost certainly true; it is but one more reason we now require another round of progressive reforms.

"My first day back and I already forgot my election promises. How about you?"

Cartoon by Earl Engleman. Reprinted with permission of Earl Engleman.

Toward a Neoprogressive, Communitarian Movement

The public's current loss of control over our political institutions calls for a new progressive movement, a major social effort to energize a package of reforms that will reduce the role of special interests in the government of our local and national communities. As Robert Putnam and William Parent, two political science professors, put it:

> At the close of this century, we are again faced with a haunting feeling that things have gone awry in our democratic institutions. The "splendid little war" in Iraq aside, an array of problems frustrates elected representatives and policy makers operating traditionally out of the two-party system. . . . It falls on all of us to ask ourselves what kind of government we want and to become participants toward that end.

The details of the reforms and the specific reasons for favoring some over others is a subject that requires an extensive, separate discussion. I have spelled this out in my book *Capital Corruption*. The following list illustrates the *kinds* of reforms that are needed:

• *Finance congressional elections with public funds such as we already do for presidential elections.* Opponents argue that such spending would add to the deficit. The simple truth is that there is no better bargain to be had in these United States. If by freeing our legislatures from the purse strings of special interests (by paying the full cost of congressional elections, which is estimated to average between $200 million and $250 million per year) we have prevented just one of the numerous special favors that our elected officials dish out to their benefactors, the public would already be way ahead. If we would succeed, say, in cutting subsidies given to farmers, about $2 billion in 1989, by about 10 percent to 15 percent we could pay for each year's election costs. Even cutting out cotton subsidies for one year (they cost $6 billion between 1986 and 1990) would pay for about five years of campaigns at the going rate. If we would forgo building one nuclear Seawolf submarine, which the Pentagon and the White House freely acknowledged in 1992 that we do not need, we would save enough money to more or less cover the costs of elections until the end of the century. After that time I would personally take on the rather undemanding responsibility of finding another sizable pot of public funds on which some special interest feeds, and that could be used to free elections from the undue influence of those with deep pockets.

• *Curb the flow of private money* into the coffers of members of Congress. Impose a total ban on PACs. Limit individual contributions to $100 per person. Allow no "bundling." Bundling occurs when a lobbyist collects checks from numerous individuals and then delivers them to a politician in the name of a corporation, a trade association, or a labor union. This allows the lobbyist to act as a PAC, whether or not he or she manages one. Thus, while corporations are prohibited from making campaign contributions, and PACs are limited to $5,000 per candidate, some sixty-one general partners of Goldman, Sachs and Company contributed almost eleven times that amount, $54,000, to the 1992 presidential campaign of Bill Clinton. IBM executives did almost as well for President Bush's reelection effort.

Unfortunately, the ACLU has opposed legislation to abolish PACs and to set spending limits on election campaigns, as it "opposes all legislatively mandated spending limits," although it does support allowing public financing of elections. It is to the credit of Nadine Strossen, the current president of the ACLU, that she opposes her organization's position on spending limits and has tried to convince its board to abandon it.

• *Reduce the cost of running for office.* Provide free time for all bona fide candidates on radio and TV. As these stations use public airwaves, the public is entitled to insist that they contribute some of their capacities to making democracy work. The campaign period and the amount that one can spend ought to be limited, as is done in the United Kingdom, to sharply curtail campaign expenditures.

In 1992 the United Kingdom managed a national election campaign that lasted, from start to finish, three weeks. A candidate for Parliament is limited to a precisely calculated amount of spending: the paltry amount of $15,000. As a member of Parliament noted: "There is no question of bending the rules; an election agent, or campaign manager, who exceeded the limit last time was fined about $1,000, dismissed from his job, and barred from participation

in politics, even from voting, for five years." He further explained
that "if I spend more, I get disqualified. So the close watch is not on
raising the money but on seeing that there is no overspending." He
adds that "$15,000 is enough, since I know that that is all my
opponents will have as well." Time is spent not on buying more
TV time, but on figuring out what to state on the "same amount of
free air time" that each candidate gets.

This British approach may be too virtuous—or too constricting—for Americans. And British candidates do cover fewer people
and smaller territories than American candidates. However, if Britain can conduct elections in less than a month and with a pittance,
we should be able to cap both the period and the expenditures, even
if at higher levels.

• *Promote disclosure of the political process.* For starters, introduce
a lobbyist registry for all congressional and executive branch offices. If every time a lobbyist visited a congressional member or
head of a government agency she or he were required to record the
visit in a book open to the public, it would curb inappropriate
lobbying without slowing legitimate representatives of public
groups. These have no reason to wish to conceal their visits. On the
contrary, they are sure to seek to highlight whom they courted on
behalf of their constituents.

A bill requiring lobbyists to file regular reports about their
activities and disclose the amount of monies they spend was introduced into Congress by Senator Carl Levin in 1992. It would get
the lobbyists' attention by fining them up to $100,000 for noncom-
pliance. Lobbyists have lobbied against it, so far successfully.

• *Enhance the enforcement of all rules, old and new.* Existing regulations are often misleading because they seem tough but are barely
enforced. Congress has rescinded the Federal Election Commission's power to conduct random audits of campaign finances. And
the agency has been further weakened by budget cuts and its staff
has been curtailed—as money spent on elections has grown rapidly.
The FEC has no legal authority to impose fines; instead it must
negotiate with the offending party to come up with an agreeable
figure.

Furthermore, the FEC moves so slowly in investigating and
negotiating that judgments are rarely made until after the election,
when it's too late to make a difference. The FEC audits of Michael

Dukakis's and George Bush's 1988 presidential campaigns weren't completed until October 1991. The investigations of Pat Robertson's and Jesse Jackson's 1988 campaigns were still pending in mid 1992.

In a 1990 study of the FEC, reporter Brooks Jackson concludes: "The FEC has failed. It has neither the will nor the means to deter wanton violators, who sometimes ridicule openly the commission's weakness. It has interpreted the law so permissively that special-interest groups may funnel money to candidates practically without limit if they wish." Instead of being a watchdog, the FEC has become a lapdog and now a laughingstock. *The New York Times,* in an editorial titled "The Campaign Sewer Overflows," chimed in that "the corruption of public financing for Presidential elections is by now obvious to everyone but the Federal Election Commission."

Of the estimated eighty thousand persons who work at lobbying Congress, only about six thousand were registered in 1991 as the law requires. Half of the lobbyists who were registered as foreign agents did not disclose who they were lobbying for. It is said that the only lobbyists who do register are those who believe that their clients are impressed with the title "registered lobbyist." Lawyers who represent foreign interests are not even required to register.

• *Enhance the role of political parties.* Channel campaign contributions (if any are to be allowed) through political parties rather than directly to individual candidates, or provide the parties with public funds—which is a more difficult medicine to stomach but may be a necessary one. Historically, American political parties have been weak, and they have grown weaker in the past generation. As a result, individual legislators, and their myriad staffers, are often free to cut deals—and to collect payoffs in the form of campaign contributions—from special interests. If there were somewhat more party discipline, at least on important policy measures, it would reduce the ability of individual legislators to cut deals. Political parties, however, have shown little ability to represent the public interest. (If you attend a typical Democratic or Republican discussion group, policy deliberation, or reception in Washington, D.C., more than half of those present are likely to be lobbyists, mainly from business groups.) It may be wise to enhance their role only if all the other measures suggested do not suffice—or if the parties reform their own ways.

• *Restore honest debates among the candidates to reduce the effect of sound bites, of what is called teledemocracy.* Many observers of the American political scene are gravely concerned about the ever-shorter time span the news media allow for candidates for public office to express their substantive positions, as distinct from cussing each other out and engaging in personal slurs. Sound bites are said to have shrunk between 1968 and 1988 from 42 seconds to 9 seconds, then shriveled even more in 1992, when many were a mere 6.5 seconds long.

Honest debates entail opportunities for the candidates to speak at longer intervals. Allow them to challenge one another, rather than rely only on questions from the press. And provide opportunities for one or more rounds of rebuttal. Call-in shows, such as "Larry King Live," allow citizens to field questions and for candidates to respond at some length.

A Pack of Reforms

Critics gleefully point out that several reform measures, which have been introduced in the recent past, have failed to stem the flood of private money from special-interest groups into legislators' campaign chests and pockets. As I see it, these reforms failed in part because they were introduced in an erratic and piecemeal fashion and because they were not sufficiently encompassing. It follows that *the suggested reforms are best implemented as one package.* The main catch, though, is not that we lack at this point full knowledge of which specific reforms will work and how they are to be combined. The main requirement stands: that sufficient political energy arise to propel the needed changes in face of long-standing and deeply entrenched opposition of strong coalitions of special-interest groups. Little that happens in Washington commands their undivided attention as much as attempts to clip their wings, not to mention file down their fangs.

There is a subtle connection between the scope of the reform package and the mobilization of our fellow citizens to energetically participate in a neoprogressive Communitarian movement: citizens cannot get truly excited about limited marginal reforms, say, reducing the contributions PACs may make from $5,000 to $2,500. They are much more likely to actively support encompassing reforms, reforms that may free our legislature from the grip of special interests and allow them to serve the community at large.

Objections

When we take on the special interests and their deep pockets, we must be ready to face layer upon layer of rationalizations, some advanced by well-meaning folks and some by self-serving ones. Both groups often argue that the presence of moneylenders in the temples of democratic government is the way things ought to be. It is not possible here to go through all the numerous arguments made (and the subpoints and asides) and to refute them. Volumes have been written on these points. However, a quick review of the key points and responses may help community members who are willing to become active in these matters.

• It is said that all that money buys is access and not actual votes. That is, all it gains is time with the legislator, to bend his or her ear, to hear out one's arguments. In *A Case for PACs,* Herbert Alexander argues that "access should not be confused with buying votes." And Bill Grove, vice-chairman of Chesapeake and Potomac Telephone Company's federal PAC, argues that a PAC contribution "helps provide an entreé for us," but that "anybody who thinks that $500 or $1,000 or even $5,000 is going to get you that much in terms of getting that candidate's vote . . . is very, very sadly mistaken."

But consider the following little episode. When Representative Robert Matsui (D-CA) inserted a provision into the 1986 tax bill that reduced the tax bill of utilities by many hundreds of millions, he received more than $60,000 in donations for his reelection campaign. When, however, he and others changed their views and tried to remove some of the special favors granted to this industry, they faced a formidable opponent: the utilities contributed about $8 million to campaign treasuries of those opposed to closing the tax loophole. Representative Matsui reports: "I have been told a number of times by [House] members . . . that my bill makes good policy sense but dangerous political sense to them. Rich in honorariums and campaign contributions, their [the utility lobbyists'] talk is pretty loud in the halls around here."

Twenty percent of 114 members of Congress surveyed by the Center for Responsive Politics openly admitted that political contributions had affected their votes. Another 30 percent said they weren't sure (50 percent claimed that contributions had no effect on them).

Assume that the following statement is the whole truth and nothing but the truth. The president of the National Association of Broadcasters explains that the $100,000 his association granted to various members of Congress helped the group to "become better acquainted personally with the members of Congress. And it's always easier to deal with someone if you're on a first-name basis." Assume for a moment that all that PACs buy is access. Still, access to busy legislators should not be bought and sold. They should be accessible to all on the basis of the urgency of their needs or on the fact that those who approach them are representing a large group of constituents—and not how high their dough piles up on congressional counters.

• Other defenders of the status quo argue that the contributions are small: "What's $5,000 between you and me?" Mobil claims that in an ad "that's hardly enough in these days of costly campaigns to 'buy' thirty seconds on TV, let alone an election." Note, though, that while $5,000 is the legal limit one PAC can allot to one member of Congress, special interests have long found two effective ways around the limit—ways that allow them to, in effect, channel as much money as they wish into election campaigns. The first way is the creation of multiple PACs by the same interest group. All you need is a patient copying machine operator and a bit of talent in generating names. Thus the dairy industry has twenty-one PACs, though some are state affiliates of larger PACs. And the oil and gas industry has more than 180 PACs. Hence the suggestion that "all" a special interest can give is $5,000 is disingenuous. You decide the amount of money you want to give, divide it into $5,000 chunks, and go to work to generate a PAC for each chunk.

Second, the Supreme Court ruled (in a decision rather difficult for nonlawyers to fathom) that although limits may be placed on what one may contribute *to* a candidate, there can be no limit on expenditures *against* the opponent(s) of a candidate, nor on so-called independent expenditures on behalf of the candidate but not coordinated with him or her.

When all is said and done, *there are now no effective limits in place.* For example, six members of the House Agriculture Committee received $20,000 or more each from various PACs of dairy groups. Wisconsin's Alvin Baldus collected $34,400. Representative Richard Nolan of Minnesota banked $37,225. Representative Jerry Huckaby received a cool $42,000. And Representative John Jenrette, Jr., gained a hefty $59,900. (These figures are from the period between January 1975 and July 1978. And all that has changed since is that the money pots have grown larger.) Note that these figures exclude contributions from individual dairymen and -women, which probably were made but are difficult to trace. It is hard to believe that special-interest groups would shell out these sums without some significant return. We already have seen that they are quite correct in anticipating more than access—that they will have a major say on numerous legislative proposals.

• Some champions of PACs argue that legislators receive money in support of positions that they would hold anyhow. A spokeswoman for the American Medical Association insisted that donations were "based on the basic philosophy of a member" and that doctors "weren't buying votes." If this were true, corporations and labor unions and such would be blowing millions away without discernible benefits. For anybody who believes such a tale, I have a lovely bridge in Brooklyn I'd like to sell him.

Moreover, special interests lay their sizable bets on members and chairs of committees central to their interests, rather than distributing them randomly among those they find to be philosophically attuned. This makes sense only if they expect specific payoffs.

A 1990 study by the nonpartisan Center for Responsive Politics found that only 11 percent of PAC contributions came from ideological or single-issue groups; 24 percent were provided by labor and 65 percent by business PACs. The study also established that contributions by most PACs were based less on ideological factors than on which committees the recipient served. For example, members of the Ways and Means Committee received an average of $35,000 each from the insurance industry PACs in 1988, when the committee was studying tax legislation that was of great concern to the industry. The same center also found that twelve members of the House Banking Committee garnered campaign contributions of more than $100,000 each from finance, insurance, and real estate interests during the 1989–1990 election cycle. (Four received more than $150,000.) Groups associated with finance, insurance, and real estate (such as the American Bankers Association, National Association of Realtors, and Independent Insurance Agents of America) deposited $3.8 million in accounts of members of the Senate Finance Committee; $2.8 million in those of members of the Senate Banking, Housing and Urban Affairs Committee; $3.9 million to members of the House Banking, Finance and Urban Affairs Committee; and $2.8 million to those on the House Ways and Means Committee. Agricultural interests dedicated $2 million to members of the House Agricultural Committee, more than PACs from other fields. And so it goes.

Moreover, it is sad to say, evidence reveals that many members of Congress are quite willing to vote against their stated philosophy when the price is right. Thus conservatives vote for government handouts and liberals for cutting regulations when the lobbies and their PACs line up. A case in point: nineteen senators and representatives well-known for their conservative, laissez-faire, antigovernment-spending positions voted for more government handouts to help PAC-backed interests.

A study by Congress Watch examined three votes: one on the financing of the Alaska pipeline; one on government subsidies for the Clinch River Breeder Reactor; and one that concerned a government subsidy to exporters. Ten members of Congress voted against their free-market position on all three occasions. Nine voted for government handouts on two of the three votes and once against them.

Similarly, Senate Minority Leader Robert Dole's publicity crowns him as a big deficit cutter. But Dole argued forcefully in support of tax incentives for the ethanol-fuel industry that would result in lost federal revenue. Approximately 70 percent of the United States's ethanol is produced by Archer Daniels Midland Company. Donations to the senator's campaigns from the company and individuals associated with it total more than $81,000. The Archer Daniels people also coughed up a generous $185,000 for a foundation that Dole set up.

Robert Hopkins, a former executive of the now defunct Commodore Savings of Dallas, Texas, was sentenced to fifteen years in prison stemming from charges of misadministration of a company-

affiliated PAC. As *The Wall Street Journal* noted about the beneficiaries of his largesse:

> The political ideology of the recipients did not appear to be a
> consideration. Mr. Hopkins contributed to a Dallas mayoral
> campaign because "the city was doing low-cost housing and
> we had some opportunities there." He gave to a campaign
> supported by liberal Jim Wright, because Mr. Wright was in
> line to be the next speaker of the House. A few months later,
> conservative Jack Kemp was beneficiary. "We felt we could
> have an input into Mr. Kemp," Mr. Hopkins told the jury [at
> his trial]. "We felt obviously he would wind up in an influen-
> tial place in the administration, and as it turned out he's sec-
> retary of HUD today, and I thought it was a very well-
> thought-out effort."

• Finally, there are some who maintain that PACs enhance democratic participation. Keith Geiger, president of the National Education Association, argues: "Abolishing PACs would greatly curtail
the political participation of ordinary citizens and once again increase the influence of rich individuals. . . ." But if PACs are abol-
ished, we should also forbid rich individuals from making sizable
campaign contributions by setting a limit of $100 on individuals'
donations to politicians (assuming individual contributions are per-
mitted at all). Moreover, PACs are not exactly organizations of the
poor, near poor, or even working-class Americans. They typically
are organizations of those who can readily spare up to $10,000 (the
contribution limit to a PAC per candidate per election cycle) *and*
whose members are often expected to make additional contributions as individuals.

A New Political Force

Arguments pro and con are sure to continue. Lists other than the
one offered here of reforms that would stem the flood of special-
interest monies into politics may well be drawn up. The main
point, though, is that whatever reforms are called for, *they will not
be advanced until there is a significant new political force, and one that has*

staying power. Public opinion, temporarily mobilized by the media, will not do.

We need first and foremost more citizens who are willing to *study* these matters systematically. Without an understanding of how special interests make their way, and the rationalizations they concoct to justify their corrupting influence, citizens will not be able to respond effectively. Second, once citizens are informed, they must make it their civic duty to *organize others* locally, regionally, and nationally to act on their understanding of what it takes to clean up public life in America.

There are already some organizations that aim in that direction. Common Cause is the main one. Congress Watch, a Ralph Nader group, is another. So is the Center for Responsive Politics. These groups are all on the side of the public interest and champion several of the needed reforms. The agendas of these organizations, especially Common Cause, tend to be carefully honed around drafting, redrafting, and promoting details of reform legislation. These are matters of significance, and citizens who are interested in these matters would do well to contribute time, energy, and funds to these organizations.

Unfortunately, Common Cause and the other organizations, which have been around for many years, have not captured the imagination of the public at large. The reasons are far from evident and may well lie in factors beyond their control. As I see it, what is missing is a broader agenda, one that goes beyond legislative reform and encompasses the deep moral issues at stake. It might also be necessary to find effective ways to communicate the reform message, measures that go beyond mailing flyers and lobbying selected members of Congress and their staffs. The environmental movement dramatized its issues by burying a new car, holding Earth Day demonstrations, and sitting in at nuclear plants. The civil rights movement stirred the nation's conscience through freedom riders, boycotts, and sit-ins in segregated restaurants. The ground for a neoconservative movement was readied by a demonstration by "hard hats" (worn by construction workers) in New York City against hippies and those who dodged the war in Vietnam.

Without such dramatic approaches, it may not be possible in our society to effectively mobilize many groups of citizens into reform movements. In effect, most societies draw on some such devices, from passion plays to mock funerals to guerrilla theater, to involve people. The specific communication tools of the new, progressive, Communitarian movement have yet to be forged. One thing, though, is clear: Books, position papers, and draft legislation are the beginning; the movement needs to move beyond those into the "three-dimensional" world to be fully effective.

In Conclusion

The state of the Union and its member communities call for a massive social movement in support of political change. Reforms will not be won merely by proposing legislation, offering amendments to reform bills, providing expert testimony, and other such inside-the-Beltway measures. Steps must be taken that highlight the nefarious connections between legislatures and the interest groups that all too often control them with campaign contributions. Legislators need to be challenged repeatedly by asking them to account for their payoffs to special interests. Local, regional, and national connections between special interests and legislators can be exposed by citizen commissions of inquiry. Call-in radio shows may be mobilized to oppose private money in public places, just as they were used to roll back the large raises that Congress legislated for itself. Pro-democracy and anti-PAC demonstrations are called for. Teach-ins on the evils of money in public life may be of service.

All this and more is to be undertaken by those members of the community who become aware of the considerable corruptions PACed special interests wreak, until cleaning up public life becomes a focus of a major social movement. This will be a movement whose leadership and cadres will be able to keep millions of Americans focused on, and committed to fighting for, lasting major reforms in local, state, and federal government. Without a major social movement, the reforms required to render public policy responsive to the public at large will not take place. Muckraking mobilizes the people only for a short period of time, after which they inevitably revert to apathy. These periods of public outrage are to be used to introduce lasting changes—above all, to establish arrangements such as much shorter election campaigns, some free media for all candidates, and public finance of election campaigns, which will curb special-interest groups after the public zeal for reform is exhausted. The ultimate goal is to replace a government by and for deep pockets with a political system that is based on the principle of "one person, one vote," one that is responsive to all the members of the community.

In Conclusion

WHAT is Communitarianism?" we are frequently asked. We are a social movement aiming at shoring up the moral, social, and political environment. Part change of heart, part renewal of social bonds, part reform of public life.

Change of heart is the most basic. Without stronger moral voices, public authorities are overburdened and markets don't work. Without moral commitments, people act without any consideration for one another. In recent years too many of us have been reluctant to lay moral claims on one another. It is a mistaken notion that just because we desire to be free from governmental controls we should also be free from responsibilities to the commons, indifferent to the community.

Which values should the renewed moral voices reaffirm? Let's start with those we all share. Nobody seriously maintains that lying is better than truth telling (other than under some rather peculiar circumstances philosophers argue about). Using force to push around other fellow human beings—whether it is a police officer indiscriminately clubbing a civilian who is already shackled or rioters pulling innocent people out of their cars—is something we deem to be unacceptable. Sexual harassment occurs, and although we may disagree about what exactly is encompassed by this term, we all agree that it should be considered morally inappropriate. And so on.

In the fifties we had a well-established society, but it was unfair to women and minorities and a bit authoritarian. In the sixties we undermined the established society and its values. In the eighties we were told that the unbridled pursuit of self-interest was virtuous. By the nineties we have seen the cumulative results. There is now near universal agreement that the resulting world of massive street violence, the failing war against illegal drugs, unbridled greed, and so on—our well-worn list of ills—is not one we wish for our children or, for that matter, ourselves. Where do we turn from here?

To shore up the moral foundations of our society, we start with the family. The family was always entrusted with laying the foundations of moral education. In the renewed communities we envision, raising children is a job not for mothers alone, but for both parents. There is no contradiction between treating women and men as equals and calling for greater attention to, investment in, and, above all, a higher valuation of children.

Second in line are the schools. They are more than places in which people acquire skills and knowledge: they are places in which to acquire—or fail to acquire—education. Education includes the reinforcement of values gained at home and the introduction of values to those children whose parents neglected their character formation and moral upbringing.

Third are the social webs that communities provide, in neighborhoods, at work, and in ethnic clubs and associations, the webs that bind individuals, who would otherwise be on their own, into groups of people who care for one another and who help maintain a civic, social, and moral order. However, for these communities to be able to make their contributions, they themselves need to be shored up. This requires a new respect for the role that institutions, such as local schools, have in sustaining communities. Government needs to refrain from usurping their functions; planners need to make spaces more community-friendly; and all of us need to invest more of ourselves in one another.

Fourth, the national society must ensure that local communities will not lock in values that we, as a more encompassing and overriding community, abhor—such as burning books. And the national society should seek to maintain encompassing bonds that keep the many vying groups from turning hateful and violent toward one another. We can readily accommodate, indeed be enriched, by the cuisines, music, and religious practices of the great variety of subcultures that make up America. But all of these subgroups must subscribe to a set of overarching values: specifically the democratic process, the Constitution and its Bill of Rights, and the commitment to be respectful of one another.

As our moral order is shored up, we need to concern ourselves with the civic order. Individuals' rights are to be matched with social responsibilities. If people want to be tried before juries of their peers, they must be willing to serve on them. If they want elected officials that respond to their values and needs, they must involve themselves in the primaries in which the candidates are chosen. Voting is not enough. They will also have to dedicate more time and energy to participating in local politics and institutions, from the community hospital to the local school board.

We need to remind one another that no rights are absolute. Even the freedom of speech, we all know, is refused to people who shout fire in a crowded theater, unless there is a fire. Testing those who have the lives of others directly in their hands for drugs, setting up sobriety checkpoints to stop murderous drunk drivers, and asking people whose blood is being tested to allow it to be checked for the HIV virus are all reasonable responses to new massive threats we must deal with in order to make the society work again.

Finally, complaining about special interests is not good enough. Don't get mad; get going. Special interests must be countered, and their money bags must be kept from corrupting our elected officials. The political energy required to reform the political system and restore the public interest to the central place it belongs cannot come from anywhere but aggrieved citizens banding together to clean up politics.

During a dinner discussion of the Communitarian agenda, Dr. Joan W. Konner, dean of the School of Journalism at Columbia University, puzzled over Communitarianism. "It appeared to be one part church sermon, one part reassertion of old values, one part political campaign, and one part social movement," she said. I could not have put it better myself. Our agenda, by necessity, is as complex and encompassing as the problems we face: beware of politicians promising simple solutions. We aim to change values, to alter mind-sets, and to promote public policy that serves the commons.

As encompassing as the new Communitarian agenda is, it requires much experimentation and elaboration. This book is only a preliminary exploration of its ideas and practicalities. Above all, the agenda requires more good people and leaders who will join with one another to further develop the messages and form the social movement without which no basic change of direction is possible.

We do not have all the answers. But we are engaged in a genuine, shared undertaking. Many of these answers must evolve out of the give and take among those who make the Communitarian movement their social, civic, and moral home. It is, I assure you, a mighty fine place to start. May we hear from you?

The Responsive Communitarian Platform: Rights and Responsibilities

The Communitarian platform was first drafted by the author. It was extensively rewritten, edited, and modified by Mary Ann Glendon and William Galston, and significant new segments were added. It was sent to a large number of colleagues for comments and revised accordingly. Seventy leading Americans endorsed it, including both conservatives and liberals. The platform was issued on November 18, 1991. Additional Communitarian position papers are being issued. For more information, contact:

> *The Communitarian Network: Gelman Library, 2130 H Street NW, Suite 714J, Washington, D.C. 20052. 202-994-7997.*

> *The only Communitarian quarterly:* The Responsive Community: Rights and Responsibilities. *1-800-245-7460.*
> *Or write* The Responsive Community, *2020 Pennsylvania Avenue NW, Suite 282, Washington, D.C. 20006.*

Preamble

AMERICAN men, women, and children are members of many communities—families; neighborhoods; innumerable social, religious, ethnic, workplace, and professional associations; and the body politic itself. Neither human existence nor individual liberty can be sustained for long outside the interdependent and overlapping communities to which all of us belong. Nor can any community long survive unless its members dedicate some of their attention, energy, and resources to shared projects. The exclusive pursuit of private interest erodes the network of social environments on which we all depend and is destructive to our shared experiment in democratic self-government. For these reasons, we hold that the rights of individuals cannot long be preserved without a Communitarian perspective.

A Communitarian perspective recognizes both individual human dignity and the social dimension of human existence.

A Communitarian perspective recognizes that the preservation of individual liberty depends on the active maintenance of the institutions of civil society where citizens learn respect for others as well as self-respect; where we acquire a lively sense of our personal and civic responsibilities, along with an appreciation of our own rights and the rights of others; where we develop the skills of self-government as well as the habit of governing ourselves and learn to serve others—not just self.

A Communitarian perspective recognizes that communities and polities, too, have obligations—including the duty to be responsive to their members and to foster participation and deliberation in social and political life.

A Communitarian perspective does not dictate particular policies. Rather, it mandates attention to what is often ignored in contemporary policy debates: the social side of human nature; the responsibilities that must be borne by citizens, individually and collectively, in a regime of rights; the fragile ecology of families and their supporting communities; the ripple effects and long-term consequences of present decisions. The political views of the signers of this statement differ widely. We are united, however, in our conviction that a Communitarian perspective must be brought to bear on the great moral, legal, and social issues of our time.

Moral Voices

America's diverse communities of memory and mutual aid are rich resources of moral voices—voices that ought to be heeded in a society that increasingly threatens to become normless, self-centered, and driven by greed, special interests, and an unabashed quest for power.

Moral voices achieve their effect mainly through education and persuasion, rather than through coercion. Originating in communities, and sometimes embodied in law, they exhort, admonish, and appeal to what Lincoln called the better angels of our nature. They speak to our capacity for reasoned judgment and virtuous action. It is precisely because this important moral realm, which is neither one of random individual choice nor of government control, has been much neglected that we see an urgent need for a Communitarian social movement to accord these voices their essential place.

Within History

The basic Communitarian quest for balances between individuals and groups, rights and responsibilities, and among the institutions of state, market, and civil society is a constant, ongoing enterprise. Because this quest takes place within history and within varying social contexts, however, the evaluation of what is a proper moral stance will vary according to circumstances of time and place. If we were in China today, we would argue vigorously for more individual rights; in contemporary America, we emphasize individual and social responsibilities.

Not Majoritarian but Strongly Democratic

Communitarians are not majoritarians. The success of the democratic experiment in ordered liberty (rather than unlimited license) depends not on fiat or force, but on building shared values, habits and practices that assure respect for one another's rights and regular fulfillment of personal, civic, and collective responsibilities. Successful policies are accepted because they are recognized to be legitimate, rather than imposed. We say to those who would impose civic or moral virtues by suppressing dissent (in the name of religion, patriotism, or any other cause), or censoring books, that their cure is ineffective, harmful, and morally untenable. At the same time divergent moral positions need not lead to cacophony. Out of genuine dialogue clear voices can arise, and shared aspirations can be identified and advanced.

Communitarians favor strong democracy. That is, we seek to make government more representative, more participatory, and more responsive to all members of the community. We seek to find ways to accord citizens more information and more say, more often. We seek to curb the role of private money, special interests, and corruption in government. Similarly, we ask how "private governments," whether corporations, labor unions, or voluntary associations, can become more responsive to their members and to the needs of the community.

Communitarians do not exalt the group as such, nor do they hold that any set of group values is *ipso facto* good merely because such values originate in a community. Indeed, some communities (say, neo-Nazis) may foster reprehensible values. Moreover, communities that glorify their own members by vilifying those who do not belong are at best imperfect. Communitarians recognize—indeed, insist—that communal values must be judged by external and overriding criteria, based on shared human experience.

A responsive community is one whose moral standards reflect

the basic human needs of all its members. To the extent that these needs compete with one another, the community's standards reflect the relative priority accorded by members to some needs over others. Although individuals differ in their needs, human nature is not totally malleable. Although individuals are deeply influenced by their communities, they have a capacity for independent judgment. The persistence of humane and democratic culture, as well as individual dissent, in Eastern Europe and the Soviet Union demonstrate the limits of social indoctrination.

For a community to be truly responsive—not only to an elite group, a minority, or even the majority, but to all its members and all their basic human needs—it will have to develop moral values which meet the following criteria: they must be nondiscriminatory and applied equally to all members; they must be generalizable, justified in terms that are accessible and understandable: e.g., instead of claims based upon individual or group desires, citizens would draw on a common definition of justice; and they must incorporate the full range of legitimate needs and values rather than focusing on any one category, be it individualism, autonomy, interpersonal caring, or social justice.

Restoring the Moral Voice

History has taught that it is a grave mistake to look to a charismatic leader to define and provide a moral voice for the polity. Nor can political institutions effectively embody moral voices unless they are sustained and criticized by an active citizenry concerned about the moral direction of the community. To rebuild America's moral foundations, to bring our regard for individuals and their rights into a better relationship with our sense of personal and collective responsibility, we must therefore begin with the institutions of civil society.

Start with the Family

The best place to start is where each new generation acquires its moral anchoring: at home, in the family. We must insist once again that bringing children into the world entails a moral responsibility to provide not only material necessities, but also moral education and character formation.

Moral education is not a task that can be delegated to baby-sitters, or even professional child care centers. It requires close bonding of the kind that typically is formed only with parents, if it is formed at all.

Fathers and mothers consumed by "making it" and consumerism, or preoccupied with personal advancement, who come home too late and too tired to attend to the needs of their children, cannot discharge their most elementary duty to their children and their fellow citizens.

It follows, that *workplaces should provide* maximum flexible opportunities to parents to preserve an important part of their time and energy, of their life, to attend to their educational-moral duties, for the sake of the next generation, its civic and moral character, and its capacity to contribute economically and socially to the commonweal. Experiments such as those with unpaid and paid parental leave, flextime, shared jobs, opportunities to work at home, and for parents to participate as volunteers and managers in child care centers should be extended and encouraged.

Above all, what we need is a *change in orientation* by both parents and workplaces. Child raising is important, valuable work, work that must be honored rather than denigrated by both parents and the community.

Families headed by single parents experience particular difficulties. Some single parents struggle bravely and succeed in attending to the moral education of their children while some married couples shamefully neglect their moral duties toward their offspring. However, the weight of the historical, sociological, and psychological evidence suggests that on average *two-parent families are better able to discharge their child-raising duties* if only because there are more hands—and voices—available for the task. Indeed, couples often do better when they are further backed up by a wider circle of relatives. The issue has been wrongly framed when one asks what portion of parental duties grandparents or other helpers can assume. Their assistance is needed in addition to, not as a substitute for, parental care. Child-raising is by nature labor-intensive. There are no labor-saving technologies, and shortcuts in this area produce woefully deficient human beings, to their detriment and ours.

It follows that *widespread divorce*, when there are children involved, especially when they are in their formative years, is indicative of a serious social problem. Though divorces are necessary in some situations, many are avoidable and are *not in the interest of the children,* the community, and probably not of most adults either. Divorce laws should be modified, not to prevent divorce, but to signal society's concern.

Above all, we should cancel the message that divorce puts an end to responsibilities among members of a child-raising family. And the best way cancel that message is to reform the economic aspects of divorce laws so that the enormous financial burden of marriage dissolution no longer falls primarily on minor children and those parents who are their principal caretakers. Just as we recognized in the 1960s that it was unjust to apply to consumers laws that were fashioned for the dealings of merchants with one another, we must now acknowledge that it is a mistake to handle divorces involving couples with young children with a set of rules that was tailored mainly to the needs and desires of warring husbands and wives alone. The principle of "children first" should be made fundamental to property settlements and support awards.

Schools—the Second Line of Defense

Unfortunately, millions of American families have weakened to the point where their capacity to provide moral education is gravely impaired. And the fact is that communities have only a limited say over what families do. At best it will take years before a change in the moral climate restores parenting to its proper status and function for many Americans.

Thus, by default, schools now play a major role, for better or worse, in character formation and moral education. Personal and communal responsibility come together here, for education requires the commitment of all citizens, not merely those who have children in school.

We strongly urge that all educational institutions, from kindergartens to universities, recognize and take seriously the grave responsibility to provide moral education. Suggestions that schools participate actively in moral education are often opposed. The specter of religious indoctrination is quickly evoked, and the question is posed: "Whose morals are you going to teach?"

Our response is straightforward: *We ought to teach those values Americans share,* for example, that the dignity of all persons ought to be respected, that tolerance is a virtue and discrimination abhorrent, that peaceful resolution of conflicts is superior to violence, that generally truth telling is morally superior to lying, that democratic government is morally superior to totalitarianism and authoritarianism, that one ought to give a day's work for a day's pay, that saving for one's own and one's country's future is better than squandering one's income and relying on others to attend to one's future needs.

The fear that our children will be "brainwashed" by a few educators is farfetched. On the contrary, to silence the schools in moral matters simply means that the youngsters are left exposed to all other voices and values but those of their educators. For, one way or another, moral education does take place in schools. The only question is whether schools and teachers will passively stand by or take an active and responsible role.

Let us note that moral education takes place least in classroom lectures (although these have a place) and is only in a limited measure a matter of developing moral reasoning. To a much greater extent, moral education is fostered through personal example and above all through fostering the proper institutional culture—from corridors and cafeteria to the parking lot and sports. In effect, the whole school should be considered as a set of experiences generating situations in which young people learn the values either of civility, sharing, and responsibility to the common good or of cheating, cutthroat competition, and total self-absorption.

Education must be reorganized to achieve a better integration between work and schooling. Educators need to search for ways to connect schooling with activities that make sense to young people; and the many businesses who employ high school students part-time ought to recognize that they are educators too. These early work experiences will either reinforce responsible habits and attitudes, or will serve as lessons in poor civics and deficient work ethics.

Within Communities

A Matter of Orientation

The ancient Greeks understood this well: a person who is completely private is lost to civic life. The exclusive pursuit of one's self-interest is not even a good prescription for conduct in the marketplace; for no social, political, economic, or moral order can survive that way. Some measure of caring, sharing, and *being our brother's and sister's keeper,* is essential if we are not all to fall back on an ever more expansive government, bureaucratized welfare agencies, and swollen regulations, police, courts, and jails.

Generally, no social task should be assigned to an institution that is larger than necessary to do the job. What can be done by families should not be assigned to an intermediate group—school, etc. What can be done at the local level should not be passed on to the state or federal level, and so on. There are, of course, plenty of urgent tasks—environmental ones—that do require national and even international action. But to remove tasks to higher levels than is necessary weakens the constituent communities. This principle holds for duties of attending to the sick, troubled, delinquent, homeless, and new immigrants; and for public safety, public health and protection of the environment—from a neighborhood crime-watch to CPR to sorting the garbage. The government should step in only to the extent that other social subsystems fail, rather than seek to replace them.

At the same time vulnerable communities should be able to draw on the more endowed communities when they are truly unable to deal, on their own, with social duties thrust upon them.

Many social goals, moreover, require partnership between public and private groups. Though government should not seek to replace local communities, it may need to empower them by strategies of support, including revenue-sharing and technical assistance. There is a great need for study and experimentation with creative use of the structures of civil society and public-private cooperation, especially where the delivery of health, educational and social services are concerned.

Last, but not least, we should not hesitate to speak up and express our moral concerns to others when it comes to issues we care about deeply and share with one another. It might be debatable whether or not we should encourage our neighbors to keep their lawns green (which may well be environmentally unsound), but there should be little doubt that we should expect one another to attend to our children and vulnerable community members. Those who neglect these duties should be explicitly considered poor members of the community.

National and local service, as well as volunteer work, is desirable to build and express a civil commitment. Such activities, bringing together people from different backgrounds and enabling and encouraging them to work together, build community and foster mutual respect and tolerance.

Americans should *foster a spirit of reconciliation*. When conflicts do arise, we should seek the least destructive means of resolving them. Adversarial litigation is often not the optimal way; mediation and arbitration are often superior. We should favor settlements that are fair and conciliatory even if we have to absorb some losses. Going for the last ounce of flesh is incompatible with community spirit. (It is said that marriage works better when each side is willing to give 75 percent and expect 25 percent, rather than each give 50 percent and expect 50 percent. The same holds for other close relations.)

We should *treat one another with respect* and recognize our basic equality, not just before the law, but also as moral agents.

Duties to the Polity

Being informed about public affairs is a prerequisite for keeping the polity from being controlled by demagogues, for taking action when needed in one's own interests and that of others, for achieving justice and the shared future.

Voting is one tool for keeping the polity reflective of its constituent communities. Those who feel that none of the candidates reflect their views ought to seek out other like-minded citizens and seek to field their own candidate rather than retreat from the polity. Still, some persons may discharge their community responsibilities by being involved in non-political activities, say, in volunteer work. Just as the polity is but one facet of interdependent social life, so voting and political activity are not the only ways to be responsible members of society. A good citizen is involved in a community or communities but not necessarily active in the polity.

Paying one's taxes, encouraging others to pay their fair share, and *serving on juries* are fully obligatory. One of the most telling ills of our time is the expectation of many Americans that they are entitled to ever more public services without paying for them (as reflected in public opinion polls that show demands to slash government and taxes but also to expand practically every conceivable government function). We all take for granted the right to be tried before a jury of our peers, but all too often we are unwilling to serve on juries ourselves.

Cleaning up the Polity

We need to revitalize public life so that the two-thirds of our citizens who now say they feel alienated or that the polity is not theirs will again be engaged in it.

Campaign contributions to members of Congress and state legislatures, speaking fees, and bribes have become so pervasive that in many areas of public policy and on numerous occasions the public interest is ignored as legislators pay off their debts to special interests. Detailed rationalizations have been spun to justify the system. It is said that giving money to politicians is a form of democratic participation. In fact, the rich can "participate" in this way so much more effectively than the poor that the democratic principle of "one person, one vote" is severely compromised. It is said that money buys only access to the politician's ear; but even if money does not buy commitment, access should not be allotted according to the depth of one's pockets. It is said that every group has its pool of money, and hence as they all grease Congress, all Americans are served. But those who cannot grease at all or not as well lose out, and so do long-run public goals that are not underwritten by any particular interest groups.

To establish conditions under which elected officials will be able to respond to the public interest, to the genuine needs of all citizens, and to their own consciences requires that the role of private money in public life be reduced as much as possible. All candidates should receive some public support, as presidential candidates already do, as well as some access to radio and TV.

To achieve this major renewal and revitalization of public life, to reinstitute the prerequisites for attending to the public interest, *requires a major social movement,* akin to the Progressive movement of the beginning of the century. For even good causes can become special interests if they are not part of such a movement, keeping their strategies and aims in constant dialogue with larger aims and multiple ends. Citizens who care about the integrity of the polity either on the local, state, or national level should band with their fellows to form a neo-progressive Communitarian movement. They should persevere until elected officials are beholden—not to special interests—but only to the voters and to their own consciences.

Freedom of Speech

The First Amendment is as dear to Communitarians as it is to libertarians and many other Americans. Suggestions that it should be curbed to bar verbal expressions of racism, sexism, and other slurs seem to us to endanger the essence of the First Amendment, which is most needed when what some people say is disconcerting to some others. However, one should not ignore the victims of such abuse. Whenever individuals or members of a group are harassed, many *non-legal measures* are appropriate to express disapproval of hateful expressions and to promote tolerance among the members of the polity. For example, a college campus faced with a rash of incidents indicating bigotry may conduct a teach-in on intergroup understanding. This, and much more, can be done without compromising the First Amendment.

Rights vs. Rightness

The language of rights is morally incomplete. To say that "I have a right to do X" is not to conclude that "X is the right thing for me to do." One may, for example, have a First Amendment right to address others in a morally inappropriate manner. Say one tells a Jew that "Hitler should have finished you all," or a black, "nigger go back to Africa," or worse. Rights give reasons to others not to coercively interfere with the speaker in the performance of protected acts; however, they do not in themselves give me a sufficient reason to perform these acts. There is a gap between rights and rightness that cannot be closed without a richer moral vocabulary—one that invokes principles of decency, duty, responsibility, and the common good, among others.

Social Justice

At the heart of the Communitarian understanding of social justice is the idea of reciprocity: each member of the community owes something to all the rest, and the community owes something to each of its members. Justice requires responsible individuals in a responsive community.

Members of the community have a responsibility, to the greatest extent possible, to provide for themselves and their families: honorable work contributes to the commonwealth and to the community's ability to fulfill its essential tasks. Beyond self-support, individuals have a responsibility for the material and moral well-being of others. This does not mean heroic self-sacrifice; it means the constant self-awareness that no one of us is an island unaffected by the fate of others.

For its part, the community is responsible for protecting each of us against catastrophe, natural or man-made; for ensuring the basic needs of all who genuinely cannot provide for themselves; for appropriately recognizing the distinctive contributions of individuals to the community; and for safeguarding a zone within which individuals may define their own lives through free exchange and choice.

Communitarian social justice is alive both to the equal moral dignity of all individuals and to the ways in which they differentiate themselves from one another through their personal decisions.

Public Safety and Public Health

The American moral and legal tradition has always acknowledged the need to balance individual rights with the need to protect the safety and health of the public. The Fourth Amendment, for example, guards against unreasonable searches but allows for reasonable ones.

Thus, while people with AIDS must be vigilantly protected from invasions of their privacy and from job and housing discrimination, the community must be allowed to take effective measures to curb the spread of the disease. Although drug dealers' civil rights must be observed, the community must be provided with constitutional tools that will prevent dealers from dominating streets, parks, indeed, whole neighborhoods. Although high school students must be protected against wanton expulsion, places of learning must be able to maintain the social-moral climate that education requires.

We differ with the ACLU and other radical libertarians who oppose sobriety checkpoints, screening gates at airports, drug and alcohol testing for people who directly affect public safety (pilots, train engineers, etc.). Given the minimal intrusion involved (an average sobriety checkpoint lasts ninety seconds), the importance of the interests at stake (we have lost more lives, many due to drunken drivers, on the road each year than in the war in Vietnam), and the fact that such measures in the past have not led us down a slippery slope, these and similar reasonable measures should receive full public support.

There is little sense in gun registration. What we need to significantly enhance public safety is *domestic disarmament* of the kind that exists in practically all democracies. The National Rifle Association suggestion that "criminals not guns kill people" ignores the fact that thousands are killed each year, many of them children, from accidental discharge of guns, and that people—whether criminal, insane, or temporarily carried away by impulse—kill and are much more likely to do so when armed than when disarmed. The Second Amendment, behind which NRA hides, is subject to a variety of interpretations, but the Supreme Court has repeatedly ruled, for over a hundred years, that it does not prevent laws that bar guns. *We join with those who read the Second Amendment the way it was written, as a Communitarian clause, calling for community militias, not individual gunslingers.*

When it comes to public health, people who carry sexually transmitted diseases, especially when the illness is nearly always fatal, such as AIDS, should be expected to disclose their illness to previous sexual contacts or help health authorities to inform them, to warn all prospective sexual contacts, and to inform all health care personnel with whom they come in contact. It is their contribution to help stem the epidemic. At the same time, the carriers' rights against wanton violation of privacy, discrimination in housing, employment, and insurance, should be scrupulously protected.

The Human Community

Our Communitarianism is not particularism. We believe that the responsive community is the best form of human organization yet devised for respecting human dignity and safeguarding human decency and the way of life most open to needed self-revision through shared deliberation. We believe that the human species as a whole would be well served by the movement, as circumstances permit, of all polities toward strongly democratic communities. We are acutely aware of the ways in which this movement will be (and ought to be) affected by important material, cultural, and political

differences among nations and peoples. And we know that enduring responsive communities cannot be created through fiat or coercion, but only through genuine public conviction.

We are heartened by the widespread invocation of democratic
principles by the nations and peoples now emerging from generations of repression; we see the institutionalization of these principles
as the best possible bulwark against the excesses of ethnic and national particularism that could well produce new forms of repression.

While it may seem utopian, we believe that in the multiplication
of strongly democratic communities around the world lies our best
hope for the emergence of a global community that can deal con-
certedly with matters of general concern to our species as a whole:
with war and strife, with violations of basic rights, with environmental degradation, and with the extreme material deprivation that
stunts the bodies, minds, and spirits of children. *Our Communitarian
concern may begin with ourselves and our families, but it rises inexorably
to the long-imagined community of humankind.*

In Conclusion

A Question of Responsibility

Although some of the responsibilities identified in this manifesto are expressed in legal terms, and the law does play a significant
role not only in regulating society, but also in indicating which
values it holds dear, our first and foremost purpose is to *affirm the
moral commitments of parents, young persons, neighbors, and citizens,* to
affirm the importance of the communities within which such commitments take shape and are transmitted from one generation to the
next. This is not primarily a legal matter. On the contrary, when a
community reaches the point at which these responsibilities are
largely enforced by the powers of the state, it is in deep moral crisis.
If communities are to function well, most members most of the
time must discharge their responsibilities because they are committed to do so, not because they fear lawsuits, penalties, or jails.
Nevertheless, the state and its agencies must take care not to harm
the structures of civil society on which we all depend. *Social environments, like natural environments, cannot be taken for granted.*

It has been argued by libertarians that responsibilities are a personal matter, that individuals are to judge which responsibilities they accept as theirs. As we see it, responsibilities are anchored in community. Reflecting the diverse moral voices of their citizens, responsive communities define what is expected of people; they educate their members to accept these values; and they praise them when they do and frown upon them when they do not. While the ultimate foundation of morality may be commitments of individual conscience, it is communities that help introduce and sustain these commitments. Hence the urgent need for communities to articulate the responsibilities they expect their members to discharge, especially in times, such as our own, in which the understanding of these responsibilities has weakened and their reach has grown unclear.

Further Work

This is only a beginning. This platform is but a point in dialogue, part of an ongoing process of deliberation. It should be viewed not as a series of final conclusions, but as ideas for additional discussion. We do not claim to have the answers to all that troubles America these days. However, we are heartened by the groundswell of support that our initial efforts have brought to the Communitarian perspective. If more and more Americans come forward and join together to form active communities that seek to reinvigorate the moral and social order, we will be able to deal better with many of our communities' problems while reducing our reliance on governmental regulation, controls, and force. We will have a greater opportunity to work out shared public policy based on broad consensus and shared moral and legal traditions. And we will have many more ways to make our society a place in which individual rights are vigilantly maintained, while the seedbeds of civic virtue are patiently nurtured.

Notes

Introduction: A New Moral, Social, Public Order—Without Puritanism or Oppression

3   study on juries and young people: Morris Janowitz, *The Reconstruction of Patriotism: Education for Civic Consciousness* (Chicago: The University of Chicago Press, 1983), 8.

3   young people have learned only half the story: *Democracy's Next Generation* (Washington, D.C.: People for the American Way, 1989), 27.

3   one in eight feels voting is included in what makes a good citizen: ibid., 74 (text), 153 (poll result).

3–4   what makes the United States special: ibid., 68 and 69.

4   mismatch of rights and responsibilities: Lawrence Friedman, *The Republic of Choice* (Cambridge, Mass.: Harvard University Press, 1990).

5   incessant issuance of new rights devalues moral claims: Richard E. Morgan, *Disabling America: The "Rights Industry" in Our Time* (New York: Basic Books, 1984).

5   survey on rights vs. privileges: Roper Organization (Roper Reports 91–3), 123.

5   comment by president of the U.S. Students Association: Tajel Shah, "Make Access to Higher Education a Right," *USA Today*, March 23, 1991, A9.

5   Santa Monica restricts crossover use of public bathrooms: Robert Reinhold, "In Land of Liberals, Restroom Rights are Rolled Back," *The New York Times,* November 15, 1991, A14.

5   San Quentin death-row inmates sue for right to procreate by artificial insemination: Daniel Seligman, "Keeping Up," *Fortune,* February 10, 1992, 145.

5–6   mother sues school district: Ronald Sullivan, "Mother Scolded for Suit over Son's Honors," *The New York Times,* November 23, 1991, 28.

6   American Bankers Association ad: *The Washington Post,* November 17, 1991, A13.

6–7   "rights talk polarizes debate": John Leo, "The Lingo of Entitlement," *U.S. News & World Report,* October 14, 1991, 22.

7   as rights talk penetrates society, impoverishment and confrontation follow: Mary Ann Glendon, *Rights Talk: The Impoverishment of Political Discourse* (New York: The Free Press, 1991).

7   rights often "masquerade as reasons": Cass R. Sunstein, *The New Republic,* September 2, 1991, 34.

7   Glendon shows many rights are treated the way we treat property: *Rights Talk,* chapter 2.

8   libertarians apply the no government idea to narcotics: for example, see James Ostrowski, "Thinking about Drug Legalization," in David Boaz, *The Crisis in Drug Prohibition* (Washington, D.C.: Cato Institute, 1990).

8   "it is no answer that streams and forest cannot speak": Christopher D. Stone, *Should Trees Have Standing?* (Los Altos, CA: William Kaufman, 1974), 17.

9   sand has rights: Katherine E. Stone and Benjamin Kaufman, "Sand Rights: A Legal System to Protect the 'Shores of the Sea,'" *Shore and Beach,* 56(July 1988): 8–14.

9   "no obligations . . . except to avoid the infliction of harm": Glendon, *Rights Talk,* 77.

10   "find in the Declaration of Independence or Bill of Rights . . .": ibid., 13.

11   ACLU opposes sobriety checkpoints: "Drunk Driving Road-blocks," Policy #217, American Civil Liberties Union.

12   Friedan: *The Feminine Mystique* (New York: Norton, 1962) and *The Second Stage* (New York: Summit Books, 1981).

12   Harrington: *The Other America* (New York: Macmillan, 1962).

13   statistics on confidence in leaders: "If You Think Congress' Popularity Is Low Now . . ." in *USA Today*, April 1, 1992, 11A. See also Seymour Martin Lipset and William Schneider, *The Confidence Gap: Business, Labor and Government in the Public Mind* (New York: The Free Press, 1983), chapter 2 (especially table 2-1).

13   *New York Times* story on Columbus: James Barron, "What Did Columbus Do to Deserve a Big Parade?" *The New York Times*, October 15, 1991, B1.

16   *BusinessWeek* on communitarianism: Elizabeth Ehrlich, "Your Rights vs. My Safety: Where Do We Draw the Line?" *BusinessWeek*, September 3, 1990, 56.

16   *Washington Post* on communitarianism: Spencer C. Rich, "Balancing Community and Individual Rights," *The Washington Post*, December 25, 1990, A17.

17   Leo on communitarianism: John Leo, "Community and Personal Duty," *U.S. News & World Report*, January 28, 1991, 17.

17   *Chronicle of Higher Education* on communitarianism: Denise K. Magner, "Probing the Imbalance Between Individual Rights, Community Needs," *Chronicle of Higher Education*, February 13, 1991, A3.

17   *Time* on communitarianism: Walter Shapiro, "A Whole Greater Than Its Parts?" *Time*, February 25, 1991, 71.

Chapter 1: The Moral Voice

24   mention of how an economy may thrive, but not necessarily: Amitai Etzioni, *The Moral Dimension* (New York: Free Press, 1988).

24   "habits of the heart": Robert N. Bellah, Richard Madsen, William M. Sullivan, Ann Swidler, and Steven M. Tipton, *Habits of the Heart* (Berkeley: University of California Press, 1985); Alexis de Tocqueville

(George Lawrence, trans.; J. P. Mayer, ed.), *Democracy in America* (New York: Anchor Books, 1969), 287.

26–27   for a fuller discussion of the I and we paradigm: Etzioni, *Moral Dimension.*

27   statistic on teens losing their virginity by age thirteen: James Patterson and Peter Kim, *The Day America Told the Truth* (New York: Prentice-Hall Press, 1991), 103.

27   statistics on Americans' self-reporting: ibid., 66, 155.

28   statistics on Americans' view of politics and politicians: "Trust in Government," *The Washington Post,* November 3, 1991, A17.

28   "den of thieves": James B. Stewart, *Den of Thieves* (New York: Simon & Schuster, 1991); money culture: Michael Lewis, *The Money Culture* (New York: Norton, 1991).

29   less discrimination now than thirty years ago: Daniel Yankelovich, "The Affluence Effect," unpublished paper presented at Brookings Institution seminar on values, 1991.

31   Gardner: John Gardner, *Building Community* (Washington, D.C.: Independent Sector, 1991), 5.

33   it is well established that working-class communities uphold their values: for example, see Jim Sleeper, *The Closest of Strangers: Liberalism and the Politics of Race in New York* (New York: W. W. Norton & Company, 1990).

34–35   "high-profile group of ethicists" quote from seminar: private communication with the author.

35   Baumgartner: M. P. Baumgartner, *The Moral Order of a Suburb* (New York: Oxford University Press, 1988), 10–11 passim.

35   bone-marrow transplants: from a conference in Paris of the Council for International Organizations of Medical Sciences, a creation of WHO and UNESCO, 1972.

38   Georgetown Law student's quote: Saundra Torry, "Affirmative Action a Flash Point at GU," *The Washington Post,* April 17, 1991, D1.

38   Stanley Fish's remarks: Transcript, "The MacNeil/Lehrer News-

Hour," June 19, 1991, 10 (from Jonathan Rauch, *Kindly Inquisitors: The New Attacks on Free Thought* [Chicago: The University of Chicago Press, 1993]).

40 *Time* magazine cover story: John Elson, "Busybodies: The New Puritans," *Time*, August 12, 1991, 20.

40–41 *The Economist* editorial: "From There to Intolerance," *The Economist*, July 20, 1991, 15–16.

41 Richard Rabinowitz of the American History Workshop points out that Puritans were full of zest of life; it was the Victorians who saw deadly sins in lust and gluttony: Transcript, "All Things Considered," National Public Radio, January 29, 1992, 10.

41 *The Crucible:* Arthur Miller, *The Crucible* (New York: Bantam Books, 1953).

42 *The Naked Maja:* Quoted by Nat Hentoff in *The Washington Post,* January 11, 1992, A19.

42–43 *Economist* comment on California kissing: "From There to Intolerance," 15.

43 *Economist* comment on "if you lose your job . . .": ibid.

44 security guard at *Los Angeles Times:* Elson, "Busybodies," 20.

44 Janice Bone: Zachary Schiller, Walecia Konrad, and Stephanie Anderson Forest, "If You Light up on Sunday, Don't Come in on Monday," *BusinessWeek,* August 26, 1991, 68.

44–45 studies on alcohol impairment: Jack G. Modell and James M. Mountz, "Drinking and Flying—The Problem of Alcohol Use by Pilots," *New England Journal of Medicine* 323(7): 455–461.

46 employee restrictions in North Miami and Atlanta and at Fortunoff's: Paula Span, "Now There's a New Hazard for Smokers: Unemployment," *The Washington Post,* November 12, 1991, A1.

46 Best Lock, Turner, U-Haul, Texas Instruments health restrictions: Schiller, Konrad, and Forest, "If You Light up on Sunday," 68, 69.

47 *The Economist* editorial: "From There to Intolerance," 15–16.

47   Glasser's letter: "Mushy Thinking on Individual Rights," letter to the editor in *The Wall Street Journal*, November 1, 1991, A15.

47   Glendon's "At the very least . . . ," quote: *Rights Talk*, 104.

48   studies on divorce: Bryce J. Christensen, "Taking Stock: Assessing Twenty Years of 'No Fault' Divorce," *The Family in America* 5(September 1991): 1–10; and Lenore Weitzman, *The Divorce Revolution: The Unexpected Social and Economic Consequences for Women and Children in America* (New York: The Free Press, 1985).

49   Glasser interview in *BusinessWeek*: Elizabeth Ehrlich, "Your Rights vs. My Safety: Where Do We Draw the Line?" *BusinessWeek*, September 3, 1990, 56.

50   Machan's "Communitarians wish to place . . ." quote: Tibor Machan, "The Communitarian Manifesto," *The Orange County Register*, May 12, 1991.

51   about 130 universities have speech codes: Mayerene Baker, "University Divided over Proposal for Speech Code," *Los Angeles Times*, May 16, 1991, B3.

51   objections to campus restrictions on free speech: Arthur Schlesinger, Jr., *The Disuniting of America: Reflections on a Multicultural Society* (Whittle Direct Books, 1991); and Dinesh D'Souza, *Illiberal Education: The Politics of Race and Sex on Campus* (New York: The Free Press, 1991).

52   Orr-Cahall resignation: Barbara Gamarekian, "Corcoran Said to Select Interim Chief," *New York Times*, January 27, 1990, 16.

52   for a discussion of the Mapplethorpe case, see Robin Cembalest, "The Obscenity Trial," *ArtNews* 89(December 1990): 136–41.

Chapter 2: The Communitarian Family

54   for an important overview of family issues, see: David Blankenhorn, Steven Bayme, and Jean Bethke Elshtain, *Rebuilding the Nest: A New Commitment to the American Family* (Milwauke, Wisc.: Family Service American, Inc., 1990).

55   Urie Bronfenbrenner says basic medical services are not enough: Urie Bronfenbrenner, "What Do Families Do?" *Family Affairs* 4(Winter/Spring 1991): 1.

55–56   two-thirds of mothers with children under eighteen are in the labor force: *Current Population Survey,* Bureau of Labor Statistics, unpublished tabulations, 1991.

57   Barbara Dafoe Whitehead says no such thing as a one-minute parent: Barbara Whithead, "The New Politics in Action—Fortifying the Family," presentation at the conference "Left and Right: The Emergence of a New Politics in the 1990s?" sponsored by the Heritage Foundation and the Progressive Foundation, October 30, 1991 Washington, D.C. (See transcript, 25.)

57   child care workers in the lowest tenth percentile for income: Richard T. Gill, Nathan Glazer, Stephen A. Thernstrom, *Our Changing Population* (Englewood Cliffs, NJ: Prentice-Hall, 1992), 278.

57   child care workers average salary: *Who Cares? Child Care and the Quality of Care in America* (Oakland, CA: Child Care Employee Project, 1989), 49.

57   Zigler says child care workers are treated like zoo keepers: Kenneth Labich, "Can Your Career Hurt Your Kids?" *Fortune,* May 20, 1991, 49.

58   children strapped into car seats all day: ibid., 49.

59   several bodies of data showing that institutionalized children become maladjusted adults: N. Baydar and Jeanne Brooks-Gunn, "Effects of Maternal Employment and Child Care Arrangements on Preschoolers' Cognitive and Behavioral Outcomes: Evidence from the Children of the National Longitudinal Survey of Youth," *Developmental Psychology* 27(November 1991): 932–946. J. Belsky and Michael J. Rovine, "Nonmaternal Care in the First Year of Life and the Security of Infant-Parent Attachment," *Child Development* 59(February 1988): 157–167. T. B. Brazelton, "Issues for Working Parents," *American Journal of Orthopsychiatry* 56(1986): 14–25. J. Belsky and D. Eggebeen, "Early and Extensive Maternal Employment in Young Children's Socioemotional Development: Children of the National Longitudinal Survey of Youth," *Journal of Marriage and Family* 53(November 1991) 1083–1110. B. E. Vaughn, K. E. Deane, and E. Waters, "The Impact of Out-of-Home Care on Child-Mother Attachment Quality: Another Look at Some Enduring Questions," pages 1–2 in I. Bretherton and E. Water, eds., *Growing Points of Attachment Theory and Research. Monographs for the Society for Research in Child Development,* 50(1985): 1–2, serial no. 209.

Some studies have found that the effects of child care are not different from parental care. For example, see K. A. Clarke-Stewart and G. G.

Fein, "Early Childhood Programs," 917–999, in P. H. Mussen, ed., *Handbook of Child Psychology*, Vol. 2 (New York: Wiley, 1983). And a few studies show that child care rather than parental care is more effective for the intellectual development of poor children. For example, see Jay Belsky, "Two Waves of Day Care Research: Developmental Effects and Conditions of Quality," 1–34, in R. C. Ainslie, ed., *The Child and the Day Care Setting: Qualitative Variations and Development* (New York: Praeger, 1984).

59   Zigler says we are cannibalizing children: Kenneth Labich, "Can Your Career Hurt Your Kids?" *Fortune,* May 20, 1991, 38.

59   University of Texas study: Deborah Lowe Vandell and Mary Anne Corasaniti, "The Relationship Between Third-Graders' After-School Care and Social, Academic, and Emotional Functioning," *Child Development* 59 (August 1988): 874.

60–61   parenting works best when there is a division of labor: for more information on family role differentiation see Morris Zelditch, Jr., "Role Differentiation in the Nuclear Family: A Comparative Study," in Talcott Parsons and Robert F. Bales, *Family, Socialization and Interaction Process* (Glencoe, Illinois: Free Press, 1955).

62   1991 study by National Center for Health Statistics on children living in single-parent families and stepfamilies: Deborah A. Dawson, "Family Structure and Children's Health: United States, 1988," Vital and Health Statistics, series 10, no. 178 (Washington, D.C.: National Center for Health Statistics, 1991).

63   poll on college freshmen's views on being well off, raising a family: American Enterprise Institute, 1990.

63   major report by National Commission on Children: *Beyond Rhetoric: A New American Agenda for Children and Families* (Washington, D.C.: National Commission on Children, 1991); Select Committee on Children, Youth, and Families, *U.S. Children and their Families: Current Conditions and Recent Trends*, 1989 (Washington, D.C.: U.S. Government Printing Office, 1989).

63–64   Duffey and Wexler greeting: private communication, December 1991.

64   parents spend only seventeen hours a week with kids: William R. Mattox, Jr., "The Parent Trap," *Policy Review,* Winter 1991, no. 5, 6–13 (cite: 6).

65   1990 Gallup poll that half of working mothers would stay home if

"money were not an issue": "Virtually All Adults Want Children, but Many of the Reasons Are Intangible," *The Gallup Poll Monthly* (June 1990): 22.

65   social scientists saying essentials are community constructs "rather than what is objectively required": see Kingsley Davis, *Human Society* (New York: Macmillan Company, 1948 and 1949), especially chapter 3.

68   letter to Ann Landers: *The Washington Post,* September 26, 1991, D9.

69   study of latchkey eighth-graders shows likelihood of substance abuse: Jean L. Richardson, et al., "Substance Use Among Eighth-Grade Students Who Take Care of Themselves After School," *Pediatrics* 84(September 1989): 556–566.

69   Richardson quote: Lawrence Kutner, "Parent & Child," *The New York Times,* October 19, 1989, C8.

69   latchkey kids score high on risk taking, anger: Kathleen M. Dwyer, Jean L. Richardson, et al., "Characteristics of Eighth-Grade Students Who Initiate Self-Care in Elementary and Junior High School," *Pediatrics* 86 (September 1990): 448–454.

69   Travis Hirschi's quote on delinquency and parents: as summed up by James Q. Wilson, *On Character* (Washington, D.C.: AEI Press, 1991), 59.

69   other studies point to connection between delinquency and parenting: see, for example, Gerald R. Patterson and Thomas J. Dishion, "Contributions of Families and Peers to Delinquency," *Criminology* 23(1985): 63–79; Larry LeFlore, "Delinquency Youths and Family," *Adolescence* 23(Fall 1988): 629–642.

70   corporations having flexible schedules (Du Pont, IBM, Knight-Ridder, Avon): Cathy Trost, "To Cut Costs and Keep the Best People, More Concerns Offer Flexible Work Plans," *The Wall Street Journal,* February 18, 1992, B1, B12.

71   others suggesting that parents who stay home should get future retraining benefits: Gill, Glazer, and Thernstrom, *Our Changing Population,* 420.

71   provisions of parental leave bill: Larry Reynolds, "Showdown Set Over Mandated Parental Leave," *Personnel* 68(6): 1–2.

71   *Working Mother* magazine's criteria for the best companies: Rick Gladstone, "Despite Slump, Family Perks Are Up," *The Washington Post,* September 18, 1991, D1.

71   Navy permits maternity leave: Alecia Swasy, "Shipboard Pregnancies Force the Manly Navy to Cope With Moms," *The Wall Street Journal,* October 3, 1991, A1.

71   effects on infants who are subject to twenty hours or more a week of nonparental care: as noted by Jay Belsky, child care expert at Penn State's College of Health and Human Development in Daniel Wattenberg, "The Parent Trap," *Insight,* March 2, 1992, 7.

72   Ruth Messinger quote: Ron Alexander, "Single Parents Meet to Share a Continuing Quest for Stability," *The New York Times,* June 20, 1981.

72–73   Mary Jane Gibson statement: Renee Loth, "Paid Leave Proposal Gains Friends, Foes," *Boston Globe,* April 11, 1989, 21.

73   definition of family as father as sole wage earner, mother a homemaker, and two children: Betty Friedan, "Feminism Takes a New Turn," *New York Times Magazine,* November 18, 1979.

73   statistics on preschool children and family type: see David Blankenhorn, "Ozzie & Harriet: Have Reports of Their Death Been Greatly Exaggerated?" *Family Affairs* 2(Summer/Fall 1989): 10. (Based on an unpublished March 1987 Bureau of Labor Statistics report.)

73   children do not see fathers after divorce: Frank F. Furstenberg, Jr., and Andrew J. Cherlin, *Divided Families: What Happens to Children When Parents Part* (Cambridge, MA: Harvard University Press, 1991).

75   quote by Douglas Besharov: private communciation.

75   "a hole in the heart": Quotation by Claire Berman, in interview by Barbara Kantrowitz, "Breaking the Divorce Cycle," *Newsweek,* January 13, 1992, 49.

75   Popenoe on the "new familism": David Popenoe, *The Responsive Community: Rights and Responsibilities* (Fall 1992): 31–39.

75   Wallerstein on adolescents after divorce: Judith Wallerstein and Sandra Blakeslee, *Second Chances: Men, Women, and Children a Decade After Divorce* (New York: Ticknor and Fields, 1989), 153–154.

76   teenagers from single-parent or stepparent homes more likely to drop out: Nan Marie Astore and Sara S. McLanahan, "Family Structure, Parental Practices, and High School Completion," *American Sociological Review* 56(1991): 309–320.

76   Princeton/Johns Hopkins study on single-parent families and GPA, attendance, etc.: ibid., 316.

76   about emotional and behavioral problems, from national health survey: Nicholas Zill and Charlotte A. Schoenborn, "Developmental, Learning, and Emotional Problems: Health of Our Nation's Children, United States, 1988," Advance Data, no. 190, Vital and Health Statistics of the National Center for Health Statistics, November 16, 1990, 9.

76   achievement and truancy among elementary students: according to a study by the National Association of Elementary School Principals in Karl Zinsmeister, "Growing Up Scared," *The Atlantic,* June 1990, 52.

76   seventy percent of juveniles in state reform institutions were children of one-parent or no-parent families: according to a study by the Bureau of Justice Statistics, ibid., 52.

76   Herzog study at Boston Medical Center: James M. Herzog, "On Father Hunger," in John Ross, Alan Gerwit, and Stanley Cath, eds., *Father and Child: Development in Clinical Perspective* (Boston: Little, Brown, 1982), 163–74.

77   "When the father leaves . . ."—many other studies show findings that lack of father has detrimental effects: for an overview, see David Blankenhorn, "The Good Family Man: Fatherhood and the Pursuit of Happiness in America," Working Paper No. 12, issued by the Institute for American Values, 1991.
        For a work that comes to dissimilar conclusions, see Paul L. Adams, Judith R. Milner, and Nancy A. Schrepf, *Fatherless Children* (New York: John Wiley & Sons, 1984); for further discussion see Sandra Scarr, *Mother Care/Other Care* (New York: Basic Books, 1984).

77   study by Glenn and Kramer at University of Texas: "The Marriages and Divorces of Children of Divorce," *Journal of Marriage and the Family* 49(November 1987): 811–825.

77   study by British psychiatrist of affective disorders: Bryan Rodgers, "Adult Affective Disorders and Early Environment," *British Journal of Psychiatry* 157(October 1990): 542-543.

77   sociologist Bernard on stepchildren: Jessie S. Bernard, *Remarriage: A Study of Marriage* (New York: Dryden Press, 1956), chapter 12.

78͵   religious leaders in California agreed to four-month waiting period before marriage: "Marriage Requirements," *Christian Century*, June 4–11, 1986, 545.

78   Modesto church waiting period and instructions: ibid., 545–546.

78   Modesto church minister quote: "Marriage Requirements," ibid., 546.

79   conflict lessons; the difference is that the partners in solid and relatively happy marriages have developed less bruising and more effective means of dealing with their differences.

79   conflicts occur in good and bad marriages: George R. Bach and Peter Wyden, *The Intimate Enemy: How to Fight Fair in Love and Marriage* (New York: Morrow, 1969).

79   Gottman and Krokoff three-year study of marriages: John M. Gottman and Loweel J. Krokoff, "Marital Interaction and Satisfaction: A Longitudinal View," *Journal of Consulting and Clinical Psychology* 57(February 1989): 47–52.

79   Gottman quote: Daniel Goleman, "Want a Happy Marriage? Learn to Fight a Good Fight," *The New York Times,* February 21, 1989, C6.

79   Markman says couples who learn to handle conflict are happier: cited in ibid.

79   Scott on "precommitment" vows: Elizabeth S. Scott, "Rational Decisionmaking About Marriage and Divorce," *Virginia Law Review*, 76 (1990): 9–94.

80   divorce breeds still more divorce: Norval D. Glenn, "The Recent Trend in Marital Success in the United States," *Journal of Marriage and the Family* 53(1991): 261–270 (cite: 268).

80   Bellah and company on the family meal: Bellah, Madsen, Sullivan, Swidler, and Tipton, *The Good Society,* 260.

80   Fagan says that families need to return to family dinner: Patrick F. Fagan, "Rebuilding the Good Society," draft dated February 22, 1991, 16.

81   Galston recommends braking mechanisms before granting divorce: William Galston, "A Liberal-Democratic Case for the Two-Parent Family," *The Responsive Community* 1(Winter 1990-91): 23.

81   Britain Law Commission's recommendation of nine-month waiting period: cited in ibid.

81   Oklahoma bill to require wait period before remarrying: *Oklahoma House Bill* 1780, 43rd Legislature, Second Session (1992).

81–82   Glendon on the differences between Europeans and Americans on divorce: Mary Ann Glendon, *Abortion and Divorce in Western Law* (Cambridge, Massachusetts: Harvard University Press, 1987).

82   no-fault divorce rewards fathers for dissolving the family: Lenore Weitzman, *The Divorce Revolution: The Unexpected Social and Economic Consequences for Women and Children in America* (New York: Free Press, 1985).

82   "Unequal division of assets"—studies that divorced men fare better economically than divorced women: income ratio: Saul Hoffman and John Holmes, "Husbands, Wives, and Divorce," *Five Thousand American Families—Patterns of Economic Progress (Volume IV)* (Ann Arbor, Michigan: Institute for Social Research, 1976); economic status: Robert Hampton, "Marital Disruption: Some Social and Economic Consequences," *Five Thousand American Families—Patterns of Economic Progress (Volume III)* (Ann Arbor, Michigan: Institute for Social Research, 1975).

82   Galston advocates sanctions: William Galston, "A Liberal-Democratic Case for the Two-Parent Family," *The Responsive Community* 1(Winter 1990–91): 25.

82–83   Ellwood says all parents have a responsibility to their children, whether they live with them or not: see David T. Ellwood, *Poor Support: Poverty in the American Family* (New York: Basic Books, 1988), especially chapter 5.

83   Ellwood calls withholding payments an offense comparable to tax evasion: ibid., 164.

83   Ellwood quote on reducing the "financial incentive to create single-parent families": ibid., 173.

83   Steuerle and Juffras suggest a $1,000 tax credit: see C. Eugene Steuerle and Jason Juffras's paper "A $1,000 Tax Credit for Every Child:

A Base of Reform for the Nation's Tax, Welfare, and Health Systems,"
Washington, D.C.: The Urban Institute, 1991.

83   percentage of income paid by family of four in 1950 and 1989:
William R. Mattox, Jr., "The Parent Trap," *Policy Review*, Winter 1991,
no. 5, 6–13 (cite: 8).

84   welfare agencies are working to maintain families in New York
City; Family Preservation program: "Raising the Children, Part II," *Re:
Rights and Responsiblilities*, December 1991/January 1992, 4.

84   interventions must include parents: Karl Zinsmeister, "Growing
Up Scared," *The Atlantic*, June 1990, 56.

85   Mason argues that marriages with children are more binding:
Mary Ann Mason, *The Equality Trap* (New York: Simon & Schuster,
1988)

85–86   Novak characterizes libertarian view of marriage: Michael Novak,
"The Family Out of Favor," *Harper's*, April 1976, 39.

86   secure but dull marriages—*Newsweek* quote and Phillips quote:
"How Marriages Can Last," *Newsweek*, July 13, 1981, 73.

86   mortality rate higher among unmarried: James S. House, Karl R.
Landis, and Debra Umberson, "Social Relationships and Health," in *Science* 241(July 1988): 540–545.

86   study of over 2,500: ibid.

86   four similar studies confirm social isolation as a mortality factor:
see James S. House, Karl R. Landis, and Debra Umberson, "Social Relationships and Health," *Science* 241 (July 1988): 540–545.

86   influence of social networks rivaling cigarette smoking . . . .: ibid.,
541.

86   living alone and heart attacks: Robert B. Case, Arthur J. Moss,
Nan Case, Michael McDermott, and Shirley Eberly, "Living Alone After
Myocardial Infarction: Impact on Prognosis," *Journal of the American Medical Association* 267(January 22/29, 1992): 515–519.

86   Kurdek study that married people are happier: Lawrence A.
Kurdek, "The Relation Between Reported Well-Being and Divorce History, Availability of a Proximate Adult, and Gender," *Journal of Marriage
and Family* 53(1991): 71–78.

86–87   another study says divorced women are more likely to abuse alcohol: Marsha Lillie-Blanton, Ellen MacKenzie, and James C. Anthony, "Black-White Differences in Alcohol Use by Women: Baltimore Survey Findings," *Public Health Reports* 106(1991): 124–134.

87   sociologists Berger and Berger define marriage: Brigitte Berger and Peter Berger, *The War Over the Family: Capturing the Middle Ground* (1983), 166–167.

Chapter 3: The Communitarian School

90   5.3 percent of students carry guns: Tom Morganthau, "It's Not Just New York . . ." in *Newsweek*, March 9, 1992, 25.

90   Number of young Americans killed by firearms: ibid.

94   Sharon Pratt Kelly on authority and discipline: Kelly said that she "think[s] that kind of authority needs to be restored, starting at the earliest possible age." She added: "Young people respond to discipline." From "Let Teachers Spank, Dixon Urges" by Mary Ann French in *The Washington Post*, April 10, 1991, A1.

94   Supreme Court letting stand Texas "short of deadly force" law is from an editorial in *Christian Science Monitor*, March 21, 1989, 20.

94–95   Coleman's study of fifty thousand plus students on discipline . . .: James Coleman, Thomas Hoffer, and Sally Kilgore, *Public and Private Schools* (Chicago: National Opinion Research Center, 1981); see also James Coleman, Thomas Hoffer, and Sally Kilgore, "Public and Private Schools," *Society* 19(January/February 1982): 4–9.

96   Richard McCloud's quote on teaching: from a letter to the editor in *The Washington Post* as quoted in Ben Wildavsky, "Can You *Not* Teach Morality in Public Schools?" in *The Responsive Community* 2(Winter 1991/1992): 54.

96   88 percent of students in public schools: U.S. Bureau of the Census, *Statistical Abstract of the United States: 1991* (Washington, D.C.: U.S. Department of Commerce, 1991), table no. 215.

96   anecdote about the Teaneck, N.J., counselor: from Ben Wildavsky, "Can You *Not* Teach Morality in Public Schools?" in *The Responsive Community* 2(Winter 1991/1992): 47.

96   Dallas, Texas, of school administrators ripping pages out of books: "Dallas, Texas," *Newsletter on Intellectual Freedom* 40(November 1991): 197.

97   Simsbury, Connecticut, incident of school canceling the play *The Shadow Box*: "Simsbury, Connecticut," *Newsletter on Intellectual Freedom* 40(November 1991): 196.

97   Piaget and Kohlberg: see, for example, Jean Piaget, *The Moral Judgment of the Child* (Glencoe, Illinois: Free Press, 1948); Lawrence Kohlberg, "Moral Development and Identification," in Harold Stevenson (ed.), *Child Psychology* (Chicago, National Society for the Study of Education: University of Chicago Press, 1963); Lawrence Kohlberg, "The Development of Children's Orientations Toward a Moral Order. Part 1: Sequence in the Development of Moral Thought," *Vita Humana* 6(1963): 11–33; Lawrence Kohlberg, "Development of Moral Character and Moral Ideology," in Martin Hoffman and Lois Hoffman (eds.), *Review of Child Development Research* (New York: Russell Sage Foundation, 1964).

98   William Raspberry's "epiphany" quote is from " 'Ethics Without Virtue' " by William Raspberry in *The Washington Post,* December 16, 1991, A23.

98–99   University of Minnesota social worker case: comments during a conference "Ethical Issues in Case Management: Invitational Working Conference" Minneapolis, Minnesota, July 11–12, 1991, during discussion.

99   Christine Hoff Sommers quote on applied ethics courses is from " 'Ethics Without Virtue' " in *The Washington Post,* December 16, 1991, A23.

99–100 whose values: for an outstanding discussion on schools reflecting our society's values, see Michael A. Rebell, "Schools, Values, and the Courts," *Yale Law & Policy Review* 7(1989).

100   Reverend Charles Fink's quote on difficulty of deciding how to interpret and teach values is from "Can You *Not* Teach Morality in Public Schools?" by Ben Wildavsky in *The Responsive Community* 2(Winter 1991/1992): 49.

100–101 professor William Damon's comments: commentary in *The Responsive Community: Rights and Responsibilities* 2(Fall 1992): 86–88.

102   Iraqi example: E. J. Dionne, Jr., *Why Americans Hate Politics* (New York: Simon & Schuster, 1991), esp. 9–10.

103   information on Baltimore's values education program is from "An Initiative from Educators: Bring Values Back to the Class" by David O'Reilly in *The Philadelphia Inquirer,* November 17, 1991, 1-A (information from 18-A).

105   discussion of Jane Elliott's class in Riceville, Iowa, is from *A Class Divided: Then and Now* by William Peters, New Haven: Yale University Press, 1987 (expanded edition); "sympathetic indifference," 16; Elliott's Friday quote on rules, 21; Elliott's quote "Long before noon . . ." 24–25; Debbie Anderson's quote, 33; Theodore Perzynski's quote, 33; student's mother's quote, 41; Susan Rolland's quote, 123; Verla Buls's quote, 124.

110   at least 22 percent of employees in eating establishments are minorities: *Current Population Survey,* Bureau of Labor Statistics, unpublished tabulations, 1991.

110   employment of minorities has risen at twice the rate for total industry growth: James E. Peters, "Bridging the Gap: Restaurant Employment of Minorities," *Restaurant Business* 88(September 1, 1989): 86.

110   statistic on Walt Whitman students saying their jobs interfere with school work: personal communication with office of the principal.

110   Charner-Fraser study on after-school work: Ivan Charner, Bryna Shore Fraser, *Youth and Work: What We Know, What We Don't Know, What We Need to Know* (Washington, D.C.: William T. Grant Foundation, 1988).
        For further discussion of the impact of teen participation in service jobs, see: Steven Waldman and Karen Springen, "Too Old, Too Fast?" *Newsweek,* November 16, 1992, 80–88.

113   unemployment information: "Unemployment Rates by Sex and Age, Monthly Data Seasonally Adjusted," *Monthly Labor Review,* March 1992, 59.

114   youth's feelings about community service is from the poll *Democracy's Next Generation* by People for the American Way, 1989, 62 (actual poll question, 154).

114   youth's reasons for not performing community service is from the poll *Democracy's Next Generation* by People for the American Way, 1989, 56 (poll question, 162).

114   statistics on the cost of a national service program: statistic of $11,000 a year is an estimate from Don Eberle of the National Service Secretariat, based on a stipend slightly less than minimum wage and including the cost of health insurance.

Chapter 4: Back to We

116   Tönnies's definition of gemeinschaft and gesellschaft: Ferdinand Tönnies, *Community and Society,* translated and edited by Charles P. Loomis (East Lansing: Michigan State University Press, 1957).

117   Sierra Club case before Supreme Court to preserve parkland: Mary Ann Glendon, *Rights Talk* (New York: The Free Press, 1991), 112.

118   social associations replacing the family: James Q. Wilson, "The Rediscovery of Character: Private Virtue and Public Policy," *The Public Interest* 81(Fall 1985): 13.

119   Jonathan Rowe to a conference in Washington: presentation at the conference "Left and Right: The Emergence of a New Politics in the 1990s?" sponsored by the Heritage Foundation and the Progressive Foundation, October 30, 1991, Washington, D.C.

120   "urban villages": Herbert Gans, *The Urban Villagers: Group and Class in the Life of Italian-Americans* (New York: The Free Press, 1962, 1982), 14–15.

120   Jim Sleeper, *Closest of Strangers: Liberalism and the Politics of Race in New York* (New York: W. W. Norton & Company, 1990).

120–121   14.4 percent of the elderly lived alone in 1950: Abraham Monk, "Aging, Loneliness, and Communications," *American Behavioral Scientist* 31(5): 534.

121   31 percent of the elderly lived alone in 1990: U.S. Bureau of the Census, Current Population Reports, series P-20, no. 450, *Marital Status and Living Arrangements: March 1990* (Washington, D.C.: U.S. Government Printing Office, 1991), table L, 12.

121   people moving less often now: Felicity Barringer, "18 percent of Households in U.S. Moved in '89," *New York Times,* December 20, 1991, A16.

122   Ray Oldenburg decries new definitions of community: cited by Deborah Baldwin, "Creating Community," *Common Cause Magazine,* July/August 1990, 17.

122   traditional communities were homogeneous: John W. Gardner, *Building Community* (Washington, D.C.: Independent Sector, 1991), 11.

122   Gardner quote: ibid.

123   Michael Milken salary: Steve Swartz, "Why Michael Milken Stands to Qualify for Guinness Book," *The Wall Street Journal,* March 31, 1989, A1.

123   rich people are not happier than poor people: Diane Swanbrow, "The Paradox of Happiness," *Psychology Today,* July/August 1989, 39.

124   happiness depends on where you live: Ronald Inglehart and Jacques-René Raber, "If You're Unhappy, This Must Be Belgium: Well-Being Around the World," *Public Opinion* 8(April/May 1985): 12.

124   rich countries are not happier than poor ones: Richard A. Easterlin, "Does Money Buy Happiness?" *The Public Interest* 30(Winter 1973): 7.

124   meaningful relationships make people psychologically healthier: For an encompassing review of the mountain of evidence, see Marc Pilisuk and Susan Hillier Parks, *The Healing Web* (Hanover, NH: University Press of New England, 1986); see also Robert I. Wuthnow, *Acts of Compassion: Caring for Others and Helping Ourselves* (Princeton: Princeton University Press, 1991).

127   books on making design pro-community: see Jane Jacobs, *The Death and Life of Great American Cities* (New York: Random House, 1961); Raquel Ramati, *How to Save Your Own Street* (New York: Doubleday, 1981); *Community Renewal Programming* (New York: Praeger, 1966); Witold Rybczynski's forthcoming work *Looking Around: A Journey Through Architecture.*

129   Jane Jacobs: ibid.

130   innovations to reduce the use of cars and create social webs: Andres Duany and Elizabeth Plater-Zyberk, "The Second Coming of the American Small Town," *Wilson Quarterly* 16(Winter 1992): 19–48.

130   Drucker on reliance on voluntary associations in the nineties: Peter F. Drucker, "It Profits Us to Strengthen Nonprofits," *The Wall Street Journal*, December 19, 1991, A14.

131   nearly half of the nation's EMTs are unpaid: John Grossmann, "Call an Ambulance . . . Quick!" *Country Journal*, July 1983, 58.

132   information on EMT staffing and training: John Grossmann, "Call an Ambulance . . . Quick!" *Country Journal*, July 1983, 52–59.

132   heart attack victims and resuscitation attempts: Robert G. Thompson, Alfred P. Hallstrom, and Leonard A. Cobb, "Bystander-Initiated Cardiopulmonary Resuscitation in the Management of Ventricular Firbrillation," *Annals of Internal Medicine* 90(May 1979): 737–40; see also W. Douglas Weaver, "Resuscitation Outside the Hospital—What's Lacking," *New England Journal of Medicine*, 325(November 14, 1991): 1437–1439.

132   Seattle information: Christina Rylko, "If You Have a Heart Attack Hope You're in Seattle," *Saturday Evening Post*, April 1988, 56–57.

Chapter 5: Rebuilding Community Institutions

136–137   Padilla clears lot in South Bronx: Sarah Bartlett, "Two Messes: One of Trash, One of Bureaucracy," *The New York Times*, November 29, 1991, A1.

138   incident in Bay City, Michigan: Robert Trojanowicz, "Community Policing Curbs Police Brutality," *Footprints* 3(Spring/Summer 1991): 1–2.

140   decentralizing Brooklyn's courts: Tina McLanus, "Brooklyn Establishes 'Community Courts,'" *Footprints* 4(Winter/Spring 1992): 15.

140   sentencing nonviolent offenders to community service is as effective as incarceration: from a study by Malcolm Feeley (UC Berkeley) and Richard Berk (UCLA) noted in "Convicts and Community Service," *Society*, November/December 1991, 3.

141   Buckley calls voting a "civic sacrament": William F. Buckley, Jr., *Reader's Digest*, October 1984.

142   satisfaction found only when we are engaged with one another: for more on this subject, see Philip Selznick, "The Idea of a Communitarian Morality," *California Law Review* 75(1987): 445–463.

143   Shelby Steele: Shelby Steele, *The Content of Our Character* (New York: St. Martin's Press, 1990).

143   L. Douglas Wilder, similar position to Steele: Lawrence Douglas Wilder, "On Our Own: The Black Family," *The Responsive Community: Rights and Responsibilities* 1(Spring 1991): 3–5.

143   Wilkins and Walters demur over Steele's assertions: Walters, comments made during a conference at George Washington University; Wilkins, see Roger Wilkins, "The Black Poor Are Different," *The New York Times,* August 22, 1989, A23.

143–144   William Julius Wilson points to the curse of either/or: see, for example, Michael Abramowitz, "Against Poverty's Odds," *The Washington Post,* December 12, 1991, B1–B2.

147   Coughlin, multiculturalism raises a series of question: Ellen K. Coughlin, "Scholars Confront Fundamental Question: Which Vision of America Should Prevail?" *The Chronicle of Higher Education,* January 29, 1992, A8.

148   Coughlin, starkly portrayed debate on multiculturalism: Ellen K. Coughlin, "Scholars Confront Fundamental Question: Which Vision of America Should Prevail?" *The Chronicle of Higher Education,* January 29, 1992, A8.

149   Charlotte Perkins Gilman's *Women and Economics*, Simone de Beauvoir's *The Second Sex*: Charlotte Perkins Gilman, *Women and Economics* (New York: Harper Torchbooks, 1966); Simone de Beauvoir, *The Second Sex* (New York, Bantam Books, 1952).

149   Lapham in *Harper's*: Lewis H. Lapham, "Who and What Is American?" *Harper's,* January 1992, 43.

150   Shanker on the new multiculturalists: Albert Shanker, "Courting Ethnic Strife," *The New York Times,* February 23, 1991, section 4, 7.

150   white traditionalists on core curriculum: "Is the Curriculum Biased?" a statement of the National Association of Scholars.

150   NAS, "the idea that students": "Is the Curriculum Biased?" a statement of the National Association of Scholars.

152   report sponsored by U.S. Labor Department on minorities in the work force: William B. Johnston (project director), *Workforce 2000: Work*

and Workers in the Year 2000 (executive summary) (Indianapolis, Indiana: Hudson Institute, 1987).

152   Riche in *American Demographics*: Martha Farnsworth Riche, "We're All Minorities Now," *American Demographics*, October 1991, 26–31; "the United States is undergoing . . ." 26; assimilation, 28.

153   June Jordan in *The Progressive*: June Jordan, "Diversity or Death," *The Progressive* (June 1990): 17.

153   *Workforce 2000* statistics: U.S. Labor Department, executive summary, *Workforce 2000: Work and Workers in the Year 2000* (Indianapolis, Indiana: Hudson Institute, 1987), 95.

153   similar projections: for example, see Peter A. Morrison, "Congress and the Year 2000: A Demographic Perspective on Future Issues," N-3279-CRS (Santa Monica, CA: The RAND Corporation, 1991).

153   minority population proportion projections: from Peter A. Morrison, *Congress and the Year 2000: A Demographic Perspective on Future Issues* (Santa Monica, CA: The RAND Corporation, 1991), 12–13; Morrison's figures are based on U.S. Census figures *Projections of the Population of the United States, by Age, Sex, and Race: 1988 to 2080* (1989) and *Projections of the Hispanic Population: 1983 to 2080* (1986).

154   competition for jobs among minorities: Lynne Duke and Richard Morin, "Demographic Shift Reshaping Politics," *The Washington Post*, August 13, 1991, A7.

154   quote from Bryce's *The American Commonwealth*: Arthur M. Schlesinger, Jr., *The Disuniting of America* (Knoxville, Tenn.: Whittle Direct Books, 1991), 7.

154   Steele argues blacks should seek advancement as individuals: Steele, *The Content of Our Character*, 173.

155   Woodrow Wilson on the melting pot: Albert Shaw, ed., *The Messages and Papers of Woodrow Wilson*, vol. I (New York: The Review of Reviews Corporation, 1924), 115–6.

155   Diane Ravitch quote: "Multiculturalism: E Pluribus Plures," in Paul Berman, ed., *Debating P.C.* (New York: Dell Publishing, 1992), 276.

156   unbounded pluralism threatens to balkanize America: Arthur M. Schlesinger, Jr., *The Disuniting of America: Reflections on a Multicultural Society* (Whittle Direct Books, 1991).

156   Berman concurs with Schlesinger: Paul Berman, "Introduction: The Debate and Its Origins," in *Debating P.C.,* 3.

157   Bayard Rustin on bilingual teaching: Quoted in William Raspberry, "Ethnocentric Excesses," *The Washington Post,* October 5, 1991, A19.

157   language extremists who say that Spanish should be the American language because we are in a Hispanic hemisphere: comment made by Arnold Torres on the "Should America Be Bilingual?" edition "The Firing Line" taped September 29, 1983.

157   poll results on "fair treatment for all": *Democracy's Next Generation II: A Study of American Youth on Race* (Washington, D.C.: People for the American Way, 1992), 57–58.

157   poll by New York State teachers union: *New York State United Teachers 1991 Education Opinion Survey: Final Report* (Albany, New York: New York State United Teachers, 1991), section II, 5, 8.

158   women in the world of Islam (Egypt, Sudan, Wahhabi): Lisa Beyer, "Life Behind the Veil," *Time,* Fall 1990, 37.

158   criminal offenders under Islam: "Sudan Seems to Shift Away from Islamic Law," *The New York Times,* February 4, 1990, 17.

158   minorities under Islam: Abdullahi A. An-Na'im, "Religious Minorities under Islamic Law and the Limits of Cultural Relativism," *Human Rights Quarterly* 9(1987), 1–18.

158   An-Na'im quote: Abdullahi A. An-Na'im, "Religious Minorities under Islamic Law and the Limits of Cultural Relativism," *Human Rights Quarterly* 9(1987), 12–13.

158   Malik's observations on Christian Arabs: Habib C. Malik, "Faith to Faith," *The New Republic,* December 31, 1990, 16.

158–159   report on Japan: Andrew Dougherty, *Japan: 2000* (Washington, D.C.: Economic Strategy Institute, 1991), 21.

159   Bank of Tokyo women must get approval to work overseas: Henny Sender, "You've Got a Long Way to Go, Baby," *Institutional Investor,* April 1991, 25. For more information on gender discrimination in the Japanese workplace: Mary Saso, *Women in the Japanese Workplace* (London: Hilary Shipman Ltd., 1990).

159   Japanese population statistics: Lee Smith, "Divisive Forces in an Inbred Nation," *Fortune,* March 30, 1987, 24.

159   discrimination against Koreans in Japan: Lee Smith, "Divisive Forces in an Inbred Nation," *Fortune,* March 30, 1987, 25.

159   Japanese "untouchables" are still discriminated against: Takagi Masyuki, "A Living Legacy of Discrimination," *Japan Quarterly,* July–September 1991, 283–290.

159   Asian scholars see support in Confucius for human rights and democracy, Chaves comment: personal correspondence, letter to Amitai Etzioni, March 5, 1992.

159   for more discussion on rebuilding communities through community institutions: see Robert N. Bellah, Richard Madsen, William M. Sullivan, Ann Swidler, Steven M. Tipton, *The Good Society* (New York: Alfred A. Knopf, 1991), especially the appendix.

Chapter 6: New Responsibilities: Public Safety and Public Health

163   contaminating drugs to make users "wretchedly ill": Paul Weyrich, "Conservatism for the People," *National Review,* September 3, 1990, 27.

163   arm every citizen with a gun: Walter E. Williams, "The Cost of Crime Has Fallen," *Conservative Chronicle,* November 7, 1990, 29.

163   quarantine all HIV carriers: see Ronald Bayer, *Private Acts, Social Consequences: AIDS and the Politics of Public Health* (New York: Free Press, 1989), 173–206.

163   suspend the Constitution until the war on drugs is won: letter to Tom Wicker, "Rights vs. Testing" in *The New York Times,* November 28, 1989, A25.

163   Chicago police superintendent says all drug dealers should be shot: *The Washington Post,* July 13, 1991, A6.

163   Houston judge favors castrating violent criminals: *Newsweek,* October 7, 1991, 8.

163   appeal of David Duke to 39 percent of Louisiana voters: Peter Applebome, "Fearing Duke, Voters in Lousiana Hand Democrat Fourth Term" in *The New York Times,* November 18, 1991, A1.

164   Guerrero of ACLU quotes Brandeis: Gene Guerrero, speech before the American Society of Industrial Security, November 8, 1989, 11.

165   Glasser warns of encroaching government power: as quoted in Herber Mitgang, "Of Rights and Rhetoric About Rights," *The New York Times,* October 30, 1991, C19.

165   ACLU opposes voluntary fingerprinting of children: "Children's Rights," *Policy Guide of the ACLU,* #272 (1986).

165–166   "possibility of access by government agencies to fingerprinting records": ibid., 363–4.

166   "fingerprinting tends to condition children to...invasions of privacy": ibid., 364.

167   115 skyjackings between 1968 and 1972: Peter St. John, *Air Piracy, Airport Security, and International Terrorism: Winning the War against Hijackers* (New York: Quorum Books, 1991), 210, 211.

167–168   twenty-four bombs killed 256 people: ibid., 213.

168   escaped convicts hijack plane from Birmingham: ibid., 20.

168   U.S. airports given sixty days to construct checkpoints: ibid., 21.

168   X-ray searches made mandatory: ibid., 21.

168   2,000 guns and 3,500 pounds of explosives found in first year: ibid., 73.

168   during first ten years, 25,000 guns confiscated: ibid., 77.

169–170   "searching . . . *all* individuals . . . is . . . inconsistent with . . . Fourth Amendment . . .": "Airport Searches," *Policy Guide of the ACLU,* #270 (1986), 359.

170   "troublesome aspect . . . is the readiness [of] most people [to] welcome such procedures": ibid.

170   250,000 Americans killed in alcohol-related crashes in 1980s: Richard K. Willard, "Yes: Checkpoints Enhance Awareness," *ABA Journal*, April 1990, 44.

170   a fatality every twenty-two minutes: "Sobriety Checkpoints," *NHTSA Facts*, 1.

170   five-hundred-thousand alcohol-related car injuries, "Sobriety Checkpoints," *NHTSA Facts*, 2.

170   alcohol-related accidents number one killer of fifteen- to twenty-four-year-olds: "Health Warning Labels on Alcoholic Beverages: A Public Health Measure Long Overdue," Center for Science in the Public Interest, March 1988.

170   two out of every five Americans will be in an alcohol-related crash: "Health Warning Labels on Alcoholic Beverages: A Public Health Measure Long Overdue," Center for Science in the Public Interest, March 1988.

171   Thirty-eight states have adopted sobriety checkpoints: National Highway Traffic Safety Administration (NHTSA), "Sobriety Checkpoint Use in the United States," August 21, 1991.

171   evaluation of New Jersey program: D. Levy, D. Shea, P. Asch, "Traffic Safety Effects of Sobriety Checkpoints and Other Local DWI Programs in New Jersey," *American Journal of Public Health* 79(1989): 291; the New Jersey effort also included educational programs.

171   checkpoints in New South Wales: R. Homel, D. Carseldine, and I. Kearns, "Drink-Drive Countermeasures in Australia," *Alcohol, Drugs and Driving* 4(1988): 113.

171   Canadian study finds that arrest rate is less effective than publicity surrounding checkpoints: G. W. Mercer, "The Relationships Among Driving While Impaired Charges, Police Drinking Driving Roadcheck Activity, Media Coverage, and Alcohol-Related Casualty Traffic Accidents," *Accident Analysis and Prevention* 17(1985): 467.

171   results of Charlottesville study: R. B. Voas, A. E. Rhodenizer, and C. Lynn, *Evaluation of Charlottesville Checkpoint Operation: Final Report*, DOT-HS-806-989 (Washington, D.C.: National Highway Traffic Safety Administration, 1985).

171   twenty-nine states may seize licenses of drivers who fail alcohol test: Jay Mathews, "New Weapon Against Drunken Drivers," *The Washington Post,* September 16, 1991, A12.

171   information on California license-sizing program: ibid.

172   90 percent of those surveyed indicate they prefer checkpoints: R. B. Voas, A. E. Rhodenizer, and C. Lynn, *Evaluation of Charlottesville Checkpoint Operation: Final Report,* DOT-HS-806-989 (Washington, D.C.: National Highway Traffic Safety Administration, 1985).

172   even those who drink and drive support the checkpoints: R. B. Voas, A. E. Rhodenizer, and C. Lynn, *Evaluation of Charlottesville Checkpoint Operation: Final Report,* DOT-HS-806-989 (Washington, D.C.: National Highway Traffic Safety Administration, 1985).

172   Kimbrough in *Daily Herald: RE: Rights and Responsibilities* (Newsletter of the American Alliance for Rights & Responsibilities), May 1990, 4.

172   Michigan ACLU's opposition to checkpoints: as quoted in Colman McCarthy, "Stop Drunks Before They Kill," in *The Washington Post,* June 23, 1990, A29.

173   drug checkpoint in Inkster: Roger Conner, "The Checkpoint at Inkster: Reasonable or Unreasonable?" *The Responsive Community* 1(Winter 1990/91): 88–91.

175   danger of allowing the camel's nose into the tent: thin edge of the wedge: Frederick Schauer, "Slippery Slopes," *Harvard Law Review* 99(1985): 361.

175   Schauer defines "slippery slopes": Frederick Schauer, "Slippery Slopes," *Harvard Law Review* 99(1985): 361–362.

175   Schauer, where do you draw the line: ibid., 378.

175–176 Glassner on antismoking legislation: quoted in Glen Evans, "Stub Out Antismoking Zealotry," *The New York Times,* May 7, 1988, 27.

176   ACLU fears what screening gates may lead to: *Policy Guide of the ACLU,* #270 (1986).

177   the discussion of notching principles benefits from a paper by William Curran, Larry Gostin, and Mary Clark, "Acquired Immunode-

ficiency Syndrome: Legal and Regulatory Policy," published by the Harvard School of Public Health, 1986. Their criteria include: 1) "true purpose" (public health vs. disguised prejudice); 2) scientific evidence of a "public health necessity"; 3) the measures themselves cannot be a source of illness; 4) the measures adopted must be related to the public health goal. Also, James F. Childress in "An Ethical Framework for Assessing Policies to Screen for Antibodies to HIV," in *AIDS and Public Policy Journal* 2(Winter 1987): 28–32, suggests four conditions that will allow "infringing" on established rules: 1) the infringing policy must be effective; 2) no alternatives must be available; 3) one must seek the least infringing rules; 4) one must disclose the policy to those being infringed upon.

178   thirty-eight Mexicans killed in the past five years by bees: Robert Johnson, "Swarms of 'Killer Bees' in Texas Imperil the Nation's Beekeepers," *The Wall Street Journal,* October 11, 1991, B1.

178–179   USDOT agrees there is a problem enough to warrant random testing of train engineers: Paul Glastris, ". . . One That Should Be the Best, *But Isn't," The Washington Monthly,* March 1988, 27–33 (cite: 31).

179   Ninth Circuit Court of Appeals upholds DOT and Federal Highway Administration rules: "Drug Tests for Transportation Workers Upheld by Appeals Court," *The Wall Street Journal,* April 29, 1991, B4.

179   court had previously upheld similar FAA regulations: "Drug Tests for Transportation Workers Upheld by Appeals Court," *The Wall Street Journal,* April 29, 1991, B4.

179   between 1975 and 1984 drugs or alcohol were "directly affecting" causes in forty-eight train accidents, accounting for thiry-seven deaths and eighty injuries: Paul Glastris, ". . . One That Should Be the Best, *But Isn't," The Washington Monthly,* March 1988, 27–33 (cite: 31).

179   of 179 train accidents in 1987, engineers in 39 cases tested positive for drugs, 34 percent more than in 1986: Peter Bensinger, *USA Today,* February 17, 1988, 8A.

179   16 people died, over 170 were injured when Amtrak train struck Conrail train in January 1987: David Gates, "Legacy of a Railroad Disaster," *Newsweek,* May 18, 1987, 8.

179   NYC motorman was speeding August 28, 1991, and derailed switching from express to local track; death, injury figures: Alan Finder,

"Transit Crews Will Now Be Tested Randomly for Drugs and Alcohol," *The New York Times*, August 30, 1991, A1, B4.

179   motorman was drunk thirteen hours after crash: Alan Finder, "Transit Crews Will Now Be Tested Randomly for Drugs and Alcohol," *The New York Times*, August 30, 1991, B4.

179   president of transit workers local agrees to random testing for drugs and alcohol: Joseph B. Treaster, "For Transit Union, a Change of Heart on Drug Testing," *The New York Times*, August 30, 1991, B4.

179   1979 study found 23 percent of railroad operating employees were problem drinkers: Paul Glastris, ". . . One That Should Be the Best, *But Isn't*," *The Washington Monthly*, March 1988, 27–33 (cite: 31).

179–180   clear and present danger from handguns; nine thousand murdered by handguns in 1988, accidents killed fourteen thousand more. Great Britain had seven handgun murders; Canada eight: "Stop the Madness; Pass Sane Gun-Control Laws," *USA Today*, October 17, 1991, 10A.

180   statistics on the AIDS epidemic: "Accelerating, Nation's AIDS Count Hits 200,000," *The New York Times*, January 17, 1992, A16.

180   more than 300,000 people die from smoking annually: Robert E. Goodin, "The Ethics of Smoking," *Ethics* 99(April 1989): 574–624 (cite: 575).

180   Goodin points out that smoking harms others: Robert E. Goodin, "The Ethics of Smoking," *Ethics* 99(April 1989): 574–624.

180   secondhand smoke accounts for 2,400 cases of lung cancer a year: Willard G. Manning, et al., "The Taxes of Sin: Do Smokers and Drinkers Pay Their Way?" *Journal of the American Medical Association* 261(March 17, 1989): 1607.

180   90 percent of smokers have tried to quit: Robert E. Goodin, "The Ethics of Smoking," *Ethics* 99(April 1989): 585.

181   a 10 percent increase in the price of cigarettes as a result of higher taxes causes a 12 percent decrease in cigarette consumption: George F. Will, "Smoking, Custom and the Law," *The Washington Post*, January 14, 1990, B7.

182   Meese wanted to do away with *Miranda* rights (two quotes): Stephen Wermiel, "Miranda Ruling Continues to Fall Under Attack; Some

Critics See It as Law Enforcement Barrier," *The Wall Street Journal*, September 8, 1987, 72.

182   Office of Legal Policy issued a position paper advocating overturning of *Miranda*: "Respecting the Vitality of *Miranda*: The Case of Preserving the Right to Remain Silent" (Washington, D.C.: The American Civil Liberties Foundation), 1.

182   Supreme Court ruled six to three that unsolicited admission of guilt did not taint second confession: Elder Witt, "Decision Trims Miranda Rule on Statements," *Congressional Quarterly*, March 9, 1985, 455.

182   police not required to tell suspect about every crime they are suspected of; Powell's quote: Elder Witt, "High Court Holds the Line on *Miranda* Rule," *Congressional Quarterly*, January 31, 1987, 196.

182–183   case in which judge filled out search warrant incorrectly: *Massachusetts* v. *Sheppard* 468 U.S. 981–993 (1984).

183   Linda Bruin in *Michigan Bar Journal*: Linda L. Bruin, "School Discipline: Recent Developments in Student Due Process Rights," *Michigan Bar Journal*, November 1989, 1066.

183–184   quote from AFT president Albert Shanker on students' rights: Albert Shanker, "Where We Stand: Discipline in Our Schools," *The New York Times*, May 19, 1991, section 4, 7.

185   ACLU opposes antiloitering ordinance in Alexandria, Virginia: L. Gordon Crovitz, "The New Civil Rights: ACLU vs. Maxine Clark," *The Wall Street Journal*, September 5, 1990, A15; see also Roger Conner, "Targeted Anti-Loitering Laws: Constitutional Violation or Community Protection?" *The Responsive Community: Rights and Responsibilities* 1(Spring 1991): 65–8.

185   curfew laws in Atlanta, Newark, Detroit: "Atlanta Sets a Curfew for Youths, Prompting Concern of Race Bias," *The New York Times*, November 21, 1990, A1, B10.

186   liberals such as Robert Kuttner advocate national ID card: Robert Kuttner, "Illegal Immigration: Would a National ID Card Help?" *BusinessWeek*, August 26, 1991, 14.

187   CDC proposal on HIV testing: Malcolm Gladwell, "CDC Urges AIDS Testing for All Hospital Patients," *The Washington Post*, September 20, 1991, A3.

188   twenty-four thousand Americans awaiting organ transplantation: Aaron Spital, "The Shortage of Organs for Transplantation," *New England Journal of Medicine* 325(October 24, 1991): 1243–1246.

188   organ donation option for patients the communitarian thing to do: James L. Nelson, "The Rights and Responsibilities of Potential Organ Donors; a Communitarian Approach," *The Responsive Community* (forthcoming).

190   the causes of crime: James Q. Wilson and Richard J. Herrnstein, *Crime and Human Nature* (New York: Simon & Schuster, 1985).

190   crime is more rampant in United States than Portugal, Chile, Spain, Indonesia, Kenya: *International Crime Statistics,* (Lyon, France: INTERPOL General Secretariat, 1990) 58, 142, 33, 56, 85, 100.

190   national violent crime rate 732 per 100,000, 284 in Utah, in 1990: Uniform Crime Reports of the United States (Washington, D.C.: Federal Bureau of Investigation, 1990), 51 and 58.

Chapter 7: Hate Speech: Nonlegal Remedies

192   Wayne Dick's satiric poster: Richard Schumacher, "Anti-Gay Poster Sparks Free Speech Controversy," *Yale Daily News,* September 3, 1986, 1.

192   one student argued that he was slandered by the poster: Stephanie Blank, " 'BAD Week' Flyer Angers Students," *Yale Daily News,* April 16, 1986, 3.

192   Dick defends himself, saying homosexuality is immoral: Richard Schumacher, "Anti-Gay Poster Sparks Free Speech Controversy," 6.

192   Dick put on probation for two years: ibid., 1.

192   executive director of Connecticut Civil Liberties Union protests: Patricia G. Barnes, "Yale Chided for Disciplining Student Who Mocked Homosexuals," *New Haven Register,* August 7, 1986, 1.

193   quote from Yale undergraduate regulations: Richard Schumacher, "Student Demands Rehearing," *Yale Daily News,* September 10, 1986, 1.

193   alumna defends Dick's punishment: Richard Schumacher, "Anti-Gay Poster Sparks Free Speech Controversy," *Yale Daily News,* September 3, 1986, 1, 6 (cite: 6).

193   Yale president Schmidt argues for free expression: Sam Conti and Richard Rothschild, "Schmidt, Others Address Dick Case," *Yale Daily News,* October 3, 1986, 1.

193   Dick acquitted in rehearing: Richard Schumacher, "Wayne Dick Acquitted," *Yale Daily News,* October 2, 1986, 1.

193   Vann Woodward's statement: ibid.

193   130 American universities have speech codes: Mayerene Barker, "University Divided over Proposal for Speech Code," *Los Angeles Times,* May 16, 1991, B3.

194   code at the University of Pennsylvania: "Colleges Take Two Basic Approaches in Adopting Anti-Harassment Plans," *The Chronicle of Higher Education,* October 4, 1989, A38.

194   sarcastic comment of Penn professor: Alan Charles Kors, "It's Speech, Not Sex, the Dean Bans Now," *The Wall Street Journal,* October 12, 1989, A16(E).

194   Tufts speech code: R. W., "Colleges Take Two Basic Approaches in Adopting Anti-Harassment Plans," *The Chronicle of Higher Education,* October 4, 1989, A38.

194   Connecticut code: R. W., "Colleges Take Two Basic Approaches in Adopting Anti-Harassment Plans," *The Chronicle of Higher Education,* October 4, 1989, A38.

194   regulations at the University of Wisconsin: "Student Nonacademic Disciplinary Procedures," Chapter UWS 17.06(2)(a)2.(c)1., University of Wisconsin System administrative code, August 1989.

194   two white University of Pennsylvania students evicted from dormitory: R. W., "Colleges Take Two Basic Approaches in Adopting Anti-Harassment Plans," *The Chronicle of Higher Education,* October 4, 1989, A38.

194   University of Michigan student punished for limerick: ibid. Students evicted from Stanford dormitory: Felicity Barringer, "Campus Battle Pits Freedom of Speech Against Racial Slurs," *The New York Times,* April 25, 1989, A1; Larry Gordon, "Stanford OKs Ban on Fighting Words," *Los Angeles Times,* May 26, 1990, A36.

194   Rutgers student punished for violating school's insult policy: Dana Milbank, "Gay Students Enjoy Programs, Protections at Rutgers University," *The Wall Street Journal,* February 3, 1992, A1.

195   Occidental College incident: "Suspension for Oral Abuse Spurs a Debate," *The New York Times,* February 16, 1992, 59.

195   Brown University expels student: Anthony DePalma, "Battling Bias, Campuses Face Free Speech Fight," *The New York Times,* February 20, 1991, B9.

195   student at SUNY-Binghamton charged with lewd behavior for putting Penthouse centerfolds on his dorm room door: John Leo, "PC Follies: The Year in Review," *U.S. News & World Report,* January 27, 1992, 22.

195   University of Toronto professor charged with sexual harassment for staring: John Leo, "PC Follies: The Year in Review," *U.S. News & World Report,* January 27, 1992, 26.

195   1986 poll indicates that Coloradans object to hate speech law: *The Denver Post*/NewsCenter 4 issues poll conducted by Talmey Associates of Boulder, Colorado, June 1986.

196   Alabamians agree that even those with unpopular views should be free to express them: *Alabama 1989: The annual report of Southern Opinion Research* (Tuscaloosa, Ala.: Southern Opinion Research, 1990), "Flag, First Amendment," 8.

196   1987 national survey on the Constitution's protection of speech: "The Constitution: 200 Years Later," CBS News/*New York Times* poll, May 1987.

196   1991 poll shows majority favors prohibiting hateful speech: Bill of Rights Survey, conducted by Research USA for the American Bar Association, July 1991.

196   1942 Supreme Court case lays down "fighting words" doctrine: *Chaplinsky* v. *New Hampshire* 315 U.S. 568, 571–72 (1942).

196   Supreme Court has not reapplied "fighting words" standard: Gerald Gunther, "Good Speech, Bad Speech—No," *Stanford Lawyer,* Spring 1990, 9.

197   St. Paul, Minnesota, hate-crime ordinance tested before Supreme Court: Linda Greenhouse, "Justices Weigh Ban on Voicing Hate," *The New York Times,* December 5, 1991, B19.

197   Scalia questions broad language of St. Paul ordinance: Linda Greenhouse, "Justices Weigh Ban on Voicing Hate," *The New York Times,* December 5, 1991, B19.

197   *St. Paul Pioneer Press* quotation: Nat Hentoff, "Looking Beyond a Burning Cross," *The Washington Post,* February 1, 1991, A23.

198   sheriff of Arlington, Virginia, tried to ban *Playboy:* Caryle Murphy, "Merchandisers Challenge Book Display Ban," *The Washington Post,* July 17, 1985, C1.

198   Justice Douglas quote: *Interstate Circuit, Inc.* v. *Dallas,* 390 U.S. 676, 707 (1968).

200   *Los Angeles Times* editorial: "Fighting Intolerance With Intolerant Speech Codes," the *Los Angeles Times,* May 13, 1991, B4.

200   Strossen of the ACLU also disparages codes: David G. Savage, "Forbidden Words on Campus," the *Los Angeles Times,* February 12, 1991, A17.

200–201   a comprehensive study: *Hate in the Ivory Tower: A Survey of Intolerance on College Campuses and Academia's Response* (Washington, D.C.: People for the American Way, 1991); "culture of denial": 6.

201   Northwestern professor defends unrestricted speech: Franklyn S. Haiman, "The Remedy Is More Speech," *American Prospect,* Summer 1991, Number 6, 30–35.

201   Scalia discusses rights and responsibilities: Antonin Scalia, "Law, Liberty, and Civic Responsibility," in Rights, Citizenship and Responsibilities: The Proceedings of Freedoms Foundation's Symposium on Citizen Responsibilities (Washington, D.C.: The Freedoms Foundation, 1984), 3,4.

201–202   Galston says language of rights is morally incomplete: William A. Galston, "Rights Do Not Equal Rightness," *The Responsive Community* 1(Fall 1991): 8.

202   quotation from Judge Learned Hand on liberty: Quoted by Philip
B. Kurland, "The Constitution and Citizen Responsibility," in *Rights,
Citizenship and Responsibilities*, op. cit., 21–2.

203   removal of Goya's *Naked Maja* at Penn State: Nat Hentoff, "Triv-
ializing Sexual Harassment," *The Washington Post,* January 11, 1992, A19.

203   the plight of Ryan White: Dirk Johnson, "Ryan White Dies of
AIDS at 18; His Struggle Helped Pierce Myths," *The New York Times,*
April 9, 1990, D10.

203   White's own words: Ryan White and Ann Marie Cunningham,
Ryan White: My Own Story (New York: Dial Books, 1991).

203   gay leader describes incident during a series of conferences on the
Bill of Rights: Fred Friendly, "That Delicate Balance," PBS special on the
Bill of Rights, produced 1992.

204   Lawrence says racist speech inflicts real harm: Charles R. Lawrence III, "The Debates over Placing Limits on Racist Speech Must Not
Ignore the Damage It Does to Its Victims," *The Chronicle of Higher Education,* October 25, 1989, B1.

204   Hentoff on incident at Arizona State: Nat Hentoff, "The Right
Thing at ASU," *The Washington Post,* June 25, 1991, A19.

205   workshops on sexual harassment at Emory: Susan Dodge, "Campus Codes That Ban Hate Speech Are Rarely Used to Penalize Students,"
The Chronicle of Higher Education, February 2, 1992, A36.

205   Ethridge approves of workshops: ibid.

205   dean of student life at Duke expresses doubt: ibid.

206   University of Maryland videotape *Still Burning: Hate in the Ivory
Tower: A Survey of Intolerance on College Campuses and Academia's Response*
(Washington, D.C.: People for the American Way, 1991), 19.

206   interactive video used at Miami University of Ohio in cultural
awareness program: "Videotape Helps Students Accept Racial Diversity,"
The New York Times, October 27, 1991, 42.

206   peer counseling, etc.: *Hate in the Ivory Tower: A Survey of Intolerance on College Campuses and Academia's Response* (Washington, D.C.: People for the American Way, 1991), 20.

Chapter 8: Communitarian Politics

209   Proxmire says you can read the phone book and be paid: Martin Tolchin, "Perils Presented by Outside Income," *The New York Times,* January 10, 1983.

209   Breaux of Louisiana retorts he can't be bought, but he can be rented: Quoted in "Struggling to Explain Washington to the Folks Back Home," interview with Pete Earley by Joan McKinney, *The Washington Post,* November 7, 1982, B3.

210   Suzanne Garment stopped counting at four hundred: statement made during meeting of Society of Professional Journalists, Alexandria, Virginia, April 4, 1992.

210   rumors about George Bush's "mistress" were cited: Joe Conason, "George Bush's Adultery Thing," *Spy,* July–August 1991, 31–38.

211   most politicians crooked, throw the rascals out: American Enterprise Institute, 1990.

211   Nichols challenges Etzioni's patriotism: Private communication, November 1982.

212   Elizabeth Drew's and Brooks Jackson's books: I and several other longtime Washington observers who have been writing along the same lines, such as Elizabeth Drew in her fine book *Politics and Money: The New Road to Corruption* (New York: Macmillan Publishing Company, 1983) and Brooks Jackson in his important book *Honest Graft: Big Money and American Political Process* (Washington, D.C.: Farragut Publishing Company, 1990); William Greider, *Who Will Tell the People: The Betrayal of American Democracy* (New York: Simon & Schuster, 1992).

212   average amount spent by House and Senate candidates in 1990: Larry Makinson, *The Price of Admission* (Washington, D.C.: The Center for Responsive Politics, 1991), 10.

212–213   top spenders in House and Senate races in 1990: ibid., 9.

214   thirty-five thousand workers qualify for TAA between 1962 and 1974: Michael R. Gordon, "Trade Adjustment Assistance Program May Be Too Big for Its Own Good," *National Journal,* May 10, 1980, 765.

214   program cost $9 million in 1973, $69.9 million by 1976, $1.5 billion in 1980: Michael Reed, "The Administration Wants to Withdraw the Carrot of Trade Adjustment Assistance," *National Journal*, May 29, 1982, 958.

214   aid goes to workers temporarily laid off: "That $1 Billion 'Surprise,' " *The Washington Post*, April 10, 1980.

214   laid-off steelworkers refuse to relocate: Robert J. Samuelson, "On Mobility," *National Journal*, August 16, 1980, 1366.

214   12 percent of Americans lived in "distressed" area in 1965: Cristie Backley, Public Affairs Office of the Economic Development Administration, private communication, March 11, 1983.

214   84.5 percent of population lives in "distressed" communities by 1979: Rochelle L. Stanfield, "EDA—The 'Perfect Vehicle' for Carter's Urban Strategy," *National Journal*, June 23, 1979, 1034.

214   EDA attempts to decertify well-off areas in 1982: Cristie Backley, Public Affairs Office of the Economic Development Administration, private communication, March 11, 1983.

215   Coelho, AFL-CIO, real estate, and Congress stories: Brooks Jackson, *Honest Graft: Big Money and the American Political Process* (Washington, D.C.: Farragut Publishing Company, rev. ed., 1990), chapter 6; "For Coelho," 105; "The obvious . . ." and "Congress dare," 109.

215   testimony of George Eads: Statement of George C. Eads before the Subcommittee on General Oversight and Renegotiation, Committee on Banking, Finance, and Urban Affairs, U.S. House of Representatives, March 10, 1983, especially 6–7.

216   a majority of Americans favor gun control laws: 86 percent of Americans favored a mandatory waiting period before an applicant for a handgun could receive it; 79 percent favored a ban on assault weapons, according to a *New York Times*/CBS News Poll, March 12, 1992.

216   about three out of four PACs have no ideological commitments: "FEC Releases 1991 Year-End PAC Count," press release, Federal Election Commission, January 10, 1992.

218   David Cohen, the disadvantaged always lose out: Gary Lee, "Tax Bills Mark Return of Hill's 'Gucci Gulch,' " *The Washington Post*, February 17, 1992, A27.

219   industry-based organizations: Deborah M. Burek (ed.), *Encyclo-pedia of Associations* (Detroit: Gale Research, Inc., 1991); see Andrew Sullivan, "Viewspeak," *The New Republic*, September 1, 1986, 13; Edward Zuckerman, *Almanac of Federal PACs: 1990* (Washington, D.C.: Amward Publications Inc., 1990), 568.

220   progun and antigun PAC contributions from 1987 to 1988: Larry Makinson, *Open Secrets* (Washington, D.C.: Congressional Quarterly Inc., 1990), 78.

220   NRA's $1.5 million "independent expenditures" in 1988: Larry Makinson, *Open Secrets* (Washington, D.C.: Congressional Quarterly Inc., 1990), 12.

220   Congress passes FTC legislative veto: "Would You Buy a Used Car from Congress?" *U.S. News & World Report,* June 7, 1982, 11.

220   cosponsors of FTC legislative veto: *Congress Gets a Tune-up: Campaign Contributions from Car Dealers to Congress after the FTC Issued Its Used Car Rule* (Washington, D.C.: Public Citizen's Congress Watch, February 1982), 1–2.

220–221   money from billboard industry flows to Capitol Hill: Carol Matlack, "Billboarding Clout," *National Journal,* October 12, 1991, 2474.

221   undercover operation investigates corruption in Arizona: Seth Mydans, "Civics 101 on Tape in Arizona, or, 'We All Have Our Prices,' " *The New York Times,* February 11, 1991, A1.

221   quotes from Walker and Raymond: ibid., B9.

221   similar investigation in South Carolina: "Two South Carolina Legislators Guilty of Corruption," *The New York Times,* March 10, 1991, 27.

222   state senate president pleads guilty to extortion in West Virginia: R. Drummond Ayres, Jr., "Corruption Cases Leave State in Search of Ethics," *The New York Times,* September 18, 1989, A14.

222   other states in which legislators have been charged with corruption: Gwen Ifill, "Scandals Cast New Light on Statehouse Ethics," *The Washington Post,* February 24, 1991, A3.

222   legislative bodies of only eleven states in session more than one hundred days a year: Wayne L. Francis, "Costs and Benefits of Legislative

Service in the United States," *American Journal of Political Science* 88(August 1985): 626–42.

222   11 percent of state legislators are full-time: *The New York Times*, June 4, 1989.

222   number of PACs in America: "FEC Releases 1991 Year-End PAC Count," press release, Federal Election Commission, January 10, 1992,

223   PAC contributions grow from 1974 to 1988: Larry Makinson, *Open Secrets* (Washington, D.C.: Congressional Quarterly Inc., 1990), 4.

223   88 percent of PAC money goes to incumbents: Robert D. Hershey, "Members' Conduct May Be in Line but Out of Step," *The New York Times*, June 21, 1988, A20.

223   "disturbing trend . . . of using huge campaign war chests"; war chest figure: "Rule by Permanent Congress," *Newsweek*, June 6, 1988, 41.

223   reelection percentages in 1986 and 1990: Larry Makinson, *The Price of Admission* (Washington, D.C.: Center for Responsive Politics, 1991), 13.

224   PACs contribute $159 million in 1989–90: Larry Makinson, *The Price of Admission* (Washington, D.C.: Center for Responsive Politics, 1991), 8.

224   PACs contributions to Democrats and Republicans: Larry Makinson, *Open Secrets: The Dollar Power of PACs in Congress* (Washington, D.C.: Congressional Quarterly Inc., 1990), 18.

224   story of David Boren's attempts at reform: Brooks Jackson, *Honest Graft: Big Money and the American Political Process* (Washington, D.C.: Farragut Publishing Company, rev. ed., 1990), 236–237.

225   PACs get together to protest Bush's call for legislation to eliminate them: James A. Barnes, "PACs' Common Front for Survival," *National Journal*, May 11, 1991, 1122.

Chapter 9: What Is to Be Done?

227–228   campaign contributions are a form of democracy: Herbert Alexander, *The Case for PACs* (Washington, D.C.: Public Affairs Council, 1983), 15.

228   Fanelli argues First Amendment basis for PACs: Joseph J. Fanelli, "PAC Overview" in Ken Clair (ed.), *The PAC Handbook* (Washington, D.C.: Fraser/Associates, 1981), 23.

228   "PACs do not derive contributions from corporations": Joseph J. Fanelli, "PAC Overview" in Ken Clair (ed.), *The PAC Handbook* (Washington, D.C.: Fraser/Associates, 1981), 24.

230   persons who form a new message: as a social scientist who has lectured and written on moral issues: see Amitai Etzioni, *The Moral Dimension* (New York: Free Press, 1988), and an article about my experiences in teaching ethics to Harvard MBAs in Amitai Etzioni, "Money, Power and Fame," *Newsweek,* September 18, 1989, 10.

230   Silent Spring: Rachel Carson, *Silent Spring* (Boston: Houghton Mifflin, 1962).

231   more recently, the multilogue dealt with questions such as what we owe the homeless and should do about those who are not covered by health insurance: see Daniel Yankelovich's new book, *Coming to Public Judgment: Making Democracy Work in a Complex World* (Syracuse, NY: Syracuse University Press, 1991).

232   Senate called the "Millionaires Club": David Graham Philips, *The Treason of the Senate* (Chicago: Quadrangle Books, 1964), 23.

232   discussion of Progressive movement: see Amitai Etzioni, *Capital Corruption: The New Attack on American Democracy* (New Brunswick, NJ: Transaction Books, 1988), chapter 9; and Richard Hofstadter, *The Age of Reform* (New York: Knopf, 1966).

232   state legislatures represented industries: William Ashworth, *Under the Influence: Congress, Lobbies, and the American Pork-Barrel System* (New York: Hawthorn/Dutton, 1981), 107.

232   Wilson's Progressive reforms: see Ernest R. May, et al., *The Progressive Era* vol. 9, Time-Life History of the United States (New York: Time/Life Books, 1964, 1974).

234   Putnam and Parent advocate reforms to reduce the role of particular interests: Robert D. Putnam and William B. Parent, "The Dawn of an Old Age?" *The Washington Post,* June 23, 1991, B5.

234   details of reforms spelled out: see Amitai Etzioni, *Capital Corrup-*

tion: The New Attack on American Democracy (New Brunswick, NJ: Transaction Books, 1988).

234   congressional elections cost $200 million to $250 million: Larry Makinson, *The Price of Admission* (Washington, D.C.: The Center for Responsive Politics, 1989), 10.

234   farm subsidies totaled about $20 billion in 1989: Dan Goodgame, "Getting Farmers off the Dole," *Time,* July 16, 1990, 26.

234   cotton subsidies cost $6 billion between 1986 and 1990: James Bovard, "Farm Subsidy Follies," *USA Today* (magazine), November 1990, 16.
       On campaign bundling, see: Mark Stencel, " 'Bundling" Skirts Campaign Gift Curbs: Corporate Contributions Outlawed, but Executives Raise Large Amounts," *The Washington Post,* April 20, 1922, A1.

235   ACLU opposes legislation to ban PACs and to set campaign spending limits: *ACLU Civil Liberties Alert,* July/August 1991, 7.

235   ACLU opposes all legislatively mandated spending limits: see, for example, the testimony of Barry W. Lynn, legislative counsel of the ACLU, regarding a constitutional amendment to regulate campaign expenditures before the Senate Judiciary Committee (Subcommittee on the Constitution), February 28, 1990. Lynn states that "notwithstanding certain limitations upheld by the Supreme Court in *Buckley* and some of its progeny, the ACLU uniformly opposes both contribution and expenditure limitations."

235   cost of parliamentary election in Britain: Dudley Fishburn, "British Campaigning—How Civilized!" *The New York Times,* March 14, 1992, 25.

235–236   "There is no question": R. W. Apple, Jr., "Campaigning in Britain: No Frills and No Glamour, Just $6,633.72," *The New York Times,* June 4, 1983, 3.
       On Carl Levin's reforms, see: Gary Lee, "Bill Targets Lobbyists' Activities: Levin Wants to Cast Light on Dealmakers," *The Washington Post,* February 28, 1992, A21.

236   Congress rescinded FEC's power to conduct random audits: Colleen O'Connor, "Who's Afraid of the FEC?" *The Washington Monthly,* March 1986, 26.

236   FEC has no legal authority to impose fines: ibid., 25.

236–237   FEC audits of Dukakis, Bush, Robertson, and Jackson: Charles R. Babcock, "FEC 1988 Audits Remain Incomplete," *The Washington Post,* February 12, 1992, A21.

237   Brooks Jackson says FEC has failed: John Dillin, "Election Commission Has Failed, Study Says," *The Christian Science Monitor,* April 11, 1990, 9.

237   *New York Times* editorial agrees: "The Campaign Sewer Overflows," *The New York Times,* November 7, 1988, A18.

237   eighty thousand lobbyists: Jeffrey H. Birnbaum, "Overhaul of Lobbying Laws Unlikely to Succeed Thanks to Opposition of Lobbyists Themselves," *The Wall Street Journal,* May 30, 1991, A16.

238   shrinkage of sound bites: James Fishkin's comments during the Teledemocracy session of The Second National Teach-in on Communitarian Thinking, held May 19, 1992, New York City, New York.

239   pros and cons of PACs: Herbert E. Alexander, *Financing Politics* (Washington, D.C.: Congressional Quarterly Press. 1976); Herbert E. Alexander, *The Case for PACs* (Washington, D.C.: Public Affairs Council, 1983); Larry Sabato, *PAC Power: Inside the World of Political Action Committees* (New York: Norton, 1984); Norman J. Ornstein and Shirley Elder, *Interest Groups, Lobbying and Policymaking* (Washington, D.C.: Congressional Quarterly Press, 1978); Amitai Etzioni, *Capital Corruption* (New Brunswick: Transaction Books, 1988).

239   "access should not be confused with buying votes": Alexander, *The Case for PACs,* 17.

239   Grove of C&P Telephone says PAC contribution provides entrée: Michael Abramowitz, "The Big Business of PACs," *The Washington Post,* February 8, 1988, WB16.

239   Matsui tries to undo 1986 tax bill damage: Brooks Jackson and Jeffrey H. Birnbaum, "Rep. Matsui Is Finding It Hard to Roll Back Break He Gave Utilities," *The Wall Street Journal,* July 13, 1989, A1.

240   survey by Center for Responsive Politics shows congressmen swayed by contributions: *The New York Times,* December 30, 1987, A10.

240   president of NAB explains that $100,000 granted to congressmen helped to get better acquainted: *The Wall Street Journal,* December 17, 1987, 64.

240   quote from Mobil Corporation ad: "PACs—The Voice of Real People" (advertisement), *The New York Times,* December 2, 1982, A31.

240   twenty-one dairy PACs: Randy Huwa, Common Cause, private communication, September 22, 1982.

240   number of oil PACs: "Energy Group Political Giving Tops $3 Million," *The New York Times,* July 18, 1982, 22.

240   *Buckley* v. *Valeo,* 424 U.S. 1 (1976).

241   contributions to six members of House Agriculture Committee between 1975 and 1978: *How Money Talks in Congress* (Washington, D.C.: Common Cause, 1979), 53.

241   AMA spokeswoman insists donations are "based on the basic philosophy of a member": Brooks Jackson, "Doctors and Dentists Prescribe Donations for Some in House," *The Wall Street Journal,* September 17, 1982, 20.

241   1990 study by Center for Responsive Politics: Richard L. Berke, "Pragmatism Guides Political Gifts," *The New York Times,* September 16, 1990, 26.

241   members of Ways and Means received an average of $35,000 each from insurance-industry PACs in 1988: ibid.

241–242   twelve House members receive more than $100,000 from finance, insurance, and real estate interests: Kenneth H. Bacon, "For Financial Firms, Banking Reform Involves Huge Stakes—and Big Donations to Lawmakers," *The Wall Street Journal,* May 28, 1991, A24.

242   finance, insurance, real estate PACs give $3.8 million to members of Senate Finance Committee: Larry Makinson, *Open Secrets: The Dollar Power of PACs in Congress* (Washington, D.C.: Congressional Quarterly Inc., 1990), 98–99.

242    $2.8 million to members of Senate Banking, Housing and Urban Affairs Committee: ibid., 88–89.

242    $3.9 million to House Banking Committee members: ibid., 122–123.

242    $2.8 million to members of House Ways and Means Committee: ibid., 154–155.

242   agricultural interests dedicate $2 million to members of House Agricultural Committee: ibid., 116–117.

242   conservative senators and representatives vote for government handouts for their PAC interests: Jay Angoff and Jane Stone, eds., *Congressional Voting Index/Money Index* (Washington, D.C.: Public Citizen, 1981), 7.

242   donations to Dole from Archer Daniels Midland: Jeffrey H. Birnbaum and Jill Abramson, "Dole, Despite Budget-Cutter Image, Seeks Tax Break Aiding Company Tied to Him," *The Wall Street Journal,* September 28, 1990, A16.

243   *WSJ* comments on Commodore Savings fiasco: Byron Harris, "A PAC of Lies: The Commodore Savings Case," *The Wall Street Journal,* July 18, 1989, A22.

243   Geiger of NEA defends PACs: Keith Geiger, "PACs and Political Participation" (advertisement), *The Washington Post,* November 3, 1991, 65.

243   PACs are typically organizations of those who can spare up to $10,000: $5,000 for the primary and $5,000 for the general election. Although many give less, there are next to no PAC members that come from the lower 40 percent of the income scale.

Acknowledgments

Barry Kreiswirth served as research assistant from the inception to the completion of the book. Aside from much digging, he made many invaluable suggestions on ways to improve the presentation of the arguments and on one public policy issue led the author to recast his position. Barbara Hoch Marcus edited the manuscript carefully twice. Sharon Pressner and Lauren Levy conducted research for several chapters. I am indebted to Trish Thomas, Steven Helland, and Pat Kellogg for comments they made on an early draft. Sarah Horton helped put the book to bed. David Groff, my editor at Crown, made numerous helpful suggestions, and Linda Abdel-Malek and Robert Teir made several very insightful comments based on their legal training. Professor Thomas Dienes tried to assist me in understanding the intricacies of the First Amendment; any failure to comprehend is completely my own doing.

Index